Martin Howells and **Keith Skinner** are both professional actors; they first met at the National Theatre. Martin Howells writes for both television and the theatre. Keith Skinner specializes in historical research for film and literary projects.

£2-

D1375478

THE
RIPPER
LEGACY

The Life and Death of Jack the Ripper

Martin Howells and Keith Skinner

SPHERE BOOKS LIMITED

SPHERE BOOKS LTD

Published by the Penguin Group
27 Wrights Lane, London W8 5TZ, England
Viking Penguin Inc., 40 West 23rd Street, New York, New York 10010, USA
Penguin Books Australia Ltd, Ringwood, Victoria, Australia
Penguin Books Canada Ltd, 2801 John Street, Markham, Ontario, Canada L3R 1B4
Penguin Books (NZ) Ltd, 182–190 Wairau Road, Auckland 10, New Zealand

Penguin Books Ltd, Registered Offices: Harmondsworth, Middlesex, England

First published in Great Britain by Sidgwick & Jackson Ltd 1987
Published by Sphere Books Ltd 1988

Extracts from documents RA Z 101/40, RA B 40/87, RA GEO VAA 6, RA GV AA6 337, RA
Queen Victoria's Journals (4 October 1888), and RA Prince of Wales's Engagement Diary 1888,
from the Royal Archives, are quoted by gracious permission of Her Majesty the Queen. Gracious
permission is also granted to quite from previously published material held under Crown
copyright.

Printed and bound in Great Britain by
Richard Clay Ltd, Bungay, Suffolk

For
Jan, Bronwen and Gareth

For
Mum and Dad

ACKNOWLEDGEMENTS

With special thanks to Shirley Richards in Australia, and our sincere gratitude to the following:

Michael Ferguson, Roger Carey Management, Sir Peter Hall, Paul Tomlinson, Dr Wendy Baron, Tom Cullen, Donald Rumbelow, Richard Whittington-Egan, David Streatfield, Alan Haywood, the Monro family, Eileen Weston, Leonard Lewis, Marjorie Henderson, David Briggs, Neil Rhind, John Ruffels, David Mickle, Jeffrey Burton, Sir James Stephen, Magnus Linklater, Roy Valentine, Christopher McLaren, Angus Macnaghten, Henry Lessore.

James Sabben-Clare (Headmaster of Winchester College), Bill Waddell (Curator of the Black Museum, Scotland Yard), Wallace Breem (Librarian, Inner Temple), Assistant Commissioner John Dellow (Chairman, Metropolitan Police Historical Society), John Back and Charles Pole-Carew (Metropolitan Police Archives), Janet Foster (District Archivist, St Bartholomew's Hospital), Elizabeth Cuthbert (Registrar, Royal Archives, Windsor).

St Arnaud and District Historical Society, Kooweerup Swamp Historical Society, East of London Family History Society, United Grand Lodge of England, Metropolitan Police Thames Division (Wapping), City of London Police Records Office.

The staff of: British Library, British Newspaper Library (Colindale), Public Record Office, Greater London Record Office and History Library, Guildhall Library, Trinity College Library (Cambridge), Manor House Library (Lee), Marylebone Library, Chiswick Reference Library, Society of Genealogists, National Meteorological Archive, London Hospital Medical College Library, Wellcome Institute.

AUTHOR'S NOTE

The authors have made every effort to trace and acknowledge the ownership of copyright in works from which they have quoted at length. If by chance any claimants to copyright have been overlooked the authors will be pleased to rectify the situation, provided they receive notification of all such claims in writing.

INTRODUCTION

As we were approaching Tower Hill station the potential horror of what we'd let ourselves in for began to dawn on us. It was a bitterly cold New Year's Day and we were about to embark with over one hundred fellow travellers on a guided walk around the back streets of Whitechapel and Spitalfields in search of a Victorian madman known only by his powerfully evocative pseudonym – Jack the Ripper.

Two hours later we stood under an old street lamp, its light already glowing yellow in the deepening gloom – a vestigial token of a rich Victorian heritage creating an appropriate atmosphere for our journey's end amidst a sea of concrete. As we stood there listening to our guide, it was interesting to note that not one of our number had departed for a more comfortable and warmer clime. After all, modern Whitechapel is a predominantly commercial, workaday area of London which bears little relation to its Victorian antecedent. None of the murder sites has survived in any recognizable form; there are certainly no plaques proclaiming that Jack the Ripper lived, murdered or bought his knives anywhere in the district where on weekdays the great markets of Spitalfields, Smithfield and Petticoat Lane – together with the thriving Bangladeshi community around Brick Lane – transfuse the area with a vibrancy far removed from the petrified desert we walked through now. What remains there were of noteworthy Victorian architecture appeared not only lifeless but insignificant, hemmed in and isolated by the effect of urban renewal.

We were asked who we thought had 'dun it', but we all shook our heads. Was it our natural reserve that had prevented us joining in the game, or was there little to choose between the catalogue of suspects that was as long as it was seemingly ludicrous: doctor, midwife, Jewish slaughterman, Polish madman, secret agent, heir to the throne of England, escaped gorilla, Cambridge aesthete, failed barrister, seaman or social reformer; Dr Barnardo, George Bernard Shaw, the Rev. Samuel Barnett or William Ewart Gladstone?

In the final analysis did it really matter who the culprit was? Wasn't it simply because he was never caught that he has excited the interest of successive generations who, for want of a more substantial culprit, have merely created from the spare parts of their nightmares a monster of Frankensteinian proportions, whose legacy is far more terrifying than the reality could ever have been, and whose continuing hold on our curiosity is assured regardless of the truth?

We may even applaud the success of countless film-makers and storytellers who have at least given form to this spectral killer, engendering in all of us an image of evil stalking the streets of London in search of blood; a shadowy caped figure disappearing into the fog, a mass murderer responsible for the dispatch of countless women. Yet the truth was that he was at work on the streets of the capital on only four occasions, and – deplorable as the wanton murder of a single individual is – he killed only five women.

Already the question is posed. It is not: Who was Jack the Ripper? Rather it is: Why has anybody bothered looking for him in the first place? – or, more precisely: Why has anybody continued looking for him after the cries for retribution and justice have clearly long since died? But look for him we do – not only through pages of print and flickering, Technicolor images, but even on the streets of modern Whitechapel itself.

Perhaps what is just as curious is the fact that we now come to add to the plethora of literature that already exists on the subject. Surely enough dry leaves have blown from countless manuscripts and magazines across the unknown grave of this madman to obscure the name on the tombstone forever, and even if his identity could be ascertained to everyone's satisfaction one last question may still prove to be the most pertinent: So what?

To begin with we were indeed idly curious readers who were cnly slowly to be brought under the spell of this anonymous Victorian magician whose enduring infamy does not – as some would have it – stem from the accidental conjunction of random elements, or from the fact that he was never caught, but from the fact that there are questions that could and should have been answered. The crimes themselves would turn out to be merely the tip of an enormous iceberg – the very existence of which could have threatened a *Titanic* on whose deck Jack the Ripper was but a passenger. But that is where our journey ends. It begins, as we have said, on the streets of Whitechapel.

In 1888 the alleys and byways of the East End were indeed gaslit (if they were lit at all), and dense, choking fogs ('London particulars', as they were known) did cloak the filthy tenements and rotting vegetation in the streets with tedious repetition. They obliterated the decaying lives of their inhabitants under a temporary blanket of oblivion and helped to lend a further air of mystery to the all-too-real events of that autumn.

Now, a century later, the true plight of the abject, poor, diseased and disenfranchised prisoners of Whitechapel's teeming ghettos has been largely forgotten. It only survives in our imagination as a silent and unseen chorus lurking behind the diabolical performance of one individual, whilst the complex tragedy of their lives has been conveniently obscured behind a ubiquitous grey blanket.

In fact there was no fog on any of the nights in question, but the sinister fusion between gaslight, mist and Victorian London is so powerful that it often goes unheralded that Jack the Ripper's second victim was actually murdered in daylight – once again the reality falls short of the legacy now firmly established in the deepest recesses of our minds. It is an inherited appreciation which has adopted anything and everything that sustains and nurtures the fantasy – including events which occurred before our main protagonist had even entered the arena.

Our interest in the death of five Victorian prostitutes has become a curiously antiseptic and painless experience, and for all our temporary discomfort on the streets of Whitechapel the retelling of the sordid results of one man's madness succeeds in entertaining and exciting our imagination against all our better judgement. We had more in common with our fellow walkers than we were at first prepared to concede. We were neither gullible nor ghoulish, but we could not deny an all-too-human fascination – not so much with the macabre aspects of the mystery, but with the puzzle itself. It was as if we had just picked up a well-worn and faded Rubik cube and, like all good puzzles we knew, there had to be a solution. Somewhere in that mesmeric Whitechapel fog we felt that an explanation could still be found – that there was ultimately an answer to the riddle. Perhaps someone had already touched the truth without being able to grasp it firmly enough to drag it into the light of day, or perhaps they had all been groping blindly in the wrong direction.

I

When Emma Elizabeth Smith, a forty-five-year-old prostitute, staggered into her lodging house at 18 George Street, Spitalfields in the early morning of 3 April 1888, she said she had been attacked and robbed by three men in Osborne Street. She had often returned battered and bruised, and on one occasion she told Mary Russell, who acted as caretaker at the lodgings, that she had been thrown out of a window. Such was the lot of this penniless widow – obliged, like so many others, to eke out an existence on the mean streets of London. Now her face was bloody and her ear virtually torn off. Mary Russell walked her to the London Hospital in Whitechapel, where it was discovered that a blunt instrument had been forcibly thrust into her vagina to such an extent that it had torn the partition between the front and the back passages. The next day Emma Smith died of peritonitis.

Four months later, on 7 August, the body of another prostitute, thirty-nine-year-old Martha Tabram (also known as Turner), was found on the first-floor landing of George Yard buildings. On her body were thirty-nine puncture wounds which had been inflicted at the same time by two different weapons – one probably a bayonet, the other a dagger. There were nine stab wounds in her throat, seventeen in the breast and thirteen in the stomach.

A friend of Tabram's, a prostitute known as Pearly Poll, testified that they had been in the company of two soldiers earlier in the evening, and PC Barrett 226 H Division, who had been on duty in George Yard the same night, said that he had seen, and spoken to, a guardsman at about 2 a.m. A Mrs Jane Gilbank and her daughter

1

had also seen the deceased talking to a private of the guards on the Sunday before the murder, but despite several identity parades which involved the Grenadier and Coldstream Guards at the nearby Tower of London, the various witnesses failed to identify any soldiers who could have been in George Yard at the appropriate time. Importantly, none came forward in order to be eliminated from the police inquiries, which was a point that one might expect to have been picked up by the press – that is, if the press had taken any real interest in the case.

The *Daily News* of 8 August carried a small paragraph at the bottom of page three headed: 'Supposed Murder in Whitechapel'. It would not have taken a Sherlock Holmes to determine that a woman found dead in a pool of blood with thirty-nine stab wounds in her body was hardly likely to have died a natural death or to have committed suicide, but the tone of the report clearly demonstrates Fleet Street's apathy. In due course *The Times*, as was usual – and as it had done in the case of Emma Smith – carried a report of the inquest. But there was no strident call for the perpetrator's apprehension, or the slightest criticism of the police for their failure to apprehend the culprit. After all, these women were prostitutes of the lowest type, surviving in a nest of filth and despair in the very bosom of London's underworld; and particularly with Emma Smith there were enough indications to suggest that she had fallen foul of a gang of muggers, or High Rips as they were called at the time.

These High Rips were often well-organized thugs who intimidated women like Emma and extorted money from them, though sometimes they were just small gangs of youths who preyed on vulnerable passers-by in just the same way that such gangs operate today. On the very morning of Martha Tabram's murder, three seventeen-year-old boys were found guilty at the Liverpool Assizes for assaulting and robbing a woman of a shawl and 3s 2d. Summing up, Mr Justice Stephen said, 'You are just the kind of people who commit the worst kind of crimes which appear to be committed in the city of Liverpool, and it is utterly intolerable that a set of rascals like you, just between boyhood and manhood, should be allowed to be a terror and a plague to decent people.' He sentenced all three to fourteen years' hard labour.

The nature of Emma Smith's injuries, the number of her assailants, and the fact that she could not or would not identify those assailants, allowed the police to make an almost certainly correct assumption that she had been attacked by one of the High

Rip gangs which had been operating in the area for some time. But what could not be foreseen by the police, press or public was that the murders of Smith and Tabram were little more than a prologue.

It was in the early hours of Friday, 31 August, three weeks after the discovery of Martha Tabram, that a forty-two-year-old prostitute called Mary Ann Nichols met someone. 'I'll soon get my doss money,' she had earlier laughed. 'See what a jolly bonnet I've got now.' Polly, as she had been known to her friends at the Lambeth workhouse, had lately enjoyed a brief period of respectable domestic service in Wandsworth before absconding with £3 of her employer's money. Now, the worse for drink and penniless, she had been turned away from her lodging house for the want of 4d. At 2.30 a.m. she had been seen at the corner of Osborne Street, where Emma Smith had been attacked, and at 3.45 her body was discovered by PC John Neil 97 J Division, less than five hundred yards away.

She must have thought her luck was in when she turned into dark Buck's Row to consummate her nefarious transaction. But instead her companion grabbed her by the neck and forced her to the ground. There was a flash of steel, and two deep slashes severed her windpipe. Tearing at her rough, brown Ulster coat her assailant attacked her stomach in a frenzy. Lifting her skirts, he stabbed her vagina and tore at her abdomen with a deep, jagged thrust which reached far enough up to cause her bowels to protrude through the wound.

Again, there was to be no panic in the streets. News that some other 'unfortunate' had come to an untimely end was received with accustomed stoicism by a populace continually faced with poverty, disease and premature – even violent – death. But at last the press was stirring from its lethargy. That evening the *Star* carried a small headline on page three: 'A Woman found horribly mutilated in Whitechapel – A Revolting Murder; Another woman found horribly mutilated in Whitechapel, Ghastly crimes by a maniac.' Other papers told much the same story.

According to *The Times* of 3 September, the police had already abandoned their earlier opinion that all the Whitechapel crimes had been committed by one or more High Rip gangs, and were now admitting their belief that the murders of Nichols and Tabram, and the unsolved murder in December 1887 of a prostitute known as Fairy Fay, were the work of a man acting alone, even though the earliest victim had not been stabbed or slashed with a knife but had

3

been impaled on an iron spike. Emma Smith's insistence that she had been attacked by a gang of men was also not enough to stop less well-informed opinion from attributing her death to the same killer. All four women, it was reasoned, were of the same class, had been killed within three hundred yards of each other, and were so poor that robbery could have formed no real motive for the crime. *The Times* then went on to say that each victim so far had been 'murdered in such a similiar fashion, that doubt as to the crime being the work of the same individual vanishes', which was patently absurd. The murders of all four women were dissimilar in as many respects as they were coincidentally alike in others.

The initial belief that several men were possibly involved in the assaults was a far more reasonable assumption. Emma Smith had been set upon by three men. Martha Tabram had been stabbed by two different weapons. Mary Nichols's throat had been slit and there were mutilations to her stomach. Only when robbery became a less acceptable explanation for the attacks did the seemingly motiveless killing of Mary Nichols suggest the possibility that a maniac could have been responsible for her death; this in turn promoted the idea that he might also have been responsible for some or all of the other unsolved murders to date. But the impression given by *The Times* that the police had whole-heartedly accepted such a notion, and abandoned the possibility that several persons could be involved, was not correct.

The *Police Chronicle and Guardian* of Saturday, 8 September ended one of its reports on the murders by saying: 'The police believe they have a clue to the perpetrators of the crime, and certain persons are being kept under surveillance. No arrest, however, is expected to be made until after the adjourned coroner's enquiry, when important evidence pointing to the murderer or murderers may be given, unless the suspected persons attempt to leave the district.' Unfortunately, this air of veiled optimism was unjustified. Even as the unsuspecting reporter's minor article was rolling off the press, another woman's fate was being decided less than a quarter of a mile away from the scene of his present attentions.

Annie Chapman was haggling with a man outside No. 29 Hanbury Street. It was 5.30 in the morning, and dawn had already broken. Half an hour later her forty-seven-year-old body was discovered in the yard at the back of the house. A strong hand had seized her by the throat and sliced into it twice, virtually severing her head. Then her killer had moved on downwards, drawing her legs up and pushing her coat and skirt out of the way as he drove a sharp-pointed knife into her stomach. He reached in and lifted the small intestines, placing them above the right shoulder. Again he used the knife – this time to remove part of the belly wall including the navel, the womb, the upper part of the vagina and the greater part of the bladder.

The Times of 10 September reassessed the situation:

> So far as we know, nothing in fact or fiction equals these outrages at once in their horrible nature and in the effect which they have produced upon the popular imagination. The circumstance that the murders seem to be the work of one individual, that his blows fall exclusively upon the wretched wanderers of the night, and that each successive crime has gained something in atrocity upon, and has followed closer on the heels of, its predecessor – these things mark out the Whitechapel murders, even before their true history is unravelled, as unique in the annals of crime. All ordinary experiences of motive leave us at a loss to comprehend the fury which has prompted the cruel slaughter of at least three, and possibly four, women. . . .

With the benefit of hindsight, it can be seen that the intuitive realization expressed in *The Times* that such a madman would probably kill more than once was correct. But the fact that the earlier murders could be considered similar enough to be attributed to the same psychopathic personality demonstrates a total lack of understanding of such a phenomenon. The *Lancet* of 15 September stated:

> The theory that the succession of murders which have lately been committed in Whitechapel are the work of a lunatic appears to us to be by no means at present well established. We can quite understand the necessity for any murderer endeavouring to obliterate by the death of his victim his future identification as a burglar. Moreover, as far as we are aware, homicidal mania is generally characterised by the one single and fatal act, although we grant this may have been led up to by a deep-rooted series of delusions. It is most unusual for a lunatic to plan any complicated crime of this kind. Neither, as a rule, does a lunatic take precautions to escape from the consequences of his act. The truth is, that under the circumstances nobody can do more than hazard a guess as to the probable condition of the mind of the perpetrator of these terrible tragedies. Until more evidence is forthcoming, it appears to us to be useless to speculate upon what can only at present be regarded as problematical.

Writing from Birmingham the following week, Dr Henry

Sutherland, a lecturer on insanity at the Westminster Hospital, was more definite:

> These murders were committed by some person or persons who were perfectly sane. . . . He was most probably a stranger to his victim, and not bound to her by ties of blood. . . . In all probability he was a poor man. . . . It is well known to experts in insanity that although the anticipation of the deed may long be cherished, yet the act itself is sudden, unexpected, uncomplicated by any subsequent mutilation, or attempt to conceal the act, and very frequently followed by some suicidal attempt. As far as we have yet heard, there have been no suicides in Whitechapel lately. And any reader of the daily papers must be aware how common is this tendency when an insane person has committed a murder.

Monomania – an excessive mental preoccupation with one thing – was also becoming an increasingly popular hook on which to hang the murderer's psychosis. The *Evening News*, among others, believed that he may well have been an epileptic, explaining: 'It is a well known fact to students of insanity that epilepsy is often induced by amatory desires of an inordinate nature.'

Whatever fragments of truth may have been embedded in such woefully inadequate understanding of serious mental disorder, the practical outcome was that police officers, coroners and the like had to rely largely on their own intuition when it came to determining a possible motive for these unprecedented crimes. But motive there had to be, as Wynne Edwin Baxter, coroner for the eastern division of Middlesex, was only too aware. Presiding at Annie Chapman's inquest, he said: 'It has been suggested that the criminal is a lunatic with morbid feeling. This may or may not be the case, but the object of the murderer appears palpably shown by the facts, and it is not necessary to assume lunacy, for it is clear that there is a market for the missing organ.'

Mr Baxter had been informed by Dr Thomas Openshaw, the Pathological Curator of the London Hospital Museum, that some months before an American had asked him to procure a number of uteri. He had been prepared to pay £20 for each specimen, and said that he intended to issue one with each copy of a publication on which he was then engaged. The American was told that his request was impossible, but he persisted and repeated his request to another institution. He wanted the organs preserved in glycerine in order to keep them in a flaccid condition.

Here then was another attempt to supply a rational motive, and once again the acceptable notion of theft for monetary gain is put forward. Mary Nichols had not been eviscerated, but it seemed quite possible that her assailant had been disturbed before he had had time to complete his grisly task. Her lower abdomen bore a deep, jagged wound; several cuts ran across the stomach and there were three or four similar cuts running down the right-hand side; but no organs were missing. This in itself did not distinguish it from Annie Chapman's murder. The cause of death in both cases – as distinct from what was to follow – was the massive loss of blood caused by two long, deep cuts which severed the main arteries in the neck and went down to the vertebrae.

Nowadays our modern comprehension of such crimes can allow for the probability that, as this was the first manifestation of the killer's sexual derangement, it had not yet reached the perverted depths it would fathom in the weeks to come. But no such knowledge was available to Mr Baxter; the evidence could only be understood within existing terms of reference. Summing up, he said:

. . . the injuries had been made by someone who had considerable anatomical knowledge and skill. There were no meaningless cuts. The organ had been taken away by one who knew where to find it, what difficulties he would have to contend against and how he should use his knife so as to abstract the organ without injury to it. No unskilled person could have known where to find it or have recognised it when it was found. For instance, no mere slaughterer of animals could have carried out these operations. It must have been someone accustomed to a post mortem room. The conclusion that the desire to possess the missing organ seems overwhelming. If the object were robbery injuries to the viscera were meaningless, for death had previously resulted from loss of blood at the neck.

Even here, it can be seen how the seeds of future argument were being sown by the way in which evidence was being presented, interpreted and accepted as fact without sufficient data to justify the conclusion.

Dr George Bagster Phillips, the divisional police surgeon who had carried out the post mortem on Chapman, had stated that the way in which the knife had been used seemed to indicate great anatomical knowledge.

It must have been a very sharp knife with a thin narrow blade and must have been at least 6in. to 8in. in length, probably longer . . . the injuries could not have been inflicted by a bayonet or a sword bayonet. They could have been done by such an instrument as a medical man used for post mortem purposes, but ordinary surgical

7

cases might not contain such an instrument. Those used by slaughtermen, well ground down, might have caused them. I think the knives used in the leather trade would not be long enough in the blade. There were indications of anatomical knowledge which were only less indicated in consequence of haste.

Mr Wynne Baxter's faith in the opinion of a divisional police surgeon with nearly twenty-five years' experience behind him was understandable, but nevertheless misguided. Two hundred years' experience would not have equipped Dr Phillips any better when it came to dealing with an event for which there was no precedent and no understanding. Testimony from equally expert witnesses in future inquests would undermine much of coroner Baxter's analysis and the efficacy of Dr Phillips's expertise. And whilst there would be a consensus of opinion on some aspects of all five murders, there would be complete divergence on others. The possible motive and the degree of skill required to commit the crimes were two of the most important and obvious areas of disagreement.

As with almost every aspect of the crimes, therefore, the potential was established for future commentators to employ the imagination of a novelist as much as the objectivity of a dedicated researcher in order to convince a sceptical public of a particular analysis and conclusion. But the truth was that none of the evidence or understanding available at the time of the murders was conclusive enough to allow a finger to be pointed at any particular group of people, let alone a specific individual.

Despite the coroner's attempt at Annie Chapman's inquest to persuade people that 'there was a market for the organ', it was generally accepted that the readily understandable motive of robbery, extortion or drunken rage did not apply. The case involved the premeditated, incomprehensible and systematic slaughter of two or more women by the same individual within three hundred yards of each other. There was distinct method in the killer's madness, and yet no apparent rhyme or reason. Confusion reigned supreme within professional circles, but the terrifying drama unfolding for the public was both uncomplicated and immediate. A monster was loose in their midst: he had dispatched at least two women so far, possibly five; the most likely assumption was that the killer would strike again.

The *Star* of Saturday, 8 September proclaimed:

London lies today under the spell of a great terror. A nameless reprobate – half beast, half man – is at large. . . . The ghoul-like creature who stalks through the streets of London, stalking down his victim like a Pawnee Indian, is simply drunk with blood, and he will have more. . . . Whitechapel is garrisoned with police and stocked with plain-clothes men. Nothing comes of it. The police have not even a clue. They are in despair at their utter failure to get so much as a scent of the criminal. . . . The people of the East-End must become their own police. They must form themselves at once into Vigilance committees.

Two days later, at a meeting of local ratepayers held in the upper room of the Crown public house in the Mile End Road, the *Star*'s suggestion beame reality. George Lusk, a master builder, was elected president, W. Harris, honorary secretary, and the landlord, Joseph Aarons, became treasurer of the sixteen-strong committee which also included a cigar manufacturer, a tailor, a picture frame maker and an actor. A Mr Albert Bachert, a twenty-eight-year-old engraver who was later to become chairman, had already written to the *Evening News* to expess his 'deepest regret and indignation at the shocking and revolting murders', and now he and his fellow citizens were to have the opportunity of making a practical contribution to the defence of the district. As it was, one man had already been singled out as a likely suspect following the murder of Mary Nichols. For a time, hopes were raised that the strange character who was supposed to prowl the streets silently after midnight in slippered feet, wearing a leather apron and carrying a sharp knife, would soon be safely under lock and key – if not actually hanging from the nearest lamp-post.

The man they were all looking for was believed to be Jewish, about five feet four or five inches tall, with black, closely cropped hair and a small black moustache. He had an unusually thick neck and small eyes that glittered from an unpleasant face that framed an excessively repellent grin. In fact he was just the kind of person to satisfy the requirements of both popular fiction and public expectations. In a few weeks the very mention of the character known as Leather-Apron would be enough to strike fear into the bravest hearts.

Anecdotes abounded. In one instance, a man was supposed to have gone into a public-house and said that he knew Leather-Apron, and the customers, leaving their drinks unfinished, fled en masse, while the landlady, speechless with terror, bolted out of the back door and ran into the police station, leaving the grim humourist in sole possession of the establishment, till and all. Another time, a passenger, finding a steamer on which he was about to take a journey inconveniently crowded, just stepped up to the man at the wheel and said, 'I am Leather-Apron', and in two seconds he had the steamer to himself, the captain and the man at the wheel being among the first to leap ashore. These anecdotes may well have been apocryphal, but at least the Victorians could never be accused of taciturnity when it came to creating their heroes and villains, and in this instance there was a desperate need to identify the monster in their midst as quickly as possible.

Unfortunately for a thirty-eight-year-old Polish Jew called John Pizer, who worked in the leather trade as a boot finisher and wore a leather apron in the course of his work, the graphic description of the wanted man appeared to fit him. The actual suspect was a small-time villain who for the past two years had apparently been blackmailing and ill-treating prostitutes in various areas of London, although he was never known to use his knife. Now his absence from Whitechapel was helping to ensure a diabolical reputation which would be further enhanced with the discovery of a leather apron in the back yard of No. 29 Hanbury Street, close to Annie Chapman's body.

From all accounts it would seem that neither Pizer nor his close family and neighbours were aware that he had ever been known as Leather-Apron, but the zealous Sergeant William Thicke of H Division – known to the locals as Johnny Upright – had known him by this name. On the morning of Monday, 10 September he knocked at No. 22 Mulberry Street, Whitechapel. Pizer came to the door himself and was promptly arrested.

The *Evening News* described the luckless Jew as a man of medium height with a florid complexion, a moustache and side-whiskers, who showed 'more than an ordinary amount of intelligence for a man of his class'. By all accounts he was an honest, hard-working man, who was not in the best of health and who hardly deserved the attention being showered on him by a hungry press. Dr Bagster Phillips's later observation at Annie Chapman's inquest – that knives in the leather trade would not have been suitable murder weapons – was made with the knowledge that Pizer had already been cleared of any involvement with the murders of Chapman or Nichols.

At the time of his arrest several sharp knives were found in the house, which must have greatly encouraged his would-be accusers, and the explanation that he was a boot finisher would have done little to dampen their spirits. Pizer's family and friends said that he had not been out of the house for the past four days, in which period of time Annie Chapman's murder had taken place. But Pizer was carted off to Leman Street police station nevertheless – as much, one suspects, for his own safety as for the well-being of the population of Whitechapel.

Within hours it became clear that John Pizer, alias Leather-Apron, was not the man they should have been looking for. At Chapman's inquest Mrs Amelia Richardson, the tenant of No. 29 Hanbury Street, explained that the apron found in the yard belonged to her son John, and that she had washed the garment and left it to dry in the yard on the Thursday before the murder. In addition, Pizer's alibis for the nights of both murders were corroborated by independent civilian witnesses, and for the night of Nichols's murder by a policeman. Pizer returned to Mulberry Street to the cheers of a large and enthusiastic crowd of well-wishers. At Annie Chapman's inquest he took the opportunity of publicly clearing his name, and then brought several successful libel actions against those newspapers which had been incautious enough to brand him as a murderer.

Again, Whitechapel held its breath. The Vigilance Committee continued to voice its concern about the inadequate gas lighting on the streets, and to press for a more effective police force. Two private detectives had been engaged to organize the dozen or so men who were nightly patrolling the lonelier parts of the district, and a request had been made to the Home Secretary, Henry Matthews, to augment the committee's funds so that a substantial reward could be offered for information leading to the arrest of the murderer. £100 had already been put up by the local Liberal Member of Parliament, Samuel Montagu, on 11 September, and later the Lord Mayor of London – acting upon the advice of Colonel Sir James Frazer, Commissioner of the City police – added a further £500 in the name of the Corporation of the City of London. The Government, however, obstinately refused to give any assistance on the grounds that offers of rewards tended to produce more harm than good.

The Vigilance Committee was furious, and resolved to make their disagreement with the Home Secretary public in the hope of mobilizing public support. In the event, all they succeeded in doing was to encourage the popular belief that the Home Secretary had not offered a reward for the simple reason that he himself was the murderer. As *The Daily Telegraph* pointed out, the public was far more ready to 'commend rather than to co-operate'; apart from subscriptions amounting to £300, money had not rolled in to support the worthwhile efforts of these few private citizens. The black clouds of misery and filth that had darkened the lives of many of Whitechapel's inhabitants were about to rain down panic and chaos, and there was little the Vigilance Committee could do about it, except witness the imminent downpour through the columns of an equally concerned press whose conscience had also been well and truly pricked by an unseen knife.

George Bernard Shaw summed up the situation, with typical Shavian wit, in a letter to the *Star* published on 24 September:

> Whilst we conventional Social Democrats were wasting our time on education, agitation and organisation, some independent genius has taken the matter in hand, and by simply murdering and dis-embowelling four women, converted the proprietory press to an inept sort of communism. The moral is a pretty one, and the Insurrectionists, the Dynamitards, the Invincibles, and the extreme left of the Anarchist party will not be slow to draw it. 'Humanity, political science, economics, and religion,' they will say, 'are all rot; the one argument that touches your lady and gentlemen is the knife.' That is so pleasant for the party of Hope and Perseverance in their toughening struggle with the party of Desperation and Death!

It is interesting that Shaw himself attributed the two earlier murders – those of Emma Smith and Martha Tabram – to the same hand. This was an increasingly popular opinion that, according to one satirical journalist of the time, arose from the fact that these murders were not in themselves the kind of crimes which sold newspapers.

> The element of romance is altogether lacking, and they are crimes of the coarsest and most vulgar brutality – not the sort of murders that can be discussed in the drawing room or nursery. The best element in the cases for newspaper purposes is that they are similar to a murder which was committed near the same spot some time previously, and this enables the talented journalist to start the idea that the four crimes are by the same hand.

Unfortunately for Whitechapel, if not Fleet Street, subsequent events were to obviate the need for any further 'creative' journal-ism. But for now the incorrect assumption that the murders of Smith, Tabram and, for that matter, Fairy Fay might have been committed by the same person was not to be altered by any official statements from the police or Home Secretary. Indeed, the authorities concerned were loath to communicate anything to the press or general public except the most basic information – a policy that was to become increasingly criticized as time went on. To begin with, however, it is clear that the CID were merely keeping an open mind on the subject: a file had been opened called simply 'Whitechapel Murders' in which the unsolved cases sat as easily as any other.

On Thursday, 27 September, three days after Shaw's letter had appeared, Scotland Yard was able to add another name to its file – not that of another victim, but the *nom de plume* of the assassin. A letter had been sent to the Central News Agency, 5 New Bridge Street, London EC:

25 Sept 1888

Dear Boss,

I keep on hearing the police have caught me but they won't fix me just yet. I have laughed when they look so clever and talk about being on the right track. That joke about Leather Apron gave me real fits. I am down on whores and I shan't quit ripping them till I do get buckled. Grand work the last job was. I gave the lady no time to squeal. How can they catch me now. I love my work and want to start again. You will soon hear of me with my funny little games. I saved some of the proper red stuff in a ginger-beer bottle over the last job to write with but it went thick like glue and I can't use it. Red ink is fit enough I hope ha ha. The next job I do I shall clip the lady's ears off and send to the police officers just for jolly wouldn't you. Keep this letter back till I do a bit more work, then give it out straight. My knife's so nice and sharp I want to get to work right away if I get a chance. Good luck.

Yours truly

JACK THE RIPPER.

Don't mind me giving the trade name. wasn't good enough to post this before I got all the red ink off my hands curse it. No luck yet they say I am a doctor now ha ha.

Whether the author was in fact the miscreant who had already brutally murdered Mary Ann Nichols and Annie Chapman on the streets of Whitechapel and Spitalfields, or whether the communication was the invention of an enterprising journalist, as Sir Robert Anderson – Assistant Commissioner, and head of the CID at the time – believed, is almost beside the point. Much has been made of certain letters by some writers who have striven to compare handwriting, or to extract meaningful clues from the author's despicable sentiments. However of the 210 letters to the Metropolitan Police still extant at the Public Record Office, there are at most only three or four that can possibly be regarded as having any value. What is important about this first letter is that the 'trade name' once again gave an alarmed public an identity on which to focus their anger and frustration. The Victorians' innate sense of theatre was well and truly satisfied with this new name, which was far more chilling than Leather-Apron. As events unfolded, this title would become capable of raising in the consciousness of successive generations a spectre that would never be exorcised.

Note also the words: 'they say I am a doctor now'. After only two murders, the idea that the perpetrator could be a medical man had already become popular. The link between fact and fiction was being forged in a way that would influence people's understanding of the mystery for the next hundred years, helping to obscure the relevance of those ten weeks in 1888.

II

On Saturday, 29 September, two days after the first 'Ripper' letter had been received, the president of the Whitechapel Vigilance Committee, George Lusk, sent a lengthy petition directly to Queen Victoria. Still smarting from the Home Secretary's refusal to offer a government reward, he was now 'praying' her to 'graciously accede' to that request.

That same night, Louis Diemschutz returned from Westow Hill market a little earlier than usual. The wet night had done nothing to encourage the sale of his cheap jewellery, and at about one o'clock in the morning he turned his pony and cart into a dark court off Berner Street which serviced the International Working Men's Educational Club, of which he had been a steward for six months. The pony kept pulling to the left as if trying to avoid something, and when the cart touched something in the dark the animal shied a little. Looking down, Diemschutz could see that the ground was not level, and with his whip he touched what he took to be a heap of dirt. It would not move. He struck a match and saw that it was a woman. He thought she must be drunk. Diemschutz went to the club and told some of the members that a woman was lying in the yard. Another man went to the yard door and struck another match. The body of the woman who lay on the ground was still warm, and blood was still oozing from her throat. She had no other injuries.

There was some confusion over her identity at the inquest, but the matter was resolved when she was recognized from a photograph by her thirty-year-old nephew, Constable Walter Frederick

Stride of the Clapham Division. Elizabeth Stride née Gustisson, a forty-five-year-old Swedish immigrant, otherwise known as Long Liz or Epileptic Annie, had married a carpenter by the name of John Thomas Stride in March 1869. Widowed in October 1884, and with no means of support, she became vulnerable to the evils that formed the very fabric of life in Whitechapel, and now she had died at the hands of its latest acquisition.

On seeing her body at the mortuary a reporter commented that 'she had a smile on her face as if she had died without a struggle'. His point of view was borne out by the fact that when she had been found she was still clutching a small bag of cachous in her left hand. What was certain was that her murderer had been disturbed. Diemschutz was probably in time to have reached out and touched the killer. But in the time it took to raise the alarm, Jack had made good his escape.

One can hardly begin to guess at the maniac's state of mind at this point. Whatever madness drove him on remained unsatisfied, his craving for blood unquenched – but not for long. He made his way towards the City and Mitre Square, where he met forty-three-year-old Catherine Eddowes. Earlier that evening she had been found lying drunk on the pavement in Aldgate High Street. Constable Lewis Robinson sat her up, but she fell down again. With some assistance he managed to take her to Bishopsgate police station where she had remained under lock and key until one o'clock.

Within three-quarters of an hour of the first murder she was dead, and this time her executioner found time to satiate his blood lust. As with his earlier victims he grabbed her by the neck, forcing her to the ground. Once her throat had been slit to the backbone, the frenzy which had brought her assailant this far rose to new heights of barbarism. He drove the knife deep into her stomach, laying open the walls from her pubis to her breastbone to draw out her intestines and dump them by her shoulder. He delved for deeper organs, and once again most of the uterus was removed together with two-thirds of the left kidney. Then he stabbed into her liver and groin before carving a diabolically clownish mask on the lifeless face of his victim. He cut off her right ear, slit her eyelids, lips and the bridge of her nose down to the cheek. He sliced off the tip of her nose, and cut a triangular flap of skin below each eye.

Then he doubled back towards Berner Street, with the City of London police in hot pursuit. In Goulston Street they discovered on a wall close to the bloody remnants of Catherine Eddowes's apron a message which read: 'The Juwes are The men That Will not be

Blamed for nothing.' Once again the Whitechapel murderer had slipped through their fingers, but at least a composite picture of the villain was beginning to emerge.

PC William Smith 452 H Division had been on his beat in Berner Street at about 12.35 a.m. and had noticed a man and a woman talking together only yards away from where Stride's body would be found at one o'clock. The twenty-six-year-old constable later confirmed that the corpse at the mortuary was the same woman. Her companion had been a man of about twenty-eight, five feet seven inches tall, respectable in appearance with no whiskers, wearing a dark cutaway coat and a dark felt deerstalker hat. And in his hand he had had a newspaper parcel about eighteen inches long by six to eight inches broad.

Ten minutes later, a respectable Hungarian Jew called Israel Schwartz was approaching the same spot when he noticed a man talking to a woman whom he later identified as Elizabeth Stride. The couple were arguing. The man threw the woman to the ground and she screamed three times, but apparently not very loudly. Schwartz crossed to the other side of the street so as not to get involved, and here he saw another man who was in the act of lighting a pipe. At this point the first man called out: 'Lipski!' Inspector Frederick George Abberline, reporting to the Home Office, explained that since a Jew named Lipski had been hanged for murder the previous year the name had become used as an insult, and, in his opinion, on this occasion it had been hurled at Israel Schwartz when he stopped to look at the man ill-using the woman. Schwartz, unable to speak a word of English and understandably alarmed, took fright and began to run away, and the man whom he had seen lighting his pipe also ran in the same direction. But whether this man was running after him or whether he had become equally alarmed, he could not say. Schwartz described the man who had been arguing with Stride as about thirty years of age and five feet five inches tall, with a fair complexion, dark hair, small brown moustache and a full face. He was broad-shouldered and was wearing a dark jacket and trousers with a black peaked cap.

Mrs Fanny Mortimer, who lived four doors from the scene of the tragedy at No. 36 Berner Street, said she had opened the door of her house at some time between 12.30 and 1 a.m. to get a breath of air:

I was standing at the door of my house nearly the whole time between half past twelve and one o'clock this [Sunday] morning and did not notice anything unusual. I had just gone indoors and was preparing to go to bed when I heard a commotion outside, and

17

immediately ran out thinking that there was another row at the Socialists' Club close by. I went to see what was the matter and was informed that another dreadful murder had been committed in the yard adjoining the clubhouse, and on going inside saw the body of a woman lying huddled up just inside the gates with her throat cut from ear to ear. A man touched her face and said it was quite warm, so that the deed must have been done while I was standing at the door of my house. There was certainly no noise made and I did not observe anyone enter the gates. It was soon after 1 o'clock when I went out, and the only man whom I had seen pass through the street previously was a young man carrying a black shiny bag who walked very fast down the street from the Commercial Road. He looked up at the Club, and then went round the corner by the Board School.

If Mrs Mortimer's evidence is taken at face value it would be conceivable that the newspaper parcel seen by PC Smith could have covered the black bag with which Mrs Mortimer's young man escaped. Could this covering have been a precaution against the bag itself becoming covered in blood? Was this how Jack the Ripper intended carrying away the selected organs of his victims?

It was a novel enough idea, except that Israel Schwartz had obviously seen two different men at the same spot ten minutes later than PC Smith, and the young man whom Mrs Mortimer had seen had almost certainly been twenty-two-year-old Leon Goldstein, who had voluntarily called at Leman Street police station to say that he had passed down Berner Street with a black bag at about that time. An hour earlier, Albert Bachert of the Vigilance Committee had got into conversation with a man in the Three Tuns Hotel in Aldgate. The stranger was a 'shabby genteel' sort of man, and was well dressed in black clothes. He wore a black felt hat and he also carried a black bag. He wanted to know what sort of loose women used the public bar and where did they go when they left. Bachert instinctively felt that he was up to no good, but at this time the black bag would have meant nothing. Bachert left him at about ten past twelve outside Aldgate railway station. Whatever the significance of this and many other such encounters, the doctor's bag had made its entrance and would now become an essential prop in the Ripper's performance, consolidating the opinion of many that he must be a medical man, and making it extremely unwise for anyone to be seen carrying such an item within five miles of Whitechapel.

Joseph Lawende, a commercial traveller, and his friends Joseph Levy and Harry Harris, were leaving the Imperial Club in Duke Street, Aldgate, at 1.30 a.m. when they noticed a man and a woman talking together in Church Passage about fifty yards from Mitre Square. The men saw no black bag, and of the three only Lawende was able to furnish the police with yet another description: a man about thirty, height five feet seven or eight, complexion fair, moustache fair, medium build; dressed in a pepper-and-salt colour loose jacket, grey peaked cloth cap and reddish neckerchief tied in a knot; he had the appearance of a sailor. The idea that Jack could have been a sailor was not new, but Lawende's description went a long way to consolidating the notion. It was a possibility that impressed Queen Victoria enough for her to write to the Home Secretary to ask if the cattle and passenger boats that regularly called at the East End docks had been searched – to which he dutifully replied that they had.

The more one looks at the likelihood of the Whitechapel murderer being a sailor, however, the less probable it becomes. To begin with, all the ships in port on the relevant days would have been easily ascertained and their crews questioned – as indeed they were. Secondly, anyone making such regular visits to the port of London would presumably have called at other destinations, and one would therefore expect similar murders to have occurred elsewhere, which was not the case. Also, it would have been almost impossible for any murderer to return to the cramped conditions of life on board without raising considerable suspicion. Most important of all is the fact that, of the three men who left the Imperial Club together, only Lawende was able to provide the police with a description, which was withheld at the inquest but eventually appeared in the *Police Gazette* alongside the equally contradictory descriptions of PC Smith and Israel Schwartz. Lawende had not seen the woman's face, and therefore asking him to identify Catherine Eddowes's corpse would have served no purpose. He was shown her clothes, however, and said he believed they were the same as those worn by the woman he had seen in the street.

Under the circumstances, one might wonder why the police gave Lawende's description so much credence, even allowing for the proximity of his man and woman to the scene of the crime. But the police themselves were clutching at straws by now, and were loath to reject anything that might open up a new line of inquiry. Even so, by the time the Acting Commissioner for the City police, Major Henry Smith, came to write his autobiography, *From Constable to Commissioner* in 1910, Lawende's description had once again metamorphosed into something more like the established portrait of a respectable gent, rather than a sailor. To all intents and purposes Smith has amalgamated various aspects of several portraits into a kind of 'Identikit':

> The description of the man given me by the German [Lawende] was as follows: Young, about the middle height, with a small fair moustache, dressed in something like navy serge, and with a deerstalker's cap – that is, a cap with a peak both fore and aft. I think the German spoke the truth, because I could not 'lead' him in any way. 'You will easily recognise him, then,' I said. 'Oh no!' he replied, 'I only had a short look at him.'

Jack the Ripper was probably not a sailor; though as an identifiable class of persons visiting seamen obviously deserved some consideration at the time. The slaughterman theory, on the other hand, was also popular and made more sense. Apart from the testimony of expert witness at the inquests, Whitechapel boasted several slaughterhouses. The cry of animals and the smell of their blood pervaded the area as it flowed into the gutters to be lapped by half-starved dogs and fat vermin. As the murders of Chapman and Eddowes had indicated a certain amount of anatomical knowledge rather than skill, a slaughterman would fit the bill perfectly.

Earlier, at Nichols's inquest on 1 September, a local surgeon named Rees Ralph Llewellyn, who had examined the body at the scene of the crime, had said: 'The murderer must have had some rough anatomical knowledge. He seems to have attacked all the vital parts.' One month later, at the inquest of Catherine Eddowes, a City of London police surgeon, Dr Frederick Gordon Brown, was asked for his opinion. He agreed that the killer had 'a great deal of knowledge of the position of the abdominal organs'. Pressing him further, the solicitor, Henry Homewood Crawford, asked: 'Would the extraction of the left kidney show great anatomical knowledge and skill?' to which the doctor again replied: 'Great knowledge of its position, for it is very easily overlooked.'

Clearly Crawford was trying to pin his expert witness down to a precise assessment of skill as opposed to mere knowledge, but Dr Brown would not be easily led. Finally he was asked: 'Would not such a knowledge be possessed by one accustomed to cutting up animals?' to which he replied, 'Yes.' Earlier, Dr George William Sequira, the first medical man to arrive at the scene of the crime, had also been asked if the assailant possessed any surgical skill, to which he had replied, 'No, I should say not.'

A practised hand or not, what was no longer in doubt was the fact that, as not all of Catherine Eddowes's uterus had been cut away, and the left kidney had been cut into, the organs would not have been of any professional use. The earlier supposition of the coroner at Annie Chapman's inquest, that someone could have been incited to kill in order to obtain valuable specimens, was now being weakened by the accumulating evidence of later events. If the murderer's objective was the removal of certain items for resale purposes, he had so far killed four women with the successful removal of the upper part of the vagina, two-thirds each of a bladder and a kidney, and just one whole uterus. These were hardly the actions of a skilled operator procuring saleable merchandise.

Robin Odell's *Jack the Ripper in Fact and Fiction*, published in 1965, was to expand the notion of Jack the Slaughterer and suggest that the killer was a Jewish ritual slaughterman, or *shochet*. Odell's argument appears as sound as any other. There are enough descriptions of the Ripper as a foreigner to allow the possibility that he could be a Jewish immigrant. The discovery of the chalked message in Goulston Street consolidated this idea. On the one hand many have argued that the anti-Semitic atmosphere in Whitechapel was almost certain to engender the belief that the monster in their midst was a Jew. Eye-witness accounts are notoriously unreliable at the best of times, and in a charged atmosphere the desire to point an accusatory finger at an offending minority is all too common. But on the other hand there was a large and growing Jewish population in Whitechapel which necessitated the kosher slaughter of animals under Talmudic law, and therefore living in the area were a number of highly trained Jewish clerics who possessed – according to Odell – an essential skill.

The author is of course making the assumption that Jack the Ripper demonstrated an unusual degree of skill in the perpetration of his crimes. But as other expert testimony would demonstrate, this was to become far from an established fact. A *shochet* possessed far more skill than was evident from the remains of Jack the Ripper's victims. Also, under Jewish law essential organs like the heart and lungs of the animal have to be examined as soon as the animal has been dispatched. If we are to accept that a man has embarked on a particular reign of terror because of some perverted religious mania – and this is inherent in Odell's argument – then we must expect him to perform the required ritual with the same dedication as he always has in the past. But most of the organs removed from the bodies were damaged in some way, and in none of the murders were the lungs or heart interfered with. Importantly, too, a *shochet*'s knife, a *khalef*, is a single-edged weapon rather like a steel ruler, and like a ruler it is cut square at the end. Expert opinion, on the other hand, was in total agreement about the kind of weapon used by the killer – a sharp-pointed knife at least five inches long. Odell is quite legitimately attempting to define the type of person that could have been responsible for the Whitechapel murders, rather than a specific individual, and in suggesting a Jewish *shochet* he is also supplying a possible motive.

Likewise William Stewart, writing in 1939, approaches the subject with the same aim in mind. In Stewart's case he plumps for Jill the Ripper, suggesting that the murders were carried out by a crazed abortionist. The idea was revamped by Arthur Butler in a series which ran in the *Sun* newspaper in 1972. In fact the notion that the assassin could have been a woman was first mooted by an eminent Victorian surgeon named Lawson Tait as early as 1889; he settled for a 'big, strong woman who had been engaged at a slaughter-house in cleaning up, and who also, now and then, had helped to cut up the meat'. But there is no evidence and it is anyway extremely unlikely that Jack the Ripper was a woman for the simple fact that such psychopathic tendencies have always been virtually unknown in women. Such conjectures remain at best a possibility and no more, just as the case against a more patrician suspect is not made appreciably stronger by the fact that he may have learnt to disembowel stags whilst hunting in Scotland.

Nevertheless the coroner, Wynne Baxter, summing up at the inquest of Annie Chapman, was to fall into the same trap by suggesting, when the available evidence was far from conclusive, that the murderer would need to know more than a mere slaughterer of animals. Even now his conclusion was: 'It must have been someone accustomed to a post mortem room', and again the inference was that someone of comparatively low status – a mortuary assistant rather than a qualified practitioner – may have been responsible for the outrages. But as can be seen from that first Jack the Ripper letter, the doctor theory was gaining ground despite the reluctance of professional men like Wynne Baxter and Henry Crawford to accept that someone of their own social standing could be reponsible for such carnage.

Within three days of the double killing the police had published and widely circulated a facsimile poster of this letter, together with a postcard sent to the Central News Agency on 30 September, only hours after the 'double event'. The card read:

I was not codding dear old Boss when I gavé you the tip. You'll hear about Saucy Jack's work tomorrow. Double event this time. Number one squealed a bit. Couldn't finish straight off. Had not time to get ears for police. Thanks for keeping last letter back till I got to work again.

JACK THE RIPPER

In the following weeks the police received literally thousands of letters, mostly signed 'Jack the Ripper', whilst others poured into the Central News Agency and the Fleet Street offices of the national press. Theories blossomed as to the character of the assassin and ways in which he might be apprehended. There were letters urging the use of bloodhounds, and others signed: 'One more unfortunate', 'A Mariner' and 'One Who Knows' from correspondents who believed that a register of strangers and a tighter control of those staying in common lodging houses ought to be implemented. Still more suggested that the police should be issued with rubber boots to avoid being heard, and 'An Old Detective' was not alone in recommending that officers should be dressed in women's clothing in order to catch the murderer red-handed. There were calls to employ the services of known spiritualists and psychics of every shade and description, and pleas to search the sewers and to close off all the 'dark unfrequented corners' that might have been 'designed purposely for murderous work'.

Again the question of rewards was raised, and much regret was expressed about the Home Secretary's apparent apathy. 'A Poor Woman' asked: 'Does this unpopular but powerful Minister think that because the victims belong to the class termed unfortunate they are of no account? What would he have done if the poor creatures had been rich and titled dames of the West-End?' One correspondent, 'Wideawake', was of the opinion that the police would never unravel the mystery unless the Government supplemented the private rewards on offer by promising a free pardon to any accomplice who would confess to a 'guilty knowledge' of the assassinations. It was indeed a radical proposition, yet one which was soon to be implemented by the same Home Secretary who had so steadfastly refused to sanction an official inducement.

Clearly, the pressure on the Government to do something about the situation was becoming intense. Not only was Jack the Ripper's continued liberty proving something of an embarrassment to the

Metropolitan police, but his activities were also drawing public attention to much wider issues, as George Bernard Shaw had so astutely pointed out. In the week following the murders of Stride and Eddowes a petition addressed to Queen Victoria had been sent to the Home Secretary by Mrs Henrietta Barnett, wife of the crusading Samuel Augustus Barnett, vicar of St Jude's, Whitechapel. It drew the Queen's attention to the vice and poverty in Whitechapel, and begged her to call on her servants in authority to implement laws which were already in existence to close the 'bad houses' within whose walls 'men and women were being ruined in body and soul'. Mrs Barnett received a somewhat sterile reply from Whitehall, which prompted a concerned Queen to request that her petitioners should know how much she personally sympathized with their objectives despite the dryness of the official answer – a clear indication that even Her Majesty was beginning to lose patience. The Home Secretary was under siege from every quarter. On 18 October two hundred Whitechapel traders sent a further petition to the Home Secretary, pleading with him greatly to increase the number of police in the district in order to remove the insecurity which was destroying commercial life. Only the omnibus companies, it would seem, were thriving in the present climate. *The Daily Telegraph* reported that many people were now taking a trip from the West End through Whitechapel and back on the tops of omnibuses, just to say that they had passed through the scene of the tragedies.

At night the area once again fell under the sinister spell of the unseen magician. Streets once busy now echoed to the measured tread of more and more plain-clothed and uniformed police. Beats were reorganized or shortened, and detectives took to disguising themselves in all manner of ways. Men lurked in the shadows to observe the known haunts of prostitutes, whilst others shadowed any suspicious person they might come across until they were sure of their innocence. One enterprising journalist who took it upon himself to dress as a woman managed to avoid detection for some hours until his masculine stride attracted the attention of an observant police constable named Ludwig. 'Stop! Are you not a man?' inquired the constable. The amateur detective admitted that he was, and the officer then asked: 'Are you one of us?' The honest reporter admitted that he was not and was subsequently marched off to Leman Street police station before being released 'to resume his proper habiliments'.

A far more viable, if irresponsible, arrangement was the actual use of women as decoys. Often they were prostitutes who were instructed not to repulse any man but to go with him in the knowledge that help was at hand should their client attempt to harm them. One such 'unfortunate' told a reporter from the *Pall Mall Gazette*: 'I have only to die once, and I'd not mind being murdered by Jack the Ripper if it led to the brute being caught. The people speak so kind and sypathisin' too about the women he has killed, and I'd not object to being ripped up by him to be talked about so nice after I'm dead. And better sudden death than sudden starvation.'

Reason was being lost to rumour and intrigue, which in itself was exciting the curiosity of a much wider audience. There had been many murders before, of course, but this was a new kind of crime – unheard of and unspeakable. A cunning monster was abroad, seeking out his victims for a very special pleasure, and even the worst excesses of cheap fiction had failed to appreciate truly the sexually motivated frenzy that was now finding ample expression on the back streets of Whitechapel and Spitalfields.

Like so many sciences, the study of human behaviour was in its infancy in the 1880s, and it would take several decades before the pioneering work of innovators like Freud and Jung would lead to our greater understanding of human sexuality – its psychological origins and its manifestations. In *Sexual Anomalies and Perversions*, published originally in 1946, Dr Magnus Hirschfield wrote: 'In genuine cases of sexual murder the killing replaces the sexual act. There is, therefore, no sexual intercourse at all, and sexual pleasure is induced by cutting, stabbing, and slashing the victim's body, ripping open her abdomen, plunging the hands into her intestines, cutting out and taking away her genitals, throttling her, and sucking her blood.' In time Jack the Ripper would become the progenitor of a whole genus of depraved killers, but in 1888 his murderous perversion was perceived as uniquely remarkable – so much so that the attention of the world was beginning to focus on this London stage.

III

At about a quarter to eleven on the morning of Friday, 9 November, a shop assistant called Thomas Bowyer, otherwise known as Indian Harry, entered Miller's Court. Close by the narrow, arched opening a ripped poster offering Mr S. Montagu's £100 for information leading to the arrest of the Whitechapel murderer added a touch of irony to the occasion. Bowyer had been sent by his employer, John McCarthy, to try to collect some overdue rent from the tenant at No. 13, a comely Irish girl from Limerick called Mary Jane Kelly. When he knocked on the door there was no answer. He knocked again, but still there was no reply. He tried the door – it was locked. A muslin curtain was drawn across the window on the end wall of the building just to the left of the door, and some rags had been stuffed into a hole where one of the two panes of glass had been broken. Bowyer put his hand through the hole and drew the curtain aside. What appeared to be two pieces of flesh were lying on a table in front of the bed, and as his eyes grew accustomed to the light the full realization of what had happened dawned on him. Bowyer ran back to his employer, who was standing on the steps of his chandler's shop at No. 27 Dorset Street, and told him what he had seen. McCarthy ran to the house himself, but the sight that now greeted him was far worse than anything that Bowyer had described.

Together the two men went to the Commercial Street police station and informed Inspector Walter Beck of what they had seen. The inspector immediately accompanied them back to Miller's Court, collecting as many constables as he could on the way. At

11.15 Dr Bagster Phillips arrived and, having satisfied himself that the mutilated corpse was not in need of any 'immediate attention', waited as other officials began to gather. At 11.30 Inspector Frederick George Abberline arrived, but as bloodhounds had already been sent for the decision was taken not to enter the room. In the City crowds had been gathering all day to enjoy the annual spectacle of the Lord Mayor's parade, but already the news from Whitechapel was beginning to cause more excitement than any of the planned festivities. At about 1.30 Superintendent Thomas Arnold arrived at the scene of the crime to instruct his anxious colleagues that, as the dogs would not now be coming, the room should be entered. Unaware that the door had not been locked with a key, or that the spring lock which automatically held it shut when it was closed to could be opened via the broken window, the superintendent ordered the door to be forced. McCarthy split it open with a pickaxe.

What had been Mary Jane Kelly was lying on the bed virtually naked, and her throat had been cut from ear to ear right back to the spinal chord. Her abdomen had been ripped open and the face slashed beyond recognition. Her nose, breasts and ears had been cut off and placed, together with flesh from her legs, on the bedside table. The left arm, like the head, was attached to her body by the skin only. Her forehead had been skinned and her thighs defleshed to the bone. Her liver and other organs had been placed between her legs, and one hand had been thrust into her stomach cavity.

Certainly the authorities were loath to let the full facts be known. This was borne out by a statement in *The Daily Telegraph* which said that it had it on good authority that 'a portion of the bodily organs was missing', even though the medical evidence given at the inquest had stated the opposite. What was not in dispute was that Mary Kelly had been three months pregnant at the time of her murder.

According to Constable Walter Dew, who later achieved fame as the inspector who arrested Dr Crippen, he had been at Commerical Street police station chatting to Inspector Beck when Thomas Bowyer had arrived with the news. Later, writing in his autobiography *I Caught Crippen*, he was to recall how Inspector Beck had staggered back from the broken window with his face as white as a sheet. 'For God's sake, Dew,' he had cried. 'Don't look.' But he ignored the order, and when his eyes had grown accustomed to the light he saw a sight which he would not forget until his dying day.

Dew may well have been a witness to the horrific discovery in

27

Miller's Court, but there are enough discrepancies in the renowned detective's colourful account to suspect him of having employed journalistic licence in the retelling of his particular involvement. Nevertheless there can be no doubt that the impact on anyone who was unfortunate enough to look into that gruesome hovel that day would defy any amount of exaggeration. Dew said he had slipped on the miasmic 'awfulness' on the floor, and he felt as if someone had given him a tremendous blow in the stomach. But the sight that was to remain most vividly with him was 'the poor woman's eyes'. They were wide open, and seemed to be staring at him with a look of terror. 'Never in my life have I funked a police duty so much as I funked this one,' he admitted; and who could have blamed him – Mary Jane Kelly's killer had done enough to ensure Jack the Ripper's notoriety for all time.

On 10 November Queen Victoria sent the following cypher telegram to her Prime Minister, Lord Salisbury: 'This new most ghastly murder shows the absolute necessity for some very decided action. All these courts must be lit, and our detectives improved. They are not what they should be. You promised, when the first murder took place, to consult with your colleagues about it.' Salisbury's reply in a similarly coded telegram began: 'At Cabinet today it was resolved to issue a Proclamation offering free pardon to anyone who should give evidence as to the recent murder except the actual perpetrator of the crime. . . .'

In recent years much has been made about Victoria's possible involvement with the Whitechapel murders, and some commentators, notably Stephen Knight, have suggested that she may even have known who the actual perpetrator was. The line in her telegram, 'You promised, when the first murder took place, to consult with your colleagues about it', was interpreted as meaning that the Queen had intimate knowledge of the first Ripper murder, that of Mary Nichols, and may even have been protecting her grandson, Prince Albert Victor.

This, however, is a complete misinterpretation of the ascertainable facts. To begin with, an entry in Victoria's private journal, dated 4 October 1888, refers to the 'dreadful murders of unfortunate women of a bad class. There were six, with horrible mutilations.' Written as this was, before the murder of Mary Jane Kelly, it clearly shows that the Queen had been concerned about the inadequate lighting in Whitechapel as early as April, when Emma Smith had been murdered. Mrs Barnett's petition had further

28

disturbed her, and now this new murder had convinced her of the need for 'some very decided action'. Writing to Henry Matthews, the Home Secretary, on the 13 November, she was to inquire further: 'Have the cattle-boats and passenger boats been examined? Has any investigation been made as to the number of single men occupying rooms to themselves? The murderer's clothes must be saturated with blood and must be kept somewhere. Is there sufficient surveillance at night?' Obviously Queen Victoria had no idea who the Whitechapel murderer was. The questions above not only testify to her genuine desire to see the perpetrator tracked down and identified as soon as possible, but demonstrate the nature of the intrigue that was now being generated by this one man's continued liberty.

In future years both amateurs and professionals would continue to try to make some sense of the complex possibilities inherent in this particular series of crimes by manipulating the imponderables at their disposal, often with amazing ingenuity. This has been more fundamental to the growth of the legend than any amount of re-examination based on the evidence available at the time.

Where did this leave us, the writers of this book? Most of those who have ventured in the past to opt for a particular suspect have been torn apart limb from limb, and their dry bones littered the path we were now on. But some survivors remained, and quite naturally we now turned our attention to them, corroborating their conclusions where we could and instigating our own areas of research where we could not.

We were not setting out deliberately to undermine the efforts of others any more than we were hoping to support a particular hypothesis, but we were not inclined to accept anything as fact unless the author's claim could be verified. So we began to spend more and more time at the Public Record Office and Newspaper Library, whilst the reading room of the British Library had become affectionately known as our club. But although we gradually came to understand the historical reality of those ten weeks in 1888 when five derelict women lost their lives at the hand of an unknown assassin, much of the truth remained shrouded in a fog. Even the number of 'events', as these appalling barbarities are euphemistically referred to, is open to question. And what about motive, and the perpetrator's evasion of discovery and arrest? Even the murderer's skill with the knife remains an unresolved topic for debate.

Reporting the findings of his post mortem on Mary Jane Kelly, Dr Thomas Bond took the opportunity of giving his opinion on the four previous murders: 'In each case the mutilation was implicated [*sic*] by a person who had no scientific nor anatomical knowledge. In my opinion he does not even possess the technical knowledge of a butcher or horse slaughterman or any person accustomed to cut up dead animals.' This view, from a lecturer on forensic medicine and consultant surgeon to the Metropolitan Police A Division, has to be taken as seriously as any other; and although there were other indications which support the still widely held belief that Jack the Ripper could have been a doctor or surgeon, the pathological evidence is far from conclusive.

The discovery of Mary Jane Kelly's murder left the nation clamouring for the perpetrator's apprehension, but it was not to be. The pitch of excitement that had been sustained for the past three months slowly began to subside until another woman was found murdered eight months later. In his autobiography *Days of My Years*, published in 1914, Sir Melville Macnaghten – who had become head of the CID in 1903 – states that 'The Whitechapel murderer committed five murders, and – to give the devil his due – no more'. (The last was Mary Jane Kelly on 9 November.) But it is difficult to accept that the murders could have ceased unless the culprit had either left the country, died or been confined in a lunatic asylum. It is certainly ludicrous to suppose that he just got better!

The first of these three schools of thought allowed the legend to infect the rest of the world. Soon America, Spain, Italy, Holland, Germany and many other countries would be able to boast their own candidate for the title. And whilst most can be readily derided, it was still a reasonable proposition that Jack might have left these shores to spread his gospel elsewhere.

The second eventuality opened up a far more wriggly can of worms. On the one hand, the possibility that Jack had died a natural or accidental death precluded any opportunity of discovering his identity. On the other hand, considering the nature of the crimes and the increasing fury of the attacks it was all too plausible that the killer's mind finally gave way and he committed suicide. Again, Macnaghten inclines to this belief, which is in itself interesting for it allows the further possibility that the police could have known (or at least suspected) the killer's identity but were ethically constrained to reveal his name after his death. This, however, does not seem likely.

The Metropolitan and City forces were desperate to salvage their reputations. Over three months this unknown madman had tested their credibility almost to destruction. Under such circumstances it is very hard to believe that they would not have issued a statement to the effect that a man suspected of being the Whitechapel murderer was now dead, and that whilst his identity would remain secret the likelihood of further atrocities was considerably reduced.

Just such a precedent was set following a series of murders in 1964–65. The circumstances surrounding the Thames nude murders were remarkably similar to those of the Whitechapel series. Six prostitutes were strangled in a series of sexually motivated killings, and their naked bodies dumped in various Thames-side areas. Then the killings stopped as suddenly as they had begun. The CID had strong suspicions as to the identity of the murderer, who had by now committed suicide; but the man's name has never been revealed, nor did the public or press expect it to be.

The third supposition, that Jack the Ripper was confined in an asylum would almost certainly mean that his guilt could be ascertained – if not immediately, then over a period of time. Once again, the coincidence of his incarceration and the cessation of the crimes would surely have allowed the authorities eventually to issue a statement.

On 7 July 1889 the body of Alice Mackenzie was found in Castle Alley, Whitechapel. She was of the same profession as the other victims, and although there was some abdominal wounding she was discovered with her throat stabbed rather than slit. Expert opinion at the time was divided, but if this had been the work of the Ripper he had obviously changed not only his *modus operandi* but also the pattern and ferocity of his attack.

Chief Commissioner James Monro, who quickly arrived at the scene, had no doubt that this was an isolated crime and not the work of the man who had butchered Mary Jane Kelly eight months earlier in a diabolical bloodbath. And unless one totally disregards the evidence inherent in the established pattern of the earlier murders, and disregards today's greater understanding of well-defined patterns of psychopathic behaviour, it seems fairly obvious that had Jack the Ripper been disturbed – and this can be the only logical explanation why he left Alice Mackenzie in a relatively respectable condition – he would almost certainly have needed to find another victim, as he did on the night of the double event.

As it turned out, no more women were to be found murdered in Whitechapel until the naked trunk of a female body was discovered underneath the Pinchin Street railway arches in September of that year. Unless one accepts, without any justification, that the cunning animal who the previous autumn had created a pattern and style of murder all of his own had changed his spots, there can be little doubt that neither of these crimes can be attributed to the Ripper.

For the same reason, poisoners like George Chapman and Dr Thomas Neill Cream must also be regarded as unlikely candidates, even though their claims have been zealously pursued by their advocates. Cream was actually in Joliet Prison, Chicago at the time, which is as good an alibi as anyone could wish for. And whereas the case against George Chapman (real name Severin Klosowski) is superficially stronger on account of the fact that he was living in Whitechapel and working as a *feldscher* – a barber-surgeon – at the time of the murders, his murderous reign almost certainly did not begin until he poisoned his first wife in 1897. His second and third wives were to end up the same way before he was eventually arrested and executed in 1903. His ability to carry on a seemingly normal heterosexual relationship with several women over a long period of time, together with the fact that he poisoned all of his victims with antimony, demonstrates an entirely different personality from the one that found such desperate expression on the streets of Spitalfields and Whitechapel.

By now we were confident that Jack the Ripper had killed only five women, with just the remotest of possibilities that either Martha Tabram and/or Alice Mackenzie could also have died by the same hand. This being so, it was intriguing to wonder why others had sought to expand the number even further. Intriguing, that is, until one considers that the final tally of Ripper victims can in itself be of considerable import to a particular hypothesis. For instance the inclusion of Alice Mackenzie's murder on 7 July 1889 automatically diminishes the argument of those whose case partly rests on 'the fact' that their Jack the Ripper was committed to an asylum, or died, or left the country shortly after the murder of Mary Jane Kelly on 9 November 1888. And by the same token the inclusion of Martha Tabram as a victim strengthens the case against George Chapman, who had a hairdressing business in George Yard at the time of her murder.

Michael Harrison must claim the current record for the greatest number of victims attributed to the Ripper by a modern writer. He has suggested that ten women were killed by the Ripper between 2 April 1888 and 22 November 1889. This author needs ten victims – or at least ten potential victims – as his particular suspect had been responsible for writing a bawdy poem in which 'Ten harlots of Jerusalem' figure prominently.

But rather than seek to increase the number – and as many as fourteen victims have been attributed to Jack in the past – it is far more reasonable to argue that the murder of Elizabeth Stride off Berner Street, just three-quarters of an hour before the body of Catherine Eddowes was discovered in Mitre Square, could have been perpetrated by someone else. The Ripper's total would thus be reduced to four. Dr Bagster Phillips was of this opinion, although it was not shared by any of his colleagues or the police. To accept this as an unrelated incident one has to allow for the considerable geographical and chronological coincidence of the two crimes, and dismiss the fact that the nature and ferocity of the attack were virtually identical with the two previous murders. Had Jack not been disturbed so soon, the scene that would have greeted Dr Bagster Phillips would probably have left him in little doubt as to its author. And when one considers the diabolical orgy of destruction that took place in Mitre Square one can readily accept that a pyschopathic killer like Jack the Ripper might well have been stimulated to a new height of frenzy by the very fact that he had been disturbed during the climax of his earlier attack on Stride.

If the Whitechapel murderer had been brought to justice – so the argument goes – his notoriety would have died with him on the gallows, and his crimes would have been seen as a series of horrific but otherwise unremarkable murders to be quickly and unregrettably relegated to a footnote in the annals of crime. But it was clear from the available literature, with which we had now familiarized ourselves, that the mystery surrounding this unknown killer had generated far more intriguing questions than just: Who was he?

Alexander Kelly's invaluable *Jack the Ripper: A Bibliography and Review of the Literature* clearly demonstrated the amount of literary and artistic attention that had been lavished on this madman for one reason or another. Apart from the two hundred or so theories and countless newspaper articles concerned with the mystery itself there were at least the same number of items of music, drama and film that derived their inspiration directly from the legend. The common denominator in all these works was still the identity – or rather the anonymity – of a killer whose life, once judicially weighed, would have been tossed into obscurity. Every relevant publication owed its existence directly or indirectly to the intrigue generated by this one man's spectral charisma, and whilst some merely documented the available evidence for the benefit of readers who wanted to make up their own minds, there were many more that promised positive identification of the culprit.

Leonard Matters's *The Mystery of Jack the Ripper*, originally published in 1929, makes one of the earliest attempts both to uncover the identity of the murderer and to supply a strong motive. As the springboard for his hypothesis Matters is obliged to rely on the unsupportable deathbed confession of a certain Dr Stanley in Buenos Aires. But it takes the reader very little effort to realize that, having researched his subject to the best of his ability, the author has been forced to resort to a plausibly dramatic but fictional account to give expression to what is little more than his own particular hunch. In this sense the book is still of interest, and possibly of value, but more than anything it was inadvertently – in its desire to uncover the truth – supplying yet another facet to the already monstrous legend.

Dr Stanley was supposed to have been an eminent Harley Street surgeon who was cast into the depths of despair following the premature death of his young wife. Only the hope of a bright future for his adored son saved the brilliant doctor from himself, and as time passed his life blossomed with his growing love for the boy. Then one day the young Stanley – handsome, talented, with a bright future before him – met a young and pretty girl called Mary Jane Kelly, from whom he soon contracted syphilis and died insane. What happens next requires little imagination. Dr Stanley sets about avenging his son's death, and, having finally contented himself by finding and ripping apart his son's paramour, he takes himself off to Buenos Aires to live out his life in peace.

One hardly needs to repeat that the above explanation is pure fantasy, but it is surprising how many elements of this story turn up in later theories. The eminent West End surgeon constantly recurs in various guises, as does the possibility that Mary Jane Kelly could have been the only intended victim of the Ripper. At least this notion would explain the cessation of the murders after her death, although it also begs the question as to why four middle-aged hags should be killed before her. If the murderer was so indiscriminate to begin with, why stop now? In trying to establish the identity of the killer, Matters has obviously fallen victim to the power of the legend he hoped to solve; but his attempt to supply a motive based on his understanding of the crimes themselves is not so easily dismissed. Again, it is an element in the mystery which constantly recurs in later works.

The scourge of syphilis was to shock the moral ranks of Victorian prudery. At the turn of the century, it was estimated that in London alone one and a half million fresh cases were reported every twelve months. Many doctors had called the disease 'the great imitator', on account of its wide range of symptoms which resembled a number of varied ailments. Syphilis was often found masquerading as chronic nephritis, cirrhosis of the liver, diseases of the aorta and many nervous conditions, particularly those in which the patient went insane. It knew no social barriers, and often resulted in madness and death. At that date there was no effective cure, and apparently no way of preventing the disease's spread. The parallel with the movement of the AIDS virus in our society today is remarkable. But admitting that there was a problem to begin with was impossible for the God-fearing, church-going Victorian middle classes, who covered the legs of their pianos and swept the filth of places like Whitechapel under their drawing room carpets rather than accept responsibility for their own human desire and weakness. Dr Stanley was no more than a projected character – a cypher for his creator's intuition; but the suggested motive for the crimes themselves could certainly have something to do with the disease that was ravaging nineteenth-century England.

In January 1987 a prostitute in London's Soho was repeatedly stabbed in the chest and abdomen. Her murderer escaped. The police statement to the media was immediate: he would probably strike again, an assessment born of a society grown used to the phenomenon of serial murders and of a police force used – unlike their Victorian counterpart – to recognizing the symptoms of an attack by a psychopath and the possible motives for the killer's malevolence toward a certain type of woman. Universally, the media declared: 'Vice Killing – Ripper hunt. Prostitute killer could be a victim of AIDS.'

In 1970 another contribution to the Ripper legend again embroiled in the saga of an eminent (and this time actual) surgeon, Sir William Withey Gull, who was Physician in Ordinary to Queen Victoria. Dr Thomas Stowell's suspect for the Whitechapel murders would turn out to be not only a syphilitic patient of Sir William's but the heir presumptive to the throne of England, HRH Prince Albert Victor Christian Edward, Duke of Clarence and Avondale. We shall look at Dr Stowell's theory more closely later, but it is intriguing to note here how elements of Matters's original theory were continuing to survive through the imaginative intuition of later writers.

According to Stephen Knight, the Whitechapel murderer had been not one but three people, most notably Sir William Gull himself, who under the veil of masonic ritual killing had finally succeeded in silencing Mary Jane Kelly, who had witnessed the illicit wedding between Prince Albert Victor and a Roman Catholic shop assistant, Annie Elizabeth Crook. His motive: quite simply to protect the Royal Family and the Establishment from a scandal it might not have survived. An eminent surgeon is again vital to Knight's plot. Syphilis plays no part in the production, but the ill-fated love affair survives, with Mary Jane Kelly being revealed as the hapless and only intended victim.

It was an astonishing tale and one which was to dominate our outlook for many months to come. 'The truth about Jack the Ripper is ugly,' proclaims the author. 'Many would rather not hear it, others will revile it. But it is the truth.' The main question was not whether Leonard Matters had inadvertently touched the truth, but was our inherited mystery the legacy of some sort of conspiracy to suppress the facts? And had Stephen Knight actually arrived in shining armour to slay the beast once and for all?

IV

Like so many 'solutions', Stephen Knight's relied on the word of a third person. In this case it was Joseph Sickert, supposedly the natural son of the artist Walter Sickert, who was already deeply incriminated in the Ripper murders if Joseph's story is true. Not only had he been responsible for bringing the Prince and Annie together, but he had to have been totally *au fait* with the circumstances of the death of the five women in a way which could only deeply incriminate him, for he lived to tell his tale to Joseph in extraordinary detail.

Three years before the publication of Knight's book in 1976, Joseph Sickert's story came to the attention of the BBC. He subsequently appeared, in August 1973, in the final episode of the six-part television series *Jack the Ripper* to tell his story for himself. Two years later, in 1975, it surfaced for the first time in print in a commendable publication called *The Ripper File* by Elwyn Jones and John Lloyd.

Based on the original television dramatization, the investigation is entrusted to the two fictional BBC Television detectives, Barlow and Watt, and although the style is essentially dramatic fiction most of the content of the book is entirely factual. It is predominantly a dossier, and as such does not try to prove a particular theory but sets great store on the available testimony of eye witnesses, medical reports and police files. In this sense Joseph's story plays a comparatively minor part in the investigation, but it is important because it lends some weight to Barlow and Watt's growing conviction that the authorities had to know more about the identity of the Whitechapel murderer than they were admitting. The following is a transcript of Joseph's original story, as told to the BBC.

My name is Joseph Sickert. My father was the painter Walter Sickert. When I was a small boy I can remember my mother telling me over and over again that I had to be careful not to say or do anything which would give the police or the authorities any reason to question me or any excuse for them to take me away. She said that my grandmother had suffered terribly at the hands of the authorities. And that a servant died in a terrible way. And that I had to be very careful. I just thought it was another story that adults tell. A sort of 'If you don't behave the bogey man will get you'.

Then when I was older, in my teens, I asked my father about the story. Eventually he told me a story that I didn't really believe. He didn't mention names but he told it as a sort of fairy story.

'Once upon a time there was a Prince, a girl the Prince loved, a baby girl, and her nurse and an artist. The Prince's mother asked the artist to show the Prince the world of art. In that world, the Prince met a Catholic girl and fell in love with her. They had a child – a girl. Then a little later they got married.

But the Prime Minister heard about the wedding and was very worried because the Prince was a Royal Prince and the bride was a poor girl and a Catholic. The bride was taken away and confined to hospital. And she died without ever seeing her Prince or her child again.

The child was looked after by a servant who disappeared, taking the child with her. But she told a friend of hers about the child she was caring for and who its father was. Important people got to hear of it. And the Royal doctor was asked to find the woman and silence her. With some other people's help he did find her and she was killed. To cover up the search for her the doctor killed the other women so that no one would ask why this one woman was killed. The child was looked after, though, by the artist and eventually they fell in love. They had a child, a boy.

That was how my father told me the story first of all. I kept on nagging him and asking questions about it and eventually I broke down his reserve. He said, 'Your grandfather was the Duke of Clarence.' I laughed and he said. 'It's no laughing matter. It's a bit of a mess because you're all bloody Catholics.' And then he told me the whole story.

When Eddy, the Duke of Clarence, was twenty, his mother [Princess Alexandra] thought it would be a good idea if he met artists and writers as well as just the usual people who made up Court circles at the time. So she arranged for him to meet the painter, Walter Sickert, whose family had been painters to her own Royal

Court of Denmark. At that time Walter Sickert lived in the Cleveland Street area. The whole area around there was a little village in itself – a mixture of artists, aristocrats, and shopkeepers – a bit like Chelsea after the War.

When Prince Edward went there during his vacation from Cambridge he was passed off as Sickert's younger brother. He also met one of the shop girls who used to model for Sickert. A girl called Ann Elizabeth Crook who worked in the tobacconist's shop. She was very beautiful. In fact, she looked like Eddy's mother. Eddy fell in love with her. She became pregnant. They also went through a ceremony of marriage at St Saviour's private chapel in 1888.

The two lovers, Clarence and Ann Elizabeth, were parted after a police raid on a party in Cleveland Street. Ann Elizabeth was in Guy's Hospital for 156 days before being put in a smaller hospital at 367 Fulham Road. She was supposed to be mentally ill. She was kept in the Fulham Road hospital until her death in 1921.

The servant girl also disappeared at the same time. Her name was Mary Kelly.

The little girl, Alice Margaret, was then looked after by old Walter Sickert with the help of various local friends. One day when she was about seven years old in 1892, a woman friend was taking her for a walk in Drury Lane. A carriage ran the child down. The driver of the carriage was recognised as John Netley, a man who had been used as an outside coachman by Clarence on his visits to Sickert. A man who would know the story of the lovers and their child – and their Irish servant girl, Mary Kelly.

The child, Alice Margaret, was fortunate. After a spell in Charing Cross Hospital she recovered from her injuries. Mary Kelly was not so lucky. She was, of course, a Catholic girl, and she was known to the nuns of the convent in nearby Harewood Place. She went first of all to their sister convent which was in the East End. What then happened was that various people high in Government and the Royal Household became very worried indeed about the possibility of news getting out that the heir presumptive to the throne of England had married, had had a child, and that the child had been born of a Catholic mother. You have to remember it was a time when the possibility of revolution was thought to be a very real one – and the problems and violence surrounding Ireland were at their height.

It was decided that Mary Jane Kelly would have to be silenced. The operation was undertaken by the driver, John Netley, who was a coachman who had regularly driven Clarence although he wasn't on the official Palace staff, and by the Royal physician, Sir William Gull.

To conceal the dangerous motive behind Mary Kelly's death – and the inquiries they were making for her, she was killed as the last of five women in a way that made it look like the random work of a madman. The child, however, survived. She was protected by Walter Sickert – and had two sons by him. The first one was Charles, who disappeared at the age of two about 1911 – I am the other son.

Looked at from this viewpoint, the story seems palpably ludicrous. The fact that the Whitechapel murders had a more profound effect on the *status quo* than the ramblings of illiterate, gin-sodden prostitutes could ever have seems to have escaped the storyteller, as indeed it must the United Grand Lodge of England. But Knight tells his tale persuasively and with great conviction. It all depends on whether one accepts the word of Joseph Sickert, which largely depends on how far his claims could be verified. This, as it happens, is precisely what Knight says he intends to do.

Nevertheless there was something very deeply disturbing in Joseph Sickert's story, and even more so in Stephen Knight's version of it. It was not because of the idea that agents of the Crown or State might resort to such measures to protect the *status quo* – far from it. Few people today would doubt the will of any powerful group to maintain its position at almost any cost, and the constant stream of examples of political expediency continues to remind us of the chasm that exists between government 'done' and government 'seen to be done'. By the same token, one could not be surprised to learn that one or two members of our Royal Family have in the past been found wanting in their moral responsibilities. The royal bastard was not an uncommon phenomenon.

What was ultimately disturbing about the story was its total illogicality. Who married them? Where is the marriage certificate? Was there a best man, bridesmaids, guests? If there was to be a scandal, it surely would be incubated by those in a position to spread the word later – Walter Sickert himself, the priest, 'Eddy's' friends. But five East End prostitutes? And masonic ritual?

Before going any further, however, it is important to mention here the discrepancies between Joseph's story and the one spread by Walter Sickert himself during his lifetime. Even Stephen Knight has to accede to its veracity, quoting Sickert's friend, Marjorie Lilly, who remembered him as 'a strange, compelling and complicated man'. She said: 'He had a passion for conversation and naturally took centre stage at any gathering without realising he did so. His fascination with the Ripper case was intense and I thought perhaps he knew the truth.' Osbert Sitwell went further and recorded Sickert's account in his introduction to *A Free House!*, an anthology of Sickert's writings:

Some years after the murders he [Walter Sickert] had taken a room in a London suburb. An old couple looked after the house and when he had been there some months the woman, with whom he often used to talk, asked him one day, as she was dusting the room, if he knew who had occupied it before him. When he said 'No', she had waited a moment and then replied, 'Jack the Ripper?' . . .

Her story was that his predecessor had been a veterinary student. After he had been a month or two in London, this delicate-looking young man – he was consumptive – took to occasionally staying out all night. His landlord and landlady would hear him come in about six in the morning and then walk about his room for an hour or two, until the first edition of the morning paper was on sale, when he would creep lightly downstairs and run to the corner to buy one.

Quietly he would return and go to bed. But an hour later, when the old man called him, he would notice, by the traces in the fireplace, that his lodger had burnt the suit that he had been wearing the previous evening. For the rest of the day the millions of people in London would be discussing the terrible new murder, plainly belonging to the same series, that had been committed in the small hours. Only the student seemed never to mention them: but then he knew no one and talked to no one, though he did not seem lonely . . . the old couple did not know what to make of it: daily his health grew worse and it seemed improbable that this gentle, ailing, silent youth should be responsible for such crimes. They could hardly credit their own senses and then, before they could make up their own minds whether to warn the police or not, the lodger's health had suddenly grown much worse and his mother, a widow who was devoted to him, had come to fetch him back to Bournemouth where she lived. . . . From that moment the murders stopped. He died three months later.

To Knight's mind, Sickert's *invented* solution served two purposes: 'It satisfied his unending need to chatter on about the Ripper and over many years it provided him with an entertaining after-dinner yarn that automatically made him the most magnetic person in any group, a position he delighted in occupying.' Knight is skating on very thin ice here. For one thing, Sickert was, in Marjorie Lilly's words, a man who 'had a passion for conversation and *naturally* [our italics] took centre stage at any gathering without realising he did so'. He was an intelligent and well-known raconteur, and not a bore. The idea that the constant repetition of this simple anecdote automatically made him the most magnetic person in any group is ludicrous, as is the idea that a man so intimately connected with the sordid affair would 'need to chatter on about the Ripper'. If Sickert's 'lodger' story was merely an invention, the retelling of it would exorcise nothing. It would surely be the most tortuous exercise to impose a set of lies on oneself and one's companions when there was no need to do so. It would only serve constantly to remind Sickert of the terrible secret he nurtured, to say nothing of alerting the very same agency that was supposed to have callously butchered five women that they had a potential blabbermouth in their midst. Furthermore, Marjorie Lilly says of Sickert, 'His fascination with the Ripper case was intense and I thought perhaps he knew the truth.' She is of course referring to Sickert's retelling of his 'lodger' story, and no other.

Quite clearly the picture is of a man fired with enthusiasm for the Ripper mystery – among others. Another intrigue was the Tichborne Claimant case, which had hit the headlines in 1871 when Walter Sickert was only eleven. Since then this affair, as much as the Whitechapel murders, had maintained its interest for him. As for Jack the Ripper, Sickert was obviously convinced that the story told by his landlords was the truth. The conviction with which the artist was able to endow the tale did indeed fascinate his audience – so much so that it has been popularly believed that it was Sickert's tale that, in 1911, inspired Marie Belloc Lowndes to write her best-selling short story, *The Lodger*. In her diary she says: '*The Lodger* was written by me as a short story after I had heard a man telling a woman at a dinner party that his mother had had a butler and a cook who married and kept lodgers. They were convinced that Jack the Ripper had spent a night under their roof.'

Where then did this leave Joseph Sickert's account? At the time of our initial research *Jack the Ripper: The Final Solution* was the most popular contribution to the Ripper bookshelves, and apart from Arthur Douglas's slender paperback, *Will The Real Jack the Ripper . . .*, published in 1979, it was also the most recent. As such, its startling revelations caught the public imagination. It received unfavourable reviews, mainly on the grounds of its inherent implausibility, but no one had yet had the chance to refute Mr Knight's claims.

To begin with, Knight addresses himself to the existence or otherwise of Annie Elizabeth Crook. At first there is no trace, until BBC researcher Karen de Groot makes a search of the Cleveland Street area. The 1888 rate book records: 'Number 6 Elizabeth Cook (Basement).' Knight is quick to point out that Joseph Sickert had already said that his grandmother's surname was often rendered as 'Cook'. Further confirmation of Annie Elizabeth Crook's residency at No. 6 Cleveland Street is found when her daughter's birth certificate is examined. Dated 18 April 1885, it records:

Sex: Girl.
Name: Alice Margaret Crook.
Place of Birth: Marylebone Workhouse.
Name of Mother: Annie Elizabeth Crook. Confectionary assistant from Cleveland Street.
Name of Father: Blank.
Informant: Annie Elizabeth Crook, 6, Cleveland Street, Fitzroy Square.

It would appear that Annie Crook and Elizabeth Cook were one and the same person, and that she was living at No. 6 Cleveland Street continuously from 1885 to that fateful day in 1888 when she, her child and her Prince were forcibly torn from each other for ever. This is the most crucial episode in the whole of Sickert's story. It is the point when the well-organized conspiracy decides to act against the wayward heir, driving Mary Jane Kelly into the East End with the infant Alice in her arms. This raid in Cleveland Street is witnessed by Walter Sickert, and Knight retells Sickert's account in vivid detail:

It was late afternoon as he [Walter Sickert] wandered into the street from Maple Street and saw a gang of ruffians lounging against the wall near Howland Street. They were all strangers, an uncommon sight in that insular community. He sensed that there was something odd in their presence, but he was too immersed in his own thoughts to isolate his suspicions. Later, too late, he realised the truth. They may have been dressed as ruffians, but in reality they were a trained body of men *imitating* the loafing classes.

Suddenly a shout went up and a street brawl began. Soon that end of the street was a morass of fighting bodies. They cried out and cursed, and the vulgar spectacle drew people from their homes and shops. Sickert still could not define his fears, but he vaguely felt the acid taste of impending misfortune when he looked up and saw the studio end of the street deserted. He made off at a brisk pace towards the studio to ensure all was well with Eddy, who was staying there at the time. Before he was half-way along the street two hansom cabs turned into the road from Tottenham Street. One drew up outside the studio, the other went directly to the corner and parked by Annie's basement at No. 6. Two men in brown tweed went into the studio, and a fat man and a woman went into the basement. Sickert knew then the meaning of the charade behind him, and he knew it was too late to do anything without bringing harm upon himself. The two men came out of the studio, leading Eddy between them.

'He knew what it was all about', said Sickert. 'I could see the fear written in his face. I stood in the shadows by the shop and looked on with an awareness of the absurd inevitability of tragedy, the same in life as on the stage. Nothing can alter the inevitable.'

The man and woman emerged almost immediately from the basement and brought Annie struggling to the street. The lovers caught a brief glimpse of each other as their captors bundled them into separate cabs. When Eddy saw her he reached into the void between them and howled lamentably. She remained silent, but his continued sobs, soon muffled under the covers of the cab, expressed the insupportable grief of them both. Then the cabs were rattling off towards Oxford Street, one turning right at the end, the other left.

Either this testimony is true, or it is not. There can be no middle way. It is a comprehensive eye-witness account passed down from father to son to scribe. In its veracity lie the veracity and integrity of its proponents and the credibility of everything else that follows.

On examining the rate books for ourselves we did indeed come across a certain Elizabeth Cook living at No. 6 Cleveland Street in 1888, but checking beyond that year we discovered that she continued to live at this address until 1893, after which her name was no longer recorded. Obviously this is not compatible with the apparent fate of Annie Elizabeth Crook if the Sickert story is true. Furthermore, the rate books record that No. 6 Cleveland Street was demolished in 1887, and it is not until April 1888 that Elizabeth Cook's name appears for the first time as a resident and ratepayer in the newly completed red-brick apartment block now called Cleveland Residences.

If Elizabeth Cook and Annie Elizabeth Crook could somehow be shown to be one and the same, it would salvage something of Joseph's story and explain how the knowledge of his grandmother living in the basement of No. 6 Cleveland Street in 1888 was possible. A search of the index volumes at St Catherine's House (the General Register Office for births, marriages and deaths) swiftly revealed the registered death of an Elizabeth Cook aged seventy-three in the Marylebone district of London. Clearly this lady was not Joseph's grandmother Annie Elizabeth Crook (who died in 1920), but was she the Elizabeth Cook who had been referred to in the rate book? We applied for Elizabeth Cook's death certificate, dated 9 January 1893. The address of the deceased was No. 6 Cleveland Residences. Now there could be no doubt: information had been included in the Sickert/Knight account of happenings outside No. 6 Cleveland Street in 1888, which were supposed to be integral elements of the original Sickert story before Knight initiated his research – evidence which therefore made the story appear more plausible than it really was. 'Sickert said she was also known as Annie Elizabeth Cook. . . . Annie lived in the *basement* [our italics] of No. 6 Cleveland Street.'

Stephen Knight had declared his intention to look objectively at Joseph Sickert's recollections, though in fact supporting evidence was only being investigated insofar as it was of value to the plot, and debilitating research was being omitted altogether. Had Knight genuinely wanted to discover the truth behind Joseph Sickert's story, he would almost certainly have discovered, to begin with, that Walter Sickert's studio in the Cleveland Street area had not been in Cleveland Street itself (No. 15) between 1885 and 1888, but nearby at No. 15 Fitzroy Street from 1922 onwards.

An examination of the creed registers of the St Marylebone Workhouse would have revealed that Annie Crook, Joseph Sickert's grandmother, was an Anglican. Her parents' marriage certificate, dated December 1863, would have shown them to be Anglican, and even Alice Margaret would be christened into the Anglican faith. One of the strongest motives for Knight's conspiracy is non-existent, even supposing that it was possible for Prince Albert Victor to have been the father in the first place which – as we were to discover from the Royal Archives – it was not. Alice Margaret Crook was born on 18 April 1885, which means that her conception would have taken place between about 18 July and 11 August 1884, at a time when Prince Albert Victor was four hundred miles away in Germany. He had departed for Heidelberg with Professor Ihre, his German tutor, as early as 18 June – having completed his first six months at Cambridge University – and he did not return to England until 18 August.

The more we now looked at *The Final Solution* the more we realized that not only were Joseph Sickert's ill-remembered fantasies founded on sand, but that many of the incidents supposed to have sprung from the clear waters of truth had been carried to the well in the first place in order to be wound up from the depths by a grateful and thirsty readership. One example was Knight's attempt to verify Joseph's claim that the coachman, John Netley, had attempted to kill his mother, as a child, by running her down. This event had been included in Joseph's original account to the BBC. The story as related in *The Final Solution* runs thus:

> One violent and unexpected postscript was that the loathsome Netley, misguidedly believing he would find favour with the powerful, continued a long campaign against Alice Margaret. If he

45

killed her, he seemed to imagine, he would remove the final blemish from the future of his masters. . . . Netley twice tried to murder the controversial infant by running her down with his cab – once in 1888 at the height of the Ripper's reign of terror and once in February 1892. On the first occasion he ran Alice Margaret down as she crossed either Fleet Street or the Strand with an elderly relative. When the cab struck her it passed right over her body. The driver was later described to Sickert by the relative, and he knew it could be none other than Netley. Sickert said that in the confusion after the second 'accident', in Drury Lane, Netley pushed through the crowd and fled to Westminster Bridge, pursued by several passers by. He threw himself into the Thames and drowned.

In Joseph's original story, as told to the BBC, only one attempt was mentioned as having been made on his mother's life – in 1892 in Drury Lane, whilst Alice was being taken for a walk by a friend. There is no mention of John Netley running away and jumping in the Thames, which, considering the fact that this is now revealed as a most startling climax to the episode, is hardly something that Joseph would have forgotten.

Knight's verification of these attempted murders comes in a later chapter entirely devoted to this shadowy coachman:

> For a long time it seemed impossible to verify the story of the two incidents, until a copy of the *Illustrated Police News* of Saturday, 6th October 1888 came to the rescue. It will be remembered that Sickert said the first attempt on Alice Margaret's life took place in Fleet Street or The Strand at the height of the Ripper murders. The report said:
>> Shortly after four o'clock on Monday afternoon a little girl was run over by a hansom cab in Fleet-street, opposite Anderton's Hotel. The child was placed in the cab and conveyed to St Bartholomew's Hospital in an insensible condition, one of the wheels having passed over her body. From the serious nature of the injuries the little sufferer is not likely to recover.

Once again Knight finds the gem he is looking for, and as he goes on to say: 'The story tallies too closely with Sickert's version of events to be coincidence.'

What any discerning reader will already be able to pick out, however, is the fact that the victim in this incident was 'placed in the cab and conveyed to St Bartholomew's Hospital' – presumably, and there is no reason to suspect otherwise, by the driver of the cab himself. It would also occur to most investigators to check the admission registers at Bart's to identify the 'little sufferer' once and for all. This Knight does, only to report: 'Police and hospital records – such as had survived two wars – were useless.' This alas, is not true. The Admission Registers for 1888 contain the following entry for Monday, 1 October:

Lizzie Madewell
Age 9.
Run over.
1, Bridge St. EC. [off Fleet Street]
Discharged – 20th Oct.

A curious parallel to this occurred in May 1984, when Joseph told the *News of the World* of his meeting with and escape from death at the hands of the Yorkshire Ripper – Peter Sutcliffe: 'Ripper Haunted My Life. . . . He drove his car at me, I had to dive clear.' Who knows, perhaps he did. But it is in this same chapter of Knight's book that we uncover the most disturbing and obvious falsehood. The author goes on to say:

When Alice Margaret grew up she married a man called Gorman, who turned out to be impotent. Her relationship with Sickert had always been close, and the desperate loneliness that descended on her with growing deafness and a marriage devoid of physical love made the step from being Sickert's ward to being his mistress a natural one. She was his lover for more than twelve years, bore him a son, Joseph, and died in 1950. Sickert himself died in 1942.

Alice Margaret did indeed marry William Gorman in July 1918. But why did Knight tell us the marriage was barren when in fact Joseph was the third of five children born to Alice Margaret Crook and William Gorman between 1921 and 1927. The answer is obvious: such a conventional marriage makes it very difficult to believe that Joseph is in fact the son of Walter Sickert, just as Joseph's mention of an illegitimate brother Charles makes it even less likely – another awkward element in Joseph's original account which has been conveniently edited.

In July 1985 Stephen Knight died, tragically, at the age of thirty-three. It is with considerable regret, therefore, that we have to say what we do now when the man responsible for the book which we criticize is no longer with us to defend his creation. Nevertheless we cannot avoid our conclusions, which are based on the evidence that presented itself to us. Had Stephen Knight's book not persuaded a great many people that it was indeed *The Final Solution* then there would be little need to examine it in such depths here. Events after the publication of *The Final Solution* only served to confirm what we already suspected. On 18 June 1978 an article appeard in the *Sunday Times* – 'Jack the Ripper "solution" was a hoax, man confesses'. Beneath the headline, Joseph Sickert admitted that most of his story was untrue. The only bit he stuck to was his belief that his mother was the illegitimate daughter of the Duke of Clarence. 'The part about Jack the Ripper was invention,' he said, and went on: 'As an artist I found it easy to paint Jack the Ripper into the story I had been told about Prince Albert Victor and my grandmother by my father when I was six years old.'

Stephen Knight had been left holding the baby, having committed himself to the only conclusion possible under the weight of Joseph's detailed revelations. None other than Walter Sickert himself must have been the third man in the conspiracy, and not Sir Robert Anderson as was originally intended. Walter Sickert had to be, as much as Sir William Gull or John Netley, Jack the Ripper.

With the gloves now off, Knight turns to Sickert's paintings to find yet more incriminating evidence between the brushstrokes. In a portrait entitled *Mrs Barrett* he sees the face of Mary Jane Kelly. In the *Camden Town Murder* series, alternatively called *What Shall We Do for the Rent?* he sees Mary Jane Kelly's own situation. *Lazarus Breaks His Fast* includes a bowl of poisoned grapes used by Gull to subdue his victims. In *Ennui* a 'gull' is supposed to be perched near the head of Queen Victoria. In *La Hollandaise* he again sees the face of Mary Jane Kelly, this time mutilated beyond recognition, similar to the featureless horror of the Scotland Yard photograph of the victim. And in a painting of King George V and Queen Mary riding in a car in which the front 'half' of the Queen is obscured by the window frame of the vehicle, the painter is supposed to have deliberately obscured the Queen's face to indicate the fact that half of her belonged to 'Eddy'. For someone desperately trying to exorcise the guilt of five murdered women, as Walter Sickert was supposed to be doing through his art, this was subtle stuff indeed – Queen Mary, as Princess May of Teck, had been engaged to Prince Albert Victor when he died, which could hardly have been of any great concern to the artist whether he was Jack the Ripper or not. The truth was that Walter Sickert had faithfully reproduced this particular composition from a press photograph which is still in existence today.

Knight's subjective misinterpretations of these and other paintings are made without any regard to the facts. Mrs Barrett was a perfectly respectable woman who was known to – among others – Marjorie Lilly; and *La Hollandaise* is a typical example of the artist's impressionistic treatment of a subject – a style evident in much of his work well before the Ripper crimes were ever committed – as Dr Wendy Baron, art historian and foremost authority on Walter Sickert, was to explain to us when we met to discuss Knight's claims.

In 1975 Stephen Knight – also recognizing Dr Baron's authority – had written to inform her that he was in the process of writing a book about Jack the Ripper based on a solution to the mystery suggested by Walter Sickert, and that, as she was the 'foremost expert on Sickert the man and Sickert the artist', he hoped for clarification on two points. Firstly: had there been any connection between Sickert and Princess Alexandra? And secondly: had there been any connection between Alexandra's Danish Royal Family and the Sickerts? Dr Baron replied:

> I suspect that your book is based on the solution to the mystery suggested by Joe rather than by Walter, Sickert. The theory expounded by Joe in the television series investigated by Barlow, which involved the Duke of Clarence and Joe's personal ancestry is, as far as I can discover, one of Joe's fantasies. Joe's father may well have been Sickert; perhaps his mother was the Duke of Clarence's daughter. I do not know. But the theory of the identity of Jack the Ripper as told to Joe by Sickert is not repeated by Sickert elsewhere. . . .
>
> There is no known connection between Sickert and Princess Alexandra. There is no evidence of any remotely intimate relationship between the Sickert family and the Danish Royal Family. . . .
>
> Sickert's titles . . . are not unfathomable, although sometimes arbitrary and naughty. Their motivation was to cock a snook at the fashion for denying the anecdotic content of art which had been instigated, in England, by Whistler with his abstract titles – harmonies and symphonies and so on. Sickert deliberately harked back to the Victorian fashion for giving pictures titles suggesting a story (*When did you last see your father?* for instance). The only difference is that Sickert began his representations for purely formal reasons and only when faced with the finished work did he think of a title which seemed to fit it. . . .

In the light of this expert testimony, it is not too surprising to discover that Dr Baron does not figure in Knight's book at all. Princess Alexandra, however, comes to know Walter Sickert nevertheless, allowing the young Prince to be introduced into his artistic circle, and the Sickerts' connection with Alexandra's Danish Royal Family is promoted as probable fact.

It must have been quite a shock for Joseph to discover the

conclusion to Knight's book, which the author had for so long kept secret. Having been allowed a free hand to mould Joseph's original clay into a remarkably detailed and extraordinary sculpture Joseph was now faced with a *fait accompli*. But it still took him two years to make his retraction, having written a postscript in the book in which he says: 'I had to admit that my father must have known more than he told me. It was a fact that I had known all along.' He continues: 'I did not see all that much of him as a child', and 'If Stephen Knight is correct in his conclusions, and I am forced to admit, reluctantly, that his reasoning is sound, I do not bear my father any malice.'

The man who had recollected in such detail the very adult and sinister account from Walter Sickert now says that he did not see all that much of him as a child. His original yarn had opened an entirely different can of worms, and he regretted it from the moment he realized what he had done. One would have to understand the particular relationship between Knight and Sickert to understand the situation fully, and why it had taken two years for Joseph to speak up, but clearly the atmosphere of mutual co-operation which had uncovered so much in the past was now over.

In the 2 July issue of the *Sunday Times* Stephen Knight defended himself against Joseph's submission.

> I am not surprised that Mr Joseph Sickert himself whose story provided the basis for my research has now tried to denounce the contents. He threatened to do this after I told him that I believed his father, Walter Sickert, had been directly involved in the killings. . . . He at first begged me not to publish my findings about his father. I had to refuse. He told me then that he would find some way of exonerating him even if it meant denying the whole story. I had been prepared for this, and before showing him the last chapter I had secured a signed statement from him that I had recounted his father's original story with complete accuracy.

Signing a statement to the effect that a story has been recounted accurately is not, of course, the same thing as saying that it is true, but no matter. It is curious that Stephen Knight felt the need to secure a statement in the first place, when his own credibility lay in the fact that he had been able to prove its veracity to his and everybody else's satisfaction regardless of anything else.

Knight says that Joseph threatened to deny the whole story, but even this is impossible to equate with the facts. Joseph's afterword in the book – written at the time Knight says he was proclaiming his intention to retract everything – is an admission, however reluctantly, that he had half known all along that his father must have known more, and that he was hoping that Knight might dispel his worst private fears. 'In the event,' he confides, 'the investigation has had the opposite effect and my fears have been confirmed.' He finishes by saying: 'None of this justifies, but it might begin to explain, why an essentially good man would do what it seems my father did.' It is hardly the statement of a man who was prepared to do anything to clear Walter Sickert's name, as Stephen Knight would have us believe.

Joseph's now admitted hoax had gone too far. The very man he admired and wished so publicly to associate with as a fellow artist was now implicated in a notorious example of human depravity and perversion – not as a chronicler, an innocent bystander, but as a butcher's assistant. And all this after he had been the one to instigate the relationship between the 'star crossed lovers', lending support to the Prince and then to the child of their union but later apparently assisting in ritual masonic murder when neither he himself, nor John Netley for that matter, was a freemason.

Before we leave the fiction that had distracted us for many months, let us at least offer a 'solution', not to the mystery of Jack the Ripper but to Joseph's romantic yarn. When we finally met, our confessed disdain for *The Final Solution* did little to hinder our conversation and Joseph rambled through his story. Not surprisingly, it varied considerably from the facts as related by Stephen Knight, with yet more intriguing elements not mentioned by Knight or by Joseph in his original BBC statement now being flicked on to the already crowded canvas of his family history. Once again we found ourselves wondering where the truth might lie, but one particular addition at least suggested a possible explanation for the development of this particular fairy story and the reason for the inclusion in it of an insignificant coachman called John Netley.

According to Joseph Sickert, he had in his possession a photograph of Netley standing by his horse-drawn cab. An older man was holding the horse's reins. If true, this would be a remarkable portrait and one wonders why it was not included in Knight's book. Unfortunately we were not allowed to see the picture for ourselves, but if it did exist the obvious question was why would Joseph Sickert have it in his possession in the first place? No direct relationship between Netley and Walter Sickert has ever been suggested, and there would seem little reason why such a photograph would pass to the artist – let alone Joseph – unless there was an entirely different reason for Joseph knowing of the existence of

Clarence's unofficial chauffeur. Could it have been John Netley who was Joseph's grandfather, rather than Clarence? And was it through Netley that Joseph's mother heard the colourful gossip of a coachman used to seeing the less acceptable face of his aristocratic fares?

Central to Joseph's story was Cleveland Street, in which – according to him – a raid took place to separate the Prince and his shop assistant (Joseph's grandmother). A raid did take place in Cleveland Street seven months after the Ripper murders, and the homosexual brothel at No. 19 was virtually opposite the confectionery shop where Annie Crook worked. According to Joseph, the photograph he had of Netley was of a 'personal' nature. Had the young coachman at some time driven Clarence to No. 19, where the Prince was known to be a visitor? Did his driver meet a pretty young shop assistant on one of his visits to the area, and did he woo her with tales of royal intrigue and indiscretion? Did he eventually father her child before deserting her and condemning her to a hard and lonely life in which Cinderella fantasies provided the only means of escape? Ultimately, was Joseph's ill-conceived hoax not of his own doing but of his mother's?

V

In the absence of more substantial testimony from the seemingly impotent police authorities it is hardly surprising that opinion and assumption have grown unchecked, to be swallowed by an increasingly thirsty public. But even though we now knew *The Final Solution* to be fiction, the initial question it had raised in our minds was still relevant. How much more was known about these murders than had been admitted? Stephen Knight was not the only person to have suggested the possibility of a conspiracy of some sort, either specific or inferred; but it came as some surprise to discover on one of our early forays at the Newspaper Library that on the evening after Mary Jane Kelly's murder the *Star* published an article which read: 'We have heard the wildest stories as to the reason which popular opinion in Whitechapel assigns for Mr Matthew's obstinate refusal to offer a reward. It is believed by people who pass among their neighbours as sensible folk that the Government do not want the murderer to be convicted, that they are interested in concealing his identity, that, in fact, they know it, and will not divulge it. Of course this is rank nonsense. . . .'

Clearly this was anathema to the respectable Victorian press. But even if they could not bring themselves to accept the possibility of such a situation, the more cynical public apparently had no difficulty in accepting that a man of some education and standing – as opposed to one of the 'loafing classes' – could have been responsible for these horrors; and looked at from a modern point of view, the conclusion that there may well have been a more sinister reason why the perpetrator had not yet been brought to justice appears not only possible but downright plausible.

Without any further information, of course, suspicion immediately falls on Scotland Yard as the most likely prime mover in any potential cover-up, and whilst only Stephen Knight has directly incriminated the Metropolitan Police in the murders themselves – originally suggesting that Sir Robert Anderson may have been involved – the police would have to be instrumental in hushing up any covert activity if a plot to keep the Ripper's identity was to succeed.

The more one begins to look at the dedicated officers who were actually entrusted with the task of finding their man on the back streets of London – men like Inspectors Abberline, Moore, Beck and Swanson – the more we can see how a conspiracy initiated at pavement level would have been almost impossible. Had any of the men of H Division arrested Jack the Ripper in the course of his duty, it would have captured the attention of every member of the public in the vicinity at the time, and of every constable in the force – to say nothing of the entire Whitechapel Vigilance Committee and the gentlemen of the press.

The reputation of London's police forces, and faith in their officers' and commanders' ability adequately to protect the public from its enemies, had been well and truly damaged long before Jack the Ripper had entered the arena. As a direct result of his activities their battered pride was to be savaged even further.

Two years earlier, when riots in Trafalgar Square had resulted in the resignation of the Metropolitan Police Commissioner, Colonel Sir Edmund Henderson, the Home Secretary, Hugh Childers, had hoped that the appointment of a more distinguished soldier would help to restore public confidence. Unfortunately he was wrong. Shortly after taking office General Sir Charles Warren appointed five more military officers to help him police London in a way which was to crystallize his style of leadership and set the tone of his ill-fated administration. On 13 November 1887, a day which was to become known as Bloody Sunday, further rioting took place in Trafalgar Square. Warren's answer to the army of socialist demonstrators who were determined to break through to the mass of unemployed squatters in almost permanent residency in the Square was the use of four thousand constables, three hundred Grenadiers and three hundred Life Guards, with a further seven thousand constables being held in reserve. But in the end the Square was cleared, and as there were to be no more demonstrations against the police, Warren – for a short time at least – had managed to earn the respect of most of his political masters.

In contrast, and as a direct result of his abrasive, military style of leadership, his public popularity declined to the point where he was generally despised by the working class. Slowly, as criticism of the police increased generally, he found himself more and more isolated, not only from the public at large but from the latest in a line of Home Secretaries (Henry Matthews) and even from the head of his own CID, Assistant Commissioner James Monro – the man who would eventually succeed him.

Warren's insistence that Scotland Yard should be totally independent of Home Office control, at least where its internal administration was concerned, was matched by the no less independent convictions of James Monro, who regarded the CID as a separate entity within the Metropolitan Police, free from the control of the Commissioner. Throughout the summer of 1888 the game of musical departments was to continue until James Monro was finally forced to resign – his position being filled by his subordinate, Robert Anderson.

Warren may have temporarily found a more co-operative Assistant Commissioner in the shape of Anderson, but at what price? According to Lord John Spencer, Viceroy of Ireland, Anderson had been 'utterly careless when employed by Brackenbury [Director of Military Intelligence] and seemed to be a weak creature in every respect'. True or not, Monro's resignation had only served further to demoralize his old department, and Anderson, already overworked and exhausted, was hard pushed to stop the rot. Only with extreme difficulty did he manage to persuade Chief Superintendent 'Dolly' Williamson not to resign in protest at the way his old chief had been treated, and what had fast become a long-running comedy of errors continued with Anderson (having told Sir Charles that he could not take up his appointment for a month as he was in dire need of a rest) leaving his new post within a week for a month's holiday in Switzerland on the night before Annie Chapman was murdered in Hanbury Street. In short, the Home Office and Scotland Yard were writing the script of their own pantomime, unaware that the part of the villain was to be played by an unknown actor who was not only destined to steal the show but would turn their inept farce into the darkest of tragedies.

Little more than a week earlier, shortly after the Ripper had appeared for the first time, James Monro, following his predetermined resignation, accepted an important appointment at the

55

Home Office. It did not escape the attention of the Central News Agency: 'The unofficial announcement of Mr Monro's appointment has caused considerable surprise at Scotland Yard and in official circles generally, and much curiosity is felt as to the duties connected with his new post. On this point the authorities absolutely refuse to give any information, but there is reason to believe that Mr Monro's work will be of a character similar to that formerly performed by Mr Jenkinson.' Later, in Parliament, the Home Secretary explained that arrangements had been made to enable him to have the benefit of Mr Monro's advice, where it might seem desirable, in matters relating to crime. But when further pressed by Edward Pickersgill, MP for Bethnal Green, on whether this meant that a new office had been created for Mr Monro, Matthews guardedly replied that he could not add anything to the answer already given.

Clearly there were changes afoot behind the scenes in Whitehall, but considering the transparent confusions also present at this time it is hardly surprising that pandemonium lay waiting around the corner, and we would not need to look for a professionally organized conspiracy to explain why Jack the Ripper was never caught. The situation could hardly have been any worse if every constable on the beat had been told to wear a red nose and baggy pants.

On the night of the 'double event' Jack had travelled from Berner Street in the East End towards the City and Mitre Square. Having finished with Catherine Eddowes he cut off a piece of her apron and, wiping his hands and the blade of his knife on the material, started to head east again before turning north into Goulston Street. An hour later, at about 2.55 a.m., PC Alfred Long 254 A Division, on duty in the street, found the discarded rag of apron in the passage between Nos 118 and 119. Above it on the wall was written in chalk: 'The Juwes are The men That Will not be Blamed for nothing.' In PC Long's opinion, the writing had only recently been done.

Soon the street was buzzing with the activity of both PC Long's Metropolitan Police colleagues and the City police. At this point Acting Commissioner Major Henry Smith was summoned from his slumbers, as he later recalled in his autobiography, *From Constable to Commissioner*:

The night of Saturday, September 29, found me tossing about in my bed at Cloak Lane Station, close to the river and adjoining Southwark Bridge. There was a railway goods depot in front, and a

56

furrier's premises behind my rooms; the lane was causewayed, heavy vans were going constantly in and out, and the sickening smell from the furrier's skins was always present. You could not open the windows, and to sleep was an impossibility. Suddenly the bell at my head rang violently. 'What is it?' I asked, putting my ear to the tube. 'Another murder, sir, this time in the City.' Jumping up, I was dressed and in the street in a couple of minutes. A hansom – to me a detestable vehicle – was at the door, and into it I jumped, as time was of the utmost consequence. This invention of the devil claims to be safe. It is neither safe nor pleasant. In Winter you are frozen; in Summer you are broiled. When the glass is let down your hat is generally smashed, your fingers caught between the doors, or half your front teeth loosened. Licensed to carry two, it did not take me long to discover that a 15 stone Superintendent inside with me, and three detectives hanging on behind, added neither to its comfort nor to its safety.

Meanwhile, back in Goulston Street Detective Constable Daniel Halse had been guarding the writing, in expectation of it being photographed, when Superintendent Arnold of the Metropolitan force arrived and decided that it should be rubbed out. His reason was that, as suspicion had recently fallen on John Pizer, the message might incite further anti-Semitism. Halse protested, but to no avail; Goulston Street was within the boundaries of the Metropolitan Police area and that was that. The single most important piece of evidence to date was about to be summarily obliterated, but not before Sir Charles Warren himself had arrived at about 5 a.m. and immediately ordered that the words be erased. Like Arnold's, his sole explanation for doing so was to defuse what was in his opinion a potentially explosive situation should the word 'Juwes' incite anti-Semitic factions in the area to riot. The officers of the City police protested and alternative courses of action were proposed. The message could be covered up; the word 'Juwes' alone could be erased, or just the top line; but to no avail. According to some commentators, Warren rubbed out the words personally.

Such crass incompetence is hard to justify. Apart from the measures suggested, it would have been possible for the police simply to cordon off the area until the essential photographs had been taken. Dawn would be breaking in less than an hour. Under such circumstances it seems incredible that the Chief Commissioner could feel so intimidated by a non-existent mob as to take such drastic action. Unfortunately, such ill-conceived and impetuous behaviour had been the hallmark of Warren's administration from the outset, and now his handling of the Whitechapel investigations was hastening the end of what had been a disastrous period of leadership for the Metropolitan Police. Five weeks later, one day before Mary Jane Kelly's murder, he resigned.

We were still none the wiser. By February 1889 the plain clothes detective force in Whitechapel had been reduced somewhat, which again raised the possibility that the authorities were in possession of vital information that allowed them to make such a decision. But on the other hand they might have been looking to reduce their numbers at the earliest opportunity, fully aware that the extra presence had been a totally ineffective deterrent and an equally inefficient device for capturing their quarry. Were the large numbers of officers and men drafted into the area becoming an increasing embarrassment, or did someone in authority already know that they were no longer required?

Whatever the truth of the situation, the uniformed policing of the area was not allowed to decline, and there is any amount of evidence available to show that, as far as the population of Whitechapel and the uniformed constables on duty in the area were concerned, there was a general acceptance that Jack could still be lurking in the shadows, waiting to strike. Initially the police were of the opinion that a gang of thugs was behind the assaults. Soon this inadequate presumption gave way to the feeling that one person alone was responsible: a local resident of low calling, or a foreigner – or both. This, together with the fact that they were almost certainly dealing with a raving lunatic, raised expectations that it was only a matter of time before such a distinct monster would be identified. Hundreds of arrests had been made of those who had vaguely fitted the stereotype, and all had been subsequently released, which led one wrily amused columnist to comment: 'The police are still on the track of the Whitechapel lady-killer, and several really remarkable clues have been obtained and followed up. The wrong man has not been arrested this week quite so frequently as he was last, and there are undoubted signs that "a clue" has at last rewarded the efforts of the police authorities.' He then goes on to mention several reports by various newspapers, all revealing a different clue and yet another 'latest' suspect – from a snuff-taking Scotsman in a kilt via a man who may have had a knife up his sleeve to a well-known dramatic author – and ends by confirming that the police did not believe the Whitechapel murders to have been committed by a baboon which had recently escaped from a ship in the East India Docks, but: 'Sir Charles Warren is understood to have said that it wanted Edgar Allan Poe at the Yard to give them something to work on.'

Such satire only further increases the likelihood that the police genuinely had no idea whom they were looking for, and were helpless to defend themselves against their constant lampooning at the hands of the press. But, as we were becoming only too aware, it wasn't that simple. Sir Robert Anderson, the man who took over as head of the CID following James Monro's resignation and subsequent appointment at the Home Office, confuses the issue by making it perfectly clear in his autobiography, *The Lighter Side of My Official Life*, that he himself was in no doubt who Jack the Ripper was:

One did not need to be a Sherlock Holmes to discover that the criminal was a sexual maniac of a virulent type; that he was living in the immediate vicinity of the scenes of the murders; and that, if he was not living absolutely alone, his people knew of his guilt, and refused to give him up to justice. During my absence abroad, the Police had made a house-to-house search for him, investigating the case of every man in the district whose circumstances were such that he could go and come and get rid of his blood-stains in secret. And the conclusion we came to was that he and his people were certain low-class Polish Jews; for it is a remarkable fact that people of that class in the East End will not give up one of their number to Gentile justice.

And the result proved that our diagnosis was right on every point. For I may say at once that 'undiscovered murders' are rare in London, and the 'Jack the Ripper' crimes are not within that category. And if the Police here had powers such as the French Police possess, the murderer would have been brought to justice. Scotland Yard can boast that not even the subordinate officers of the department will tell tales out of school, and it would ill become me to violate the unwritten rule of the service. So I will only add here that the 'Jack the Ripper' letter which is preserved in the Police Museum at New Scotland Yard is the creation of an enterprising journalist.

Having regard to the interest attaching to this case, I am almost tempted to disclose the identity of the murderer and of the pressmen who wrote the letter above referred to. But no public benefit would result from such a course, and the traditions of my old department would suffer. I will merely add that the only person who ever had a good view of the murderer unhesitatingly identified the suspect the instant he was confronted with him; but he refused to give evidence against him.

In saying that he was a Polish Jew I am merely stating a definitely ascertained fact. And my words are meant to specify race, not religion. For it would outrage all religious sentiment to talk of the religion of a loathsome creature whose utterly unmentionable vices reduced him to a lower level than that of the brute.

Taken at face value, Anderson's opinion is remarkable indeed. It is a confidently asserted statement of fact from one of the men closest to the Whitechapel murder investigations. Unfortunately, Anderson gives enough away in his statement for any serious Ripperologist to realize that he is talking about John Pizer, the Polish Jew known as Leather-Apron who had been the talk of the town during the period of Anderson's leave of absence in Switzerland.

Donald Rumbelow points out in his book that, as Pizer had already been accused and acquitted shortly after the second murder, it is astonishing that Anderson could be so emphatic about his guilt. He asks: 'Is he really saying that the police knew the identity of the murderer and let him commit three more murders without bringing him to justice?' Obviously this could not be the case. At this point a more pragmatic approach suggests going back to the alternative explanation – Anderson must have been referring to another Polish Jew.

Unfortunately, however, an article which appeared in *The Times* on Wednesday, 12 September put it beyond all reasonable doubt that Sir Robert's suspect was John Pizer and nobody else, as it reported the very incident referred to when Jack the Ripper was 'unhesitatingly identified by a witness who then refused to give evidence against him':

A half Spaniard and half Bulgarian, who gave the name of Emanuel Delbast Violenia, waited on the police with respect to this enquiry. He stated that he, his wife, and two children tramped from Manchester to London with a view of being able to emigrate to Australia, and took abode in one of the lodging houses in Hanbury Street. Early last Saturday morning, walking alone along Hanbury Street, he noticed a man and a woman quarrelling in a very excited manner. Violenia distinctly heard the man threaten to kill the woman by sticking a knife into her. They passed on, and Violenia went into his lodging. After the murder he communicated what he had seen to the police. At 1 o'clock yesterday afternoon Sergeant Thicke, assisted by Inspector Cansby, placed about a dozen men, the greater portion of whom were Jews, in the yard of Leman Street Police station. Pizer was then brought out and allowed to place himself where he thought proper among the assembled men. He is a man of short stature, with black whiskers and a shaven chin. Violenia, who had been accommodated in one of the lower rooms of the station-house, was then brought up into the yard. Having keenly scrutinized all the faces before him, he at once, without any hesitation or doubt whatever, went up to Pizer and identified him as the man whom he heard threaten a woman on the night of the murder. . . . It was then decided, with the approval of Detective-Inspector Abberline, that Violenia should be taken to the Whitechapel mortuary to see whether he could identify the deceased woman as the one he had seen in Pizer's company early on Saturday morning. The result is not announced, but it is believed that he was unable to identify her. Subsequently, cross-examination so discredited Violenia's evidence that it was wholly distrusted by the police, and Pizer was set at liberty.

Rumbelow quite rightly points out that not only does this article absolutely confirm the identify of Anderson's suspect, but it also shows the real reason why Violenia was genuinely unable to give evidence against Pizer. At the very least, Annie Chapman had not been the woman Pizer had quarrelled with. In fact, it was far more probable that Violenia had mistakenly picked out the unfortunate boot finisher in the first place. Pizer already had an alibi for the time concerned, and when he was selected at the identity parade he said: 'I don't know you; you are mistaken.' Rumbelow's conclusion is that Anderson must be relating a story received at third hand, and as such it can be ignored. But on this point we have to disagree.

Certainly, Anderson had to have received most of his information about John Pizer indirectly, simply because he was out of the country for much of the time in which Pizer's ill-deserved notoriety was being established. But that hardly explains how this high-ranking officer could be so assured in his convictions, particularly when Pizer had been proved innocent beyond any shadow of doubt. Robert Anderson had to know more about the Whitechapel murder investigations than almost any other man, including Charles Warren. He had, after all, been the head of the CID for the last three months of Warren's administration, when the police investigation into the murders was at its height, and he was to continue as head of the same department for the next three years, with his old friend James Monro as Commissioner. It was incredible that a man in his position could be so emphatic about the identity of the murderer when all his evidence can be shown to be founded on sand. No other police officer of his day echoes his sentiments. Henry Smith leaves us in no doubt about his feelings on the matter:

> Sir Robert does not tell us how many of 'his people' sheltered the murderer, but whether they were two dozen in number, or two hundred, or two thousand, he accuses them of being accessories to these crimes before and after their commital. Surely Sir Robert cannot believe that while the Jews, as he asserts, were entering into

this conspiracy to defeat the ends of justice, there was no one among them with sufficient knowledge of the criminal law to warn them of the risks they were running.

Sir Robert talks of the 'Lighter Side' of his 'Official Life'. There is nothing 'light' here; a heavier indictment could not be framed against a class whose conduct contrasts most favourably with that of the Gentile population of the Metropolis. . . .

Sir Robert Anderson spent, so he tells us, the day of his return from abroad and half the following night 'in reviewing the whole case'. A more fruitless investigation, looking to all he tells us, it would be difficult to imagine.

In the light of all our research we have no hesitation in echoing Commissioner Smith's sentiments, but are still left wondering about Anderson's 'definitely ascertained fact'.

In 1892, eighteen years before the publication of Anderson's autobiography, Sir Melville Macnaghten – who was his assistant at the time – officially closed the file on the Whitechapel murders without any public explanation. But his superiors' later insistence that the murderer's identity was known at least gave us some explanation – that is, until we realized that Sir Melville, rather than concurring with Anderson's opinion, was supposed to have had his own views regarding the identity of the killer.

Seventy years after certain rumours had begun to circulate that Jack the Ripper might have been a respectable gent – a 'toff', the kind of man who may well have gone unchallenged on the streets of Whitechapel – we discovered that, according to writers Tom Cullen and Daniel Farson, Macnaghten's favoured suspect was no low-class foreign Jew, or itinerant labourer, but a quietly respectable schoolteacher and barrister – Montague John Druitt.

In 1959 writer and television interviewer Dan Farson included the subject of Jack the Ripper in his television series *Farson's Guide to the British*, and the deluge of correspondence he received as a result encouraged him to investigate the mystery further in preparation for a two-part television documentary. By pure chance Mr Farson stumbled on to a version of Macnaghten's notes which were in the possession of Sir Melville's daughter, Christabel, Lady Aberconway. These notes, however, are not the same as Scotland Yard's but a typewritten transcript of Melville Macnaghten's original rough handwritten jottings – from which, presumably, he made his final draft.

Farson was unaware at the time that the official version was not only securely locked away in the bowels of Scotland Yard, but that it varied in important detail from the typewritten notes which he used in his television programme. It was not until the BBC Television series *The Ripper File*, however, that the contents of the official papers become known to a wider audience. Sir Melville's 'official' notes, written in response to a series of articles which appeared in the *Sun* newspaper throughout the week of 13 February 1894, had claimed that a relatively harmless fetishist called Thomas Cutbush was Jack the Ripper, and Macnaghten's papers were intended to lay to rest the non-existent case against Cutbush. Importantly, they were intended for internal perusal only.

In both sets – the verifiable and the missing originals – three men were named as possible Rippers, but according to Lady Aberconway's typewritten copy Macnaghten said:

> No one ever saw the Whitechapel murderer (unless possibly it was the City PC who was on a beat near Mitre Square) and no proof could in any way ever be brought against anyone, although very many homicidal maniacs were at one time or another suspected. I enumerate the cases of three men against whom the police held very reasonable suspicion. Personally, and after much careful and deliberate consideration, I am inclined to exonerate two of them.

And in conclusion, he admitted: 'But I have always held strong opinions regarding him [the third suspect] and the more I think the matter over, the stronger do these opinions become. The truth, however, will never be known, and did indeed at one time lie at the bottom of the Thames, if my conjectures be correct.'

Unfortunately for Messrs Cullen and Farson, the official version read thus:

> (1) A Mr M.J. Druitt, said to be a doctor & of good family – who disappeared at the time of the Miller's Court murder & whose body (which was said to have been upwards of a month in the water) was found in the Thames on 31st December – or about seven weeks after that murder. He was sexually insane and from private information I have little doubt but that his own family believed him to have been the murderer.

In both versions, information about the other two suspects is identical:

> (2) Kosminski – a Polish Jew – & resident in Whitechapel. This man became insane owing to many years indulgence in solitary vices. He had a great hatred of women, specially of the prostitute class, & had strong homicidal tendencies; he was removed to a

lunatic asylum about March 1889. There were many circumstances connected with this man which made him a strong 'suspect'.

(3) Michael Ostrog, a Russian doctor, and a convict, who was subsequently detained in a lunatic asylum as a homicidal maniac. This man's antecedents were of the worst possible type and his whereabouts at the time of the murders could never be ascertained.

In deference to Lady Aberconway, Farson only revealed the initials of Macnaghten's suspect – M.J.D. But by 1965 author Tom Cullen, quite independently of Farson, had completed his own research, having seen Lady Aberconway's notes for himself. In his book *Autumn of Terror* he gives the full name of Macnaghten's first suspect as Montague John Druitt.

According to both Cullen and Farson, Sir Melville's impression of Mr M.J. Druitt was:

. . . a doctor of about forty-one years of age and of fairly good family, who disappeared at the time of the Miller's Court murder, and whose body was found floating in the Thames on 3 December, i.e. seven weeks after the said murder. The body was said to have been in the water for a month, or more – on it was found a season ticket between Blackheath and London. From private information I have little doubt but that his own family suspected this man of being the Whitechapel murderer; it was alleged that he was sexually insane.

If Macnaghten actually did write this, it makes one wonder how much information he could have had at his disposal when such basic statistics about his suspect are incorrect. Druitt was not a forty-one-year-old doctor, but a thirty-one-year-old barrister; and although the Scotland Yard version does not mention Druitt's age or the contents of his pockets, he still remains a medical man.

Whatever the explanation, the most important question to try to answer first was: Did Macnaghten really believe Druitt to be the Ripper, as the typewritten notes clearly indicate, or was he merely putting forward, by way of example, the names of three men – 'any one of whom would have been more liable than Cutbush to have committed this series of murders'.

In Cullen and Farson's version, Sir Melville, 'after much careful and deliberate consideration', is inclined to exonerate two of the named men and suggests that the truth 'did at one time lie at the bottom of the Thames'. If Macnaghten actually wrote this, his information about Druitt must have been deeply incriminating. But, even if this was the case, why would such information need to be so closely guarded?

Druitt has always been regarded as a relatively unimportant individual: a man alone, a failed barrister and schoolteacher. He was not even a freemason – at least, not according to information received from the United Grand Lodge of England. And if he was Jack the Ripper, the proposition that some sort of conspiracy may have been initiated to conceal his identity was only worth considering if the motive for such a drastic course of action could be discovered. Rumours of a cover-up have abounded since the very first, as can be seen from the article in the *Star*, and all our research to date had inclined us to the belief that more was known about the events of that autumn than had ever been admitted by the authorities of the day. The case against Macnaghten's drowned barrister/schoolteacher was obviously worth a closer look, despite the fact that public knowledge of his possible guilt would not seem to have warranted the covert protection of others at the time, or necessitated a continued blanket of silence long after the event.

VI

All the evidence so far had pointed to the fact that the Metropolitan Police were completely at a loss to know how to deal with the unique criminal phenomenon they were witnessing. Having no idea where to look for whom, they were powerless to calm the hysteria that was destroying their credibility. Sir Melville Macnaghten, who concurred with Anderson's opinion regarding the 'Dear Boss' letter – even to the point of suspecting the actual correspondent – recalls in his memoirs the very real public alarm induced by the events themselves, and in so doing tries to offer some explanation for his colleagues' failure to catch their man:

> No one who was living in London that autumn will forget the terror created by these murders. Even now I can recall the foggy evenings, and hear again the raucous cries of the newspaper boys: 'Another horrible murder, mutilation, Whitechapel.' Such was the burden of their ghastly song; and, when the double murder of the 30th September took place, the exasperation of the public at the non discovery of the perpetrator knew no bounds, and no servant-maid deemed her life safe if she ventured out to post a letter after ten o'clock at night. . . . And yet this panic was quite unreasonable. The victims, without exception, belonged to the lowest dregs of female humanity, who avoid the police and exercise every ingenuity in order to remain in the darkest corners of the most deserted alleys.

The victims were indeed pitiful creatures – squalid paupers anaesthetizing themselves against the sordid reality of their lot with cheap gin. The black and rust-coloured bonnet laced with velvet that Mary Ann Nichols had been so proud of was to serve as her wreath as it lay by her still body. Her pockets contained only a handkerchief, a comb and a bit of broken glass. So too with Annie Chapman: a piece of coarse muslin, a pocket comb and paper case, a torn piece of envelope and a screw of paper containing two pills. Elizabeth Stride owned little more: a key, a small piece of lead pencil, two combs – one broken, a metal spoon, some buttons and a hook. Catherine Eddowes was rich by comparison: on her body were found a short clay pipe and an old, red cigarette case with white metal fittings, a matchbox, an old pocket handkerchief, a thimble, a bone-handled table knife and a small packet of tea and sugar.

Their dereliction was almost complete. Gap-toothed hags in their mid-forties, they looked more like women in their sixties – pathetic cast-offs still hopeful of selling their limited charms for the price of a bed or a crust or another tot of gin. Mary Jane Kelly, the fifth and final victim, was different from the others only in that she was a comparatively attractive twenty-five-year-old not yet ravaged by time or the decay brought about by disease or malnutrition. But she was nevertheless a far cry from the cupid-lipped beauty of the French postcard and Victorian boudoir so often associated with the crimes in question.

Sir Melville is commenting, of course, not only with the benefit of hindsight but from his secure and privileged position as a leading figure – and indeed a man – in Victorian life. In the circumstances it seems hardly fair to censure the more respectable but equally vulnerable servant girl for seeing the four murders to date as primarily crimes against her sex in general. After all, the perpetrator's *modus operandi* was only just being established; and without such benefit of hindsight it would surely have been foolhardy to assume where or whom this deranged killer might next strike.

As the weeks, months and years passed, the public image of the Metropolitan Police slowly recovered under the excellent leadership of men like James Monro, and Edward Bradford who was to succeed him. But there never would be any official explanation to help exorcise the ghost of Jack the Ripper. Any attempt to heal the humiliating wounds inflicted by his unseen knife were to be left on the whole to one or two eminent officers after retiring from their public duties, of whom Sir Melville is among the most important. His clear, authoritative statement on the number of Ripper murders was based on considerable knowledge and understanding of the crimes, but his attempts to defend his colleagues' failure to apprehend the villain are less assured, and of necessity perfunctory.

In saying that the victims were 'the lowest dregs of female humanity, who avoid the police and exercise every ingenuity in order to remain in the darkest corners of the most deserted alleys', inferring that they were as much to blame as anyone for the felon's continued liberty (a view which echoed Chief Commissioner Charles Warren's opinion), he is being misleading.

Buck's Row was dimly lit by a solitary gas lamp at the far end, but it was hardly a dark corner or a deserted alley. From a newspaper sketch made at the time, and from the testimony of PC John Neil, the first policeman on the scene, it is clear that Nichols's body lay on the open pavement in full view of the surrounding houses. Mrs Emma Green, who lived next door to the murder spot with her daughter and two sons, heard nothing during the night. Mr Walter Perkins, who lived on the opposite side of the road with his wife, also heard nothing. What Mrs Green, Mr and Mrs Perkins, the watchman at a nearby tar factory and another watchman in a wool depot in Buck's Row all agreed was that it had been an unusually quiet night. Even so, the street was used by market porters on their way to work, and it was regularly patrolled by a police constable every half hour. According to Dr Ralph Llewellyn, the murderer might have taken four or five minutes to inflict such damage before slipping away unheard and unseen. It was clearly a brazen assault.

It should also be remembered that when Mary Nichols was last seen staggering drunkenly towards the Whitechapel Road in the early hours of Friday 31 August 1888 she was not seeking out the shadows but more concerned with finding the price of a bed. 'I'll soon get my doss money,' she had laughed. She needed to be noticed rather than not, and had little to fear from the policeman on the beat who was only too aware of her plight and that of a thousand more like her on the streets of Whitechapel, who were inevitably forced to consummate their transactions against a wall or in the dark stairway of a tenement. Undoubtedly such a venue would serve as well for murder as for illicit sex. But in the normal course of events it was the client who risked being set upon and robbed by the woman's accomplices in such a place if he strayed too far from friends and a better-lit thoroughfare. In this event the felons would still be taking some risk, but a lookout could minimize the possibility of discovery or pursuit. But it was not so in the case of Nichols's attacker, who almost certainly acted alone.

For Annie Chapman, Macnaghten's 'dark and deserted alley' on Saturday, 28 September meant the back yard of No. 29 Hanbury

Street, less than half a mile from Buck's Row. The yard was often used by prostitutes as it afforded some degree of privacy, but it had to be entered via the internal passageway of the house itself, which led not only into the yard but also to the common staircase of the building. The house was let room by room, and on this particular night it was occupied by seventeen people.

By 4 a.m., with the night's activities only just beginning to abate, the market porters were already up and about their business and No. 29 was also stirring. Mr Thompson, who occupied the second-floor front room with his wife and adopted daughter, left for work at about this time. Another resident, Mrs Amelia Richardson, called 'Good morning' to him. With the opening of Spitalfields Market at five o'clock, the end of Hanbury Street, where the murder had occurred, was blocked with market vehicles, and market attendants were busy regulating the traffic. The whole area was bustling with people facing up to the long hours of the Victorian working day. At 5.30 a.m. Annie was seen talking to a man in a brown deerstalker hat. At 6 a.m. her body was discovered in the yard by another resident, Mr John Davis. At about twenty past five a carpenter named Albert Cadosch, who lived next door at No. 27, went into his back yard. He heard a voice quite near him, which he thought was probably coming from No. 29. He went back into the house for a moment, and on returning to the yard heard a 'sort of fall' against the fence that divided the yard of No. 29 from No. 27; however he thought no more of it and left for work. As mentioned earlier, all this was taking place in broad daylight, with the murder occurring at least twenty-five minutes after sun-up. And yet the killer was able to make good his escape with the missing organs of his victim concealed about his bloody person.

The double event of 30 September, and the final murder on 9 November, continue to support the view that Jack's exploits were gathering momentum not only in their barbarity but also in their audacity. In the first instance the murderer's unabated lust drove him on to his second victim in Mitre Square regardless of the extra risk imposed by an already alerted constabulary. At 1.30 a.m. City PC Edward Watkins found the Square empty. When he returned some twelve to fourteen minutes later, the body of Catherine Eddowes was discovered in the most appalling state. The possibility of being disturbed or even captured in the course of such lengthy butchery was obviously considerable. Indeed, it is possibly what happened during his attack on Mary Anne Nichols, and definitely what happened in the case of Elizabeth Stride just forty-five minutes earlier. Even now the culprit found time to stop in a doorway to scribble a message in chalk before making his final exit.

Six weeks later his dissection of Mary Jane Kelly (although perpetrated indoors) constituted the most gross and time-consuming butchery imaginable. Sara Lewis, who was visiting her friend Mrs Keyler at the time, had been unable to sleep and was sitting in a chair in her friend's room directly opposite Kelly's when she heard a woman's voice shout 'Murder!' quite loudly, but as there was only one cry she took no notice. It was about 4 a.m. The neighbour directly above Mary Jane Kelly, Elizabeth Prater, also heard a low cry of 'Murder!' at about the same time. She thought it had come from the court outside, little realizing that directly beneath her a fire had been stoked in the small grate in Mary Jane's room to enable her assailant to see more clearly to finish his devilish handiwork. The heat from the fire had been so intense that it had burnt off the spout and handle from a tin kettle. More importantly, the amount of light from the fire would have increased the risk of drawing attention to the room in an otherwise dark courtyard; and again it would have been daylight when the killer left the tiny cul-de-sac by the only available exit, a narrow archway which measured barely two feet across.

Such boldness is guaranteed to excite the imagination, tempting exaggeration and distortion – the very life blood of folklore and myth. In the case of criminal legend it is often a series of crimes rather than a single event that captures sustained public attention and endows the perpetrator with almost superhuman powers. Robin Hood, Dick Turpin, Jesse James, Bonnie and Clyde, and Al Capone are all legendary characters whose notoriety has rested on the number of their deeds rather than their anonymity. Their ability continually to evade the agencies of law and order lies at the heart of their appeal.

The earliest description of the probable culprit had been given by Elizabeth Long, who was passing down Hanbury Street on her way to Spitalfields Market minutes before Annie Chapman was murdered. She was on the right-hand side of the street when she passed a man and woman talking on the pavement. They were both leaning against the shutters of No. 29. She later identified the dead woman as the woman she had seen. She didn't see the man's face except to notice that he was dark. He was wearing a brown deerstalker hat and, she thought, a dark coat, but she couldn't be sure. She couldn't say what age he was – but he looked over forty.

He looked a little taller than the woman. He looked like a foreigner. He had a shabby genteel appearance. He said to her, 'Will you?' and she replied, 'Yes.'

This brief dialogue, which was also overheard by a Mrs Durrell, marks this account as being particularly important. From the testimony of other witnesses it is certain that Annie Chapman must have been murdered some time between 5.30 and 6 a.m. The fact that she had agreed to do her client's bidding makes it extremely unlikely that she could have gone with someone else in the short time left to her. Mrs Durrell did not think she could identify the couple, and unfortunately Elizabeth Long's recollections demonstrate an all too human ability to fill in certain gaps with information which is little more than assumption. She didn't see his face, and she couldn't say what age he was – but he looked over forty, and he looked like a foreigner.

William Marshall, a labourer resident at 64 Berner Street, had seen Elizabeth Stride talking to a rather stout, middle-aged man at about a quarter to midnight, an hour and a quarter before her murder. Half an hour before the body was discovered, PC Smith had seen her talking to a different man who had been carrying a newspaper parcel. Ten minutes later Israel Schwartz saw Stride with yet another man. Half an hour later still, Joseph Lawende had seen a man and a woman talking close to where Catherine Eddowes would be discovered.

Nevertheless despite this total confusion the hybrid impression of a possible murderer was a man five feet seven or eight inches tall, with a shabbily respectable appearance, wearing a deerstalker hat and dark clothes, and sporting a moustache but no side whiskers – a man with a foreign (Jewish) appearance. The consensus of opinion made him a little younger than Elizabeth Long had thought – a man in his thirties. But the most remarkable description – at least, the most remarkable available at the time – was given by one George Hutchinson following the fifth and final murder, that of Mary Jane Kelly. It was made all the more remarkable by the fact that, due to the seemingly inordinate haste with which her inquest was conducted, Mr Hutchinson had not had time to come forward before the proceedings had been closed. At 6 p.m. on 12 November he walked into Commercial Street police station and made the following statement to Inspector Abberline:

About 2 a.m. 9th, I was coming by Thrawl Street, Commercial Street, and just before I got to Flower and Dean Street I met the

71

murdered woman Kelly, and she said to me, 'Hutchinson will you led me sixpence.'

I said, 'I can't I have spent all my money going down to Romford.' She said, 'Good morning – I must go and find some money.' She went away toward Thrawl Street.

A man coming in the opposite direction to Kelly tapped her on the shoulder and said something to her, they both burst out laughing. I heard her say alright to him and the man said, 'You will be alright for what I have told you.' He then placed his hand around her shoulders. He also had a kind of a small parcel in his left hand with a kind of a strap round it. I stood against the lamp of the Queens Head Public House and watched him. They both then came past me and the man hung down his head with his hat over his eyes. I stooped down and looked him in the face. He looked at me stern. They both went into Dorset Street. I followed them. They both stood at the corner of the court for about three minutes. He said something to her. She said, 'Alright my dear come along you will be comfortable.' He then placed his arm on her shoulder and gave her a kiss. She said she had lost her handkerchief. He then pulled his handkerchief a red one out and gave it to her. They both went up to the Court together. I then went to the court to see if I could see them but could not. I stood there for about three quarters of an hour to see if they came out. They did not so I went away.

The description Hutchinson then gave of the man was as follows:

. . . about 34 or 35, height 5ft 6ins, complexion pale. Dark eyes and eye lashes. Slight moustache curled up each end and hair dark. Very surley looking. Dress, long dark coat, collar and cuffs trimmed with astrakan and a dark jacket under, light waistcoat, dark trousers, dark felt hat turned down in the middle, button boots and gaiters with white buttons, wore a very thick gold chain with linen collar, black tie with horse-shoe pin, respectable appearance, walked very sharp, Jewish appearance.

This fascinating and atmospheric account is crammed full of potentially valuable detail, but the most important question to be answered was this. How much had Hutchinson really seen, and how much of his portrait was fanciful?

Substitute a top hat for the soft felt one, a cape for the overcoat, and for the first time we have a portrait of the archetypal Ripper – a black, bat-like creature descending on the innocent and inevitably female flesh of its victims is, as manifested in Bram Stoker's Gothic masterpiece *Dracula*, an essentially Victorian image. The wicked landowner or mill-owner abusing his privilege and power to secure sexual satisfaction over vulnerable womanhood was a socially acceptable, even erotic, metaphor. Now, it seemed, life was copying art. The public perception of Jack the Ripper and the sexually reprehensible villain of Victorian melodrama were – and still are – to all intents and purposes the same.

Another witness, Sara Lewis, had gone to Miller's Court to visit Kelly's neighbour, Mrs Keyler, at about 2.30 a.m. She saw a man standing outside a lodging-house door close to Miller's Court. This would tally exactly with Hutchinson's stated movements, and it would therefore be reasonable to assume that this was in fact Hutchinson.

He had known Kelly for about three years. He 'knew her very well, and had been in her company a number of times'. As Barlow and Watt had pointed out in the BBC investigation, if this meant he had slept with her it would be quite natural for him to take an extra interest in the man who was picking her up. In fact, most writers have tended to accept Hutchinson's testimony whole-heartedly. Certainly Inspector Abberline did, and the stranger's respectable and foreign appearance, height, age, moustache and lack of side whiskers would seem to confirm that Hutchinson had given the police the best description of Jack the Ripper yet. If it varied to any great extent from earlier descriptions it was mainly in the fact that this time Jack really was 'dressed to kill'.

Equally curious, however, was the fact that the man had apparently been carrying a 'kind of small parcel . . . with a kind of strap round it', and in later interviews given to the press Hutchinson would recall that this eight-inch-long package had looked as thought it was covered in dark American cloth. Black American cloth is indeed the material commonly associated with doctor's bags nowadays, but in the 1880s such bags were far more widely used than is often realized. Nevertheless the notion that Jack the Ripper was a respectable-looking man who possessed anatomical skill, and the association of George Hutchinson's American cloth with the medical profession, was for many virtual proof that Jack the Ripper was either a doctor or a surgeon – a possibility which encouraged one contemporary correspondent to end his seedy epistle to the police with a circumspect 'Jack the Ripper, MD'.

One wonders, of course, how much George Hutchinson's later inclusion of American cloth in his description had in itself been influenced by popular rumour at the time, but no matter. The intriguing element is the fact that on only two occasions was the possible killer seen carrying anything, and in both cases this was described as a parcel, not a bag. PC Smith had seen a man holding a newspaper parcel; Hutchinson had seen a man with an American cloth parcel.

Where did all this lead us? The composite portrait of our felon was vague but largely consistent: a respectable-looking, moustached man of about thirty, five feet seven or eight inches tall, who may have also had a Jewish appearance. Whoever he was, public patience had all but evaporated with the discovery of the atrocity in Miller's Court, and the question on everybody's lips was not so much who was he, but why hadn't he been caught?

Soon after Chapman's murder on 8 September rumours had begun to circulate that the murderer was not a mere foreigner or one of the loafing classes, but a man of respectable calling – a man with anatomical knowledge, cunning and clever, but someone who didn't readily fit the accepted portrait of the depraved killer so crudely portrayed week after week in the pages of the *Illustrated Police News*. Edward John Goodman, writing in *Sala's Journal* in November 1892, expresses the opinion that he had intuitively felt from the very beginning:

> If the truth were known – the so called 'Jack The Ripper' would probably be . . . no vulgar ruffian, repulsive in appearance, and destitute of education, but 'a most repectable' person, mild and suave, or cheerful and plausible, in manner, of superior culture and intelligence, possibly a very popular man in his own circle – what is commonly called 'a good fellow' – in short the very last person whom ordinary folks would have suspected of such deeds as his.

With Hutchinson's evidence the image of the 'toff', a man of education, influence and money, was consolidated. The public perception of the murderer had taken an irrevocable turn, and the mystery itself had become more potent as a result. This was the last sort of person that would ever have been suspected at the outset, and may even explain the ease with which the culprit had obviously been able to gain the confidence of his victims and evade any troublesome inquiries from the policeman on the beat.

Now at least the general public were alert to the possibility, and whilst Jack the Ripper continued to run the gauntlet of ever-increasing police and vigilante activity, the expectation that he would eventually be apprehended must have been high. No doubt the risk of capture did not escape Jack either; it was almost certainly an essential element in the performance of his bizarre rituals, for there can be no question that, had he chosen his victims at random from any number of other boroughs, varying the pattern of his attacks, the possibility of capture would have been considerably reduced. Had he continued to operate in such a small area increasingly saturated with uniformed and plain clothes police he might well have chanced his luck too far, but in the ten short weeks of his 'reign' it should be understood that the odds were always in his favour.

The Victorian policeman had very little to aid him in the execution of his duty beside his five senses and the support of his fellow officers. Forensic science was in its infancy and fingerprinting was not to be adopted by New Scotland Yard until 1901. The reality facing Jack's beleaguered hunters was described by a Philadelphia journalist, R. Harding Davis, who toward the end of August 1889 spent a night touring the area in the company of Detective Inspector Henry Moore of H Division.

'I don't think you will be disappointed in the district [said the inspector]. After a stranger has gone over it he takes a much more lenient view of our failure to find Jack The Ripper, as they call him, than he did before. . . . I might put two regiments of police in this half mile of district and half of them would be as completely out of sight and hearing of the others as if they were in separate cells in a prison. To give you an idea of it, my men formed a circle around a spot where one of the murders took place, guarding they thought, every entrance and approach, and within a few minutes they found fifty people inside the lines. They had come in through two passageways which my men could not find. And then, you know these people never lock their doors, and the murderer has only to lift the latch of the nearest house and walk through it and out the back way.'

It was obviously a hopeless situation for the men of H Division. The efficient policing of such a veritable rat's nest of humanity was, for any amount of conscious dedication, largely a matter of containment rather than prevention. In those dense groups of tenements interlaced with dark stinking alleys – some measuring no more than two feet across – a police officer dared not enter without considerable personal risk. Quite clearly Jack the Ripper's brinkmanship and the failure of the authorities to apprehend him were not incompatible.

And yet men like Sir Melville Macnaghten, Assistant Commissioner Robert Anderson and other highly placed officials gave a clear indication in their respective autobiographies that the police investigation was more advanced than was ever admitted at the time. Their conclusions were based either on the same shreds of evidence that less informed investigators have sifted through for the past century or on privileged information that was known only to a few and which has for one reason or another remained secret. Did Scotland Yard discover too late who Jack the Ripper was? If so, how? And why not admit it? Has there been a conspiracy of silence surrounding these abominable crimes, or have researchers been innocently playing blind man's buff for the last hundred years?

Whatever the truth, the inability – or was it reticence? – on the part of the Victorian authorities publicly to communicate their feelings at the time has helped to create the legend.

As time passed, a phantom began to haunt the back streets of Whitechapel – a spectre who could rise to claim any number of future unsolved atrocities for himself, and who was also capable of assuming a new identity at the stroke of a writer's pen. When 'Saucy Jack' walked into the night he also walked into history, and now, one hundred years on from the actual events, the legacy we have inherited is a well-established part of English folklore, a nineteenth-century enigma to be put on the same shelf as other curios from our Victorian past. Most questions were still waiting to be answered, as they had been from the very beginning, and it seemed to us from what we had learnt so far that one or two more were still waiting to be asked. For there was one further possibility to explain the sudden end to that reign of terror which brought the Metropolitan Police to their knees. It was not the fact that the instigator might have left the country, died a natural death, committed suicide or wasted away in an asylum – but that he himself had been murdered.

VII

On Tuesday evening, 16 October 1888, the forty-nine-year-old president of the Whitechapel Vigilance Committee, George Lusk, received what was almost certainly a genuine communication from Catherine Eddowes's murderer. Enclosed with the message in a three-inch cardboard box were the remains of a human kidney which Dr Openshaw of the London Hospital stated was a left female kidney taken within the last three weeks from a woman about forty-five years of age. The kidney was at an advanced stage of Bright's disease (otherwise known as a 'nutmeg' kidney, often associated with heavy gin drinking), a complaint from which Eddowes was known to have suffered. Furthermore, one inch of renal artery (a blood vessel approximately three inches long in all) was still attached to the kidney; there had been two inches of renal artery left inside Catherine Eddowes. Henry Sutton, senior surgeon at the London Hospital, who examined the organ with Dr Openshaw, said he would stake his reputation that it had been put in spirits within a few hours of removal from the body, possibly indicating that whoever had possessed the kidney for the past two weeks had not only known what to preserve the specimen in but that he had ready access to the preservative. The accompanying letter read:

Mr Lusk,
   Sir I send you half the Kidne I took from one woman prasarved it for you tother piece I fried and ate it was very nise I may send you the bloody knif that took it out if you only wate a whil longer.
   signed Catch me when you can Mishter Lusk.

From hell

Mr Lusk

    *Sor I send you half the
Kidne I took from one women
prasarved it for you tother piece
fried and ate it was very nise I
may send you the bloody knif that
took it out if you only wate a whil
longer.*

    *Signed   Catch me when
              you Can
            Mishter Lusk —*

• •

The letter suggests that a man of some learning might well be
deliberately setting out to appear semi-literate. The spelling of
'Knif' and 'whil' show that the author is perfectly at ease with the
silent 'k' and 'h', whilst being hopeless when it comes to phonetically
logical words such as mister – which he gives as 'Mishter'. Then
again other tricky words are spelt correctly – 'piece', 'fried' and
'signed'. It also seemed to us that the whole timbre of the
communication was peculiarly English. The spelling of 'prasarved'
and 'tother piece' and the general phrasing give the impression of a
ham actor enjoying himself too much, writing almost in dialect like

some deranged Long John Silver – overdoing it, in fact, at the point where subtlety could have won the day. Jack was taunting his would-be captors, confident that, for now at least, he was safe. The point was, did the authorities ever get any closer? Were there reasons why Jack's real identity could never be revealed? Had a cover-up been initiated in order to avoid a damaging scandal?

Eighty-five years after the chalked message in Goulston Street was obliterated by Sir Charles Warren, the BBC put forward in their television dramatization the most incredible explanation for such apparent lunacy. Sir Charles was one of the country's leading freemasons, and as such would have found particular significance in the spelling of the word 'Juwes'. The word relates to a part of the ceremony at which an apprentice mason is received into the brotherhood. A hand is drawn across his throat in a symbolic cut to indicate to the initiate the penalty for revealing masonic secrets.

Masonic tradition holds that three men murdered Hiram Abiff, the Masonic Grand Master and builder of Solomon's temple. The three men were Jubela, Jubelo and Jubelum, known collectively as the 'Juwes'. Eventually the culprits were brought before Solomon, who decreed that all three should be executed in the manner they themselves suggested, namely:

Jubela: O that my throat had been cut across, my tongue torn out, and my body buried in the rough sands of the sea, at low water mark, where the tide ebbs and flows twice in twenty-four hours. . . .

Jubelo: O that my left breast has been torn open and my heart and vitals taken from thence and thrown over my left shoulder. . . .

Jubelum: O that my body had been severed in two in the midst, and divided to the north and south, my bowels burnt to ashes in the centre and the ashes scattered by the four winds of heaven. . . .

Does this explain the Chief Commissioner's unprecedented visit to Goulston Street and the extraordinary action he took once he had got there? Did he recognize in the hand of the murderer the hand of a fellow mason? It was a startling premise, and once which Stephen Knight used to effect when such a possibility was grafted on to Joseph Sickert's story.

It is certainly intriguing to wonder what might have ensued had the possibility of a conspiracy been further investigated at the time, but the discovery of Alice Mackenzie's body in July 1889 would have made the idea of a conspiracy look less tenable than ever. The inability (or reticence) on the part of all the agencies and individuals involved in the original investigation to come clean has undoubtedly fanned the flames of rumour and intrigue, and it is only too easy to see how an arcane society like the Brotherhood of Freemasons can provide a ready scapegoat for all manner of potential conspiracies. In recent years this powerful society, with a membership of more than seven hundred thousand in the United Kingdom, has come under considerable attack – not least from Stephen Knight, whose best-selling book *The Brotherhood* stirred up a hornet's nest. The arguments for and against freemasonry are now voiced more vociferously than ever before, and there can be little doubt that with so much adverse publicity a great many people – rightly or wrongly – believe that the society very often uses its influence unfairly, if not actually in sinister ways. It is not our intention to condemn or condone the motives of individual freemasons or evaluate the benefit or otherwise of freemasonry on our modern society. Our concern is Victorian England and the possibility that some form of corporate secrecy has been instrumental in denying to a concerned public the full facts surrounding the murder of five East End prostitutes.

The current vogue of 'If in doubt, hang it on the freemasons' goes nowhere towards explaining the events of the autumn of 1888. Joseph Sickert's tale of royal indiscretion, much embellished by Stephen Knight, is no more than a yarn, as Sickert himself admitted. Without this testimony the motive for a masonic conspiracy is non-existent. Also, if Prince Albert Victor had been involved in any way with the Whitechapel murders we could readily appreciate the necessity for the Royal Family and its loyal servants within the Victorian Establishment to suppress the truth, and this might well have included high-ranking freemasons within the civil service and police force; but the proposition that the murders were actually carried out according to masonic ritual by rational – if somewhat misguided – individuals working in concert is demonstrably ludicrous.

To begin with, even if one accepts the existence of a strong enough motive to necessitate the dispatch of five illiterate prostitutes, there is no reason for bizarre rituals to have been carried out which would only have drawn attention to the crimes. Also, from the evidence presented to us it is perfectly clear that such retribution is reserved for fellow masons who have betrayed their trust – as Jubela, Jubelo and Jubelum had done. The fact that the victims were women further obviates the need for such ceremony: women are barred from taking part in any masonic ritual, including – one must assume – being executed in a manner reserved for the Brotherhood's most despised traitors.

Even if it is allowed that in exceptional circumstances certain misguided individuals would be prepared to carry out such barbaric acts, it is perfectly reasonable to assume that they would be at pains to get the ritual right. After all, what is a ceremony if the necessary procedures are not carried out with meticulous care? 'O that my left breast had been torn open and my heart and vitals taken from thence and thrown over my left shoulder. . . .' In the two cases in which Jack the Ripper's victims had been disembowelled the entrails had been placed over the right shoulder, not the left, and in no instance had the heart of the victim been interfered with. Indeed the incisions were made low down in the abdominal area, indicating far more reasonably a perverted sexual motive and an obsession with the internal female organs.

As so often occurs when trying to establish a motive for these murders, the obvious and most likely explanation for a potentially important clue is dismissed in favour of a more sensational conclusion. In this instance no one who wants to persuade us of masonic involvement cares to think of the reality too closely. At the risk of appearing grossly flippant, it has to be said that anyone standing or kneeling over a disembowelled corpse with several pounds of bloody intestines in his hand would have to put them somewhere before being able to butcher the deeper organs. One of the easiest places to deposit them would surely be on the ground in front of the assailant, by the head of the victim.

What then are we left with? A dozen or so words scrawled in chalk in 'a good schoolboy hand' close to the bloodstained remains of Catherine Eddowes's apron. One of them, 'Juwes', may have masonic connotations. We also know that Sir Charles Warren was a leading freemason of his day. But this is a long way from establishing that Jack the Ripper was a freemason, and even further away from demonstrating that he was protected from detection and arrest by his fellow masons.

More relevant still is the question of whether or not these words can actually be attributed to Jack the Ripper in the first place. The truth is that nobody can honestly say. Since the message was erased, the only evidence to link the communication to the apron is the opinion of Constable Long, who discovered both. He assumed the message had been recently chalked, as he felt certain it would have been erased by one of the many people living in the building soon after being written. But we can hardly accept this as proof of authorship. Nine months later, we discovered, this unfortunate constable would be dismissed from the Metropolitan Police for being found drunk on duty, which should be enough to suggest to some future researcher that he wrote the message himself! An entertaining suggestion perhaps, but the important point is that PC Long's admirable faith in the residents' social responsibility was hardly conclusive evidence, whatever his condition was at the time.

The 'writing on the wall' is yet another example of how we come to inherit aspects of these murders as proven fact simply because they excite our imaginations to new possibilities. That is not to say that Jack the Ripper *couldn't* have written the words – simply that he may not have. If the murderer had chalked the message, then it had already been on the wall for nearly an hour by the time it was discovered; and unless we believe that the tenants of No. 118 Goulston Street always came rushing out with buckets and cloths to attend to offending graffiti we have to accept that this particularly obtuse and ungrammatical prose may have been there in the darkened hallway for any part, or all, of that night. The mis-spelling of 'Juwes' could merely be a coincidence, having more likely been written by a semi-literate foreigner. This would at least explain the double negative, which clouds the meaning of the message in a manner unlikely to be employed by a native English speaker.

What is the alternative? Someone – a high-ranking freemason, or someone who has acquired some knowledge of freemasonry deliberately, leaves a sign to inform other masons of his credentials. This in itself would be unnecessary if a conspiracy to murder had been initiated by high-ranking freemasons with the sanction of their Brotherhood. All the murders would have been carried out according to masonic law, and high-ranking masons like Sir Charles Warren would already be aware of the nature of the crimes. Obliterating the word 'Juwes' would also serve no real purpose as only the initiated would be aware of its significance, and in any case the spelling was to become public knowledge because Mr Crawford's cross-examination of PC Long's testimony was soon to be widely reported in the press.

It is worth remembering, too, that the argument about whether or not the writing should be erased was initiated not by Warren but by the first Metropolitan Police officer to arrive at the scene. This was Superintendent Arnold, who, only too aware of Warren's paranoia where potential civil unrest was concerned, must have guessed what his commanding officer would want to have done in the circumstances. In the event he was to be proved correct. After some argument with the City police, Warren had the offending slogan rubbed out. He may even have felt the need to support his officer's earlier stand against City police opinion. There was, after all, considerable rivalry between the two forces, and Warren was not a man to lose an opportunity to impress his authority.

It is possible – just – that Jack the Ripper could have been a freemason. But if he was, he was an insane freemason working alone, whose motives were a product of his own diseased psychology. He would have been a homicidal maniac first and a freemason second, and any ritualistic element in his crimes would have been a symptom of his own sexual fantasies and desire. His insatiable craving to find ultimate satisfaction in the warm blood and internal organs of his victims was driving him further and further into the abyss. The carnage in Miller's Court amply demonstrates this. It was not an attempt to fulfil the prerequisites of a pagan rite, but an orgy of destruction embarked upon by a man in torment. Such a man had no reason to expect protection from a Brotherhood whose strict rules of morality and conduct he so blatantly profaned, and even less reason to suppose that Warren, whose career was soon to lie in ruins as an indirect result of the Ripper's exploits, would not be happy to present this particular masonic head to the Home Secretary on a platter.

If we accept Major Smith's opinion that the writing on the wall was probably written to throw the police off the scent, to divert attention from the Gentiles and throw it upon the Jews, then it was just as likely that, even if it had contained a masonic cipher, it could have been left by someone who knew something of the secret society and who also wished to confuse his pursuers. Someone who was close enough to the bosom of the Victorian Establishment to know something of its inner workings, perhaps? Someone who may have recognized in his own perversion the enactment of a childish oath and therefore used his knowledge of the 'Juwes' as soon as the opportunity presented itself? In doing so, the perpetrator would be mocking his peers, from whom he had become more and more estranged. He would know, and delight in, the fact that his revelation would cause great consternation among masonic circles within the civil, political and police hierarchies.

This in itself was entirely plausible – after all, there is a considerable element of mockery in the crimes themselves, which shows not only a blatant contempt for human life but a similar disposition towards the law and its ability to do anything about the situation. But what sort of a man are we talking about here – the son of a freemason perhaps? Or someone who belonged to one of the professions closely associated with membership of this particular society, such as the Metropolitan Police itself, the civil service or the legal profession? Could Jack the Ripper have been not a doctor of medicine but a doctor of law – a judge, perhaps, or a barrister? Someone like Macnaghten's barrister/schoolteacher?

This is, of course, pure conjecture. There was not the slightest evidence to support such a claim, but having indulged ourselves thus far there was another aspect in all this which was also worth considering. The message in Goulston Street had been written in chalk on a black wall, and, according to Detective Constable Halse, 'in a good schoolboy hand'. The inference is clear, as W.P. Hayden realized when he wrote to Dan Farson. The sort of person who would naturally write like this and also carry chalk in his pocket would quite likely turn out to be a schoolteacher – someone just like Montague John Druitt.

On 8 November, the day before Mary Jane Kelly's murder, Warren finally resigned – but not, as is often believed, as a direct result of the failure to apprehend the Whitechapel murderer. In November 1888 *Murray's Magazine* published an article by Warren entitled 'The Police of the Metropolis'. According to Charles Warren's grandson, Watkin Wynn Williams, writing in 1941, this article was immediately made the object of the strongest public censure by the Home Secretary, Matthews, who also drew Warren's attention to a Home Office Circular of 27 May 1879 which forbade the police to discuss departmental affairs with the press. Warren immediately countered by writing to Matthews's Private Secretary, Evelyn Ruggles-Brise:

> I never heard of the circular you sent nor do I consider it in any way refers to the Commissioner of Police any more than to any of the other Police Magistrates.
>
> I should certainly not have accepted the post of Commissioner if I had been told that my mouth was to be shut all round and the truth concerning the police was not to be known.

Obviously the relationship between Warren and Matthews was at breaking point, and with James Monro taking up residency in Whitehall the writing really was on the wall for the besieged Commissioner.

In fact Warren had discussed his resignation with the Home Secretary as early as March 1888, and he tendered it in August. When he finally did go it was not so much because of the magazine article but because of the ever-increasing lack of *entente* between himself and the Home Office, and the public's ever-decreasing confidence in his leadership.

Throughout the period of his administration, General Sir Charles Warren had consistently shown himself to be a square peg in a round hole – a military man who genuinely believed that violent revolution lurked at every street corner. He may have been misguided in trying to create a police force based on traditional military codes of practice, but he was in many ways simply reflecting the wishes of successive Home Secretaries. James Monro would in fact be the first civilian to command the Metropolitan Police, and, by 1930, of the ten men who had been appointed Chief Commissioner seven would have been ex-army officers.

According to Watkin Wynn Williams, Warren had worked night and day and never spared himself a moment in his efforts to follow up the criminal, which may well have been true. But, whatever his own commitment to the investigation, it was clearly not going to be enough to rescue his ailing career. The inability of his police force to apprehend the Whitechapel murderer under his leadership was being increasingly perceived as a personal failure by those who were desperately trying to find a scapegoat; apart possibly from the Home Secretary Warren was best placed to carry the can. Any decision he now took was almost certain to result in further ridicule, however unjust, and his public standing was at such a low ebb by the time of Elizabeth Stride's and Catherine Eddowes's murders that nothing short of Jack the Ripper's capture would have enabled him to survive the storm.

By October Scotland Yard was receiving about twelve hundred letters a day, offering various suggestions as to how the White-chapel murderer could be apprehended. About two-thirds urged the use of bloodhounds. On 1 October 1888 *The Times* reminded its readers that twelve years earlier a murderer in Blackburn had been successfully tracked and caught with the help of trained dogs, and it now asked whether they should not once more be employed. The following day Percy Lindley, a bloodhound breeder from Essex, wrote to say that if a couple of trained dogs had been put on the scent of the murderer while fresh they might well have done what the police had failed to do.

Sir Charles Warren immediately wrote to Mr Lindley to satisfy himself about certain aspects of the hound's supposed talents before arranging for a series of trials to take place. At seven o'clock on the morning of Monday, 8 October, two dogs called Barnaby and Burgho – the property of a man named Edwin Brough of Wyndgate, near Scarborough – were tested in Regent's Park; despite a heavy coating of hoar frost both dogs did their job well.

They were tested for a second time in the evening in Hyde Park, and againe in Hyde Park in the early hours of Tuesday morning – this time in the presence of the Commissioner. In two runs Sir Charles himself became the hunted man, and once more the dogs did enough to encourage him to believe in their potential value.

Although some people – including Warren – doubted the ability of the hounds to follow a trail in the crowded streets of Whitechapel, it is clear that he was prepared to consider any radical proposal if it had a chance of success. And yet such a seemingly laudable initiative – which had been largely encouraged by popular demand – only gave the press further ammunition with which to ridicule him, as this contemporary lampoon shows:

> *They brought him the bloodhounds the best to be found,*
> *And the 'tecs' and the dogs sought the murderer's ground;*
> *Then the bow-wows were loosed, and with noses to earth,*
> *They trotted away 'mid the bystanders' mirth.*
>
> *The bloodhounds grew gay with the fun of the chase,*
> *And they ran like two thoroughbreds running a race;*
> *They leapt o'er the wall, and they swam o'er the stream,*
> *Their tongues lolling out and their eyeballs agleam.*
>
> *But Warren and Matthews kept up with them still –*
> *They followed through valley, they followed o'er hill;*
> *Then darkness came down, and afar in the haze*
> *Hound, Warren, and Matthews were lost to our gaze.*
>
> *And never since then, though they're much overdue,*
> *Have those hounds or officials returned to our view;*
> *But a legend relates that in lands far away*
> *They are still running on in pursuit of their prey.*
>
> *And at eve, when the citizens gather to drink,*
> *They speak of the lost ones, and say, with a wink,*
> *'Twas an excellent thing to put hounds on the track,*
> *Since it took off two men who are not wanted back.*

Even before the Hyde Park trial had taken place, Warren had issued strict instructions that the body of any future murder victim was not to be removed until trained bloodhounds were sent for and given the chance to track the killer. A month later, on the day after

Warren finally resigned, a handful of Metropolitan Police officers found themselves standing outside No. 13 Miller's Court. It had been drizzling for most of the morning, and by eleven o'clock, when Mary Jane Kelly's body was discovered, the surrounding streets had been used by so many people that it would probably have been impossible for any animal to track a specific quarry across such busy, paved and wet ground. Nevertheless the dutiful officers sent for the dogs, totally unaware that they were unavailable: Barnaby and Burgho had been taken back to Scarborough by their owner who had been unable to get a firm commitment from Scotland Yard to buy or even insure the animals whilst they were in police service.

Once again the press justifiably ridiculed Scotland Yard's ineptitude. But, to be fair to the officers who were at the sharp end of the Ripper investigation, the Criminal Investigation Department was hardly dry behind the ears when one of the most cunning criminal maniacs in history arrived to test its mettle in an unprecedented series of crimes. The small detective force at Scotland Yard, which had been formed in 1842, consisted of only two inspectors and six sergeants, and it was not until 1878 that this department was enlarged and given its own Assistant Commissioner.

For four years James Monro had been in charge of a CID in which he had won universal support and respect from his colleagues. He was a good detective and a loyal captain to his men, and at this time he also carried considerable favour with the Home Secretary. His experience was never more required at the helm than now, when the Whitechapel murderer was about to begin his reign of terror. But it was not to be. He had left for an unspecified post at the Home Office just hours before Hurricane Jack's arrival, and he would return to the bridge just in time to see the tempest pass.

A retired Commissioner, Henry Smith, was to state confidently: 'There is no man living who knows as much of these murders as I do.' He then goes on to say that, in spite of his boast, he doesn't have the faintest idea who the murderer was. His inference is clear. If *he* didn't know the identity of the killer, then nobody else did either. But he can hardly be regarded as the greatest authority on this series of crimes when he was directly involved only in the investigation of Catherine Eddowes's murder, the only one to take place within the jurisdiction of the City police.

James Monro, however, was far better placed in the scheme of things. Even though he was not officially connected with the investigations after his discreet move to the Home Office in August, it was soon to become clear to us that he still kept in close contact with the officers of his old department for the three months of his absence. By the end of November he would be picking up the pieces of Warren's administration, fully cognizant of the CID's operations throughout the Ripper period. After all, since August Monro had been effectively overseeing his old department from a desk in Whitehall, at a time when the CID were ultimately and directly responsible to the Home Office into which Monro had been conveniently drafted.

The relationship between the Home Office and Scotland Yard at this time was so complex that it was far more likely that Henry Smith was not a party to all the available information, and may certainly have been kept ignorant of the more sensitive aspects of the case. The strong, Metropolitan, right arm of the law was often accused of not knowing what its left arm in the City was doing, and vice versa – never more so than during the Whitechapel murder investigations.

Every indication so far had led us to the conclusion that the Metropolitan Police officers involved with the day-to-day running of the Whitechapel murder investigation were doing their best to catch Jack the Ripper, and would continue to do so long after he had left the scene. Far more plausible, therefore, was the notion that the killer's identity had somehow become known at a higher level, and once his whereabouts had been ascertained his discreet arrest would have been undertaken by selected officers and men. But in this instance we might well have expected a more concerted effort on the part of Scotland Yard to placate a concerned public who were becoming increasingly tiresome. 'Why hasn't Jack the Ripper been caught?' was the one question that every senior officer in the Metropolitan Police would dearly love to have answered convincingly, and their inability to answer it has been directly responsible for creating the very legend we now come to examine.

Had a conspiracy been initiated at the highest level within Scotland Yard it would undoubtedly have been ideal to use someone like Anderson's Polish Jew as a scapegoat. But nobody was used like this. Instead we are left with a Pandora's box of possibilities, intrigues and questions, with each Commissioner or Assistant Commissioner individually contributing to the uncoordinated defence of the police force. When one considers the situation at Scotland Yard at the time – the constant battle with the Home Office; Monro and Warren's resignation; and Anderson's sojourn in Switzerland at the height of the investigation – it would be an understatement to conclude that the Metropolitan Police was not in the best state to deal with Jack the Ripper, let alone any subsequent conspiracy.

There was, however, a third possibility – that the identity of the Whitechapel murderer was known at an even higher level than the operational departments of the Metropolitan Police, and that only one or two senior police officers were aware of the real circumstances surrounding the ending of the atrocities after the death of Mary Jane Kelly. We already have reason to question Sir Robert Anderson's unconvincing testimony, and can see how he would have been one of two men most likely to be party to privileged information. The other had to be the mutual friend of both Anderson and Macnaghten, and the man who had enjoyed both the confidence of the CID and the Home Office – James Monro.

VIII

James Monro, CB, died on Wednesday, 28 January 1920, in his eighty-first year. The son of an Edinburgh solicitor, he was educated in Scotland and Berlin before passing into the Indian Civil Service in 1858. In 1863 he married, and in 1877 became the Inspector General of Police, a post which he was to hold for the next six years. According to his obituary in *The Times*, 'He had an exceptional share of most of the gifts needed for this department of the public service, especially in the detective branch, and became a veritable terror to the criminal classes of Bengal and, later, of London. His memory for facts and faces, names, and detail of cases was extraordinarily tenacious.'

In 1884 he retired from the Indian service to become Assistant Commissioner of the Metropolitan Police. After his resignation as Chief Commissioner on 12 June 1890 he returned to India, and with about a dozen helpers established a medical mission at Ranaghat, some forty miles from Calcutta. The neighbourhood suffered greatly from the ravages of fever and malaria, and people flocked in thousands to the settlement; here medical relief was given daily at considerable expense to Monro, the only condition imposed being attendance at a religious service. In 1905 he returned to England for the last time and settled in Cheltenham. During his lifetime he had written two published works. The first, in 1886, was a report on the history of a Metropolitan Police department known as the Convict Supervision Office; the second in 1921 took the form of three lecturers on the Second Coming and was entitled *The Blessed Hope*.

Clearly James Monro was a man of firm Christian faith with an innate sense of duty and public service, but he was also the man who had to have known more about the Whitechapel murders than anybody else. Unfortunately, for whatever reasons he seemed not to have committed his knowledge or opinion to print. However, the discovery of a letter published in the *Radio Times* in August 1973, in response to the BBC television series about the murders, resuscitated our flagging conviction. The final paragraph read:

> My grandfather had his own views on the identity of the Ripper, but came back into office too late to deal with the case as he would have wished. He bequeathed his notes on the affair to his eldest son who died in 1928, and it is possible that some cousins of mine may retain them to this day.
>
> Christopher Monro
>
> Shrewsbury

All our attempts to trace Christopher Monro anywhere in the Shrewsbury area failed, but at least the letter to the *Radio Times* had provided sufficient information for us eventually to contact some other living descendants of the late Commissioner – but still no sign of Christopher. James Monro's granddaughter very kindly offered to inquire about his whereabouts on our behalf, and suggested we contacted another relative, in Scotland. Here we discovered Commissioner James Monro's handwritten memoirs, written in 1903 for the benefit of his children, safely tucked away at the back of a cupboard in an Edinburgh suburb, unseen by anyone outside the immediate family.

But when we read the papers we found not a single mention of Jack the Ripper or any associated murder investigation. Understandably we were disappointed, but at the same time we realized that the papers were nevertheless extremely valuable, not just from a historical point of view but because they were still relevant to our investigations. The fact that Monro didn't mention, even in passing, the most celebrated series of crimes of the century could suggest that he had purposely avoided the subject; after all, his obituary in *The Times* had spoken of his 'memory for facts and faces, names, and detail of cases' being 'extraordinarily tenacious'. And now, when he had purposely created an ideal opportunity to tell his children about his life in the Metropolitan Police, he had chosen not to mention the most celebrated murder investigation in British criminal history.

Writing to his son, Charlie, Monro explains how a recent article in *The Times*, relating to the appointment of a new Commissioner of Police in March 1903, has prompted him to put down something for his children so that they should know something of the life their father led while in the Metropolitan Police, and the reasons which made him resign as Commissioner in June 1890. Monro is quick to point out that *The Times* was correct in saying that he had resigned not as a result of a quarrel between himself and the Home Secretary, but out of self-sacrifice on behalf of the interests of the police. And he stresses that he had no reason to resign had he chosen to remain in office. All he had to do was to tell his men that he had done everything he could for them in trying to improve their pensions, but in the end Government would not comply with their demands.

But he also recognizes that this would not have been honest. Every Monday he regularly talked to all new recruits and had made a point of telling them that they were no longer Thomas Smith or Robert Jones – they were PC 300 or PC 301. Their private life was gone, and they were now members of a great force and servants of the public, a position in which they had to sacrifice themselves – and that in all matters they had to put away private considerations.

Now, when faced with his own teaching, what was he to do? As a man of firm Christian conviction and great moral courage he really had no choice. His stand against the unfair conditions being imposed on his men was a question of right and wrong, not of mere expediency, and as such he knew he had to resign. 'Had I not done so,' says the Commissioner, 'I should have felt myself to be a coward. And I could never have looked my recruit in the face, and preached to him the duty of self-sacrifice, without condemning myself as one who had been called on to make such a sacrifice of self, and had refused to do so.'

According to Monro, every effort was made to induce him to withdraw his resignation, including an attempt by the Prince of Wales, but he could not be persuaded. 'There was but one course open which was consistent with right and honour – and that was the path of self sacrifice for my men.' Largely as a result of his efforts his men eventually received almost all that they had asked for, and although one senses a certain puritanical pride in this final justification of his sacrifice it is also abundantly clear that the Commissioner was a man of unimpeachable integrity. However, he goes on to answer the charge of occasional indiscretion levelled at him:

But, says the *Times*, 'Mr Monro albeit a strong man was not always discreet.' I am not so presumptuous as to imagine for a moment that I have always done things as they ought to have been done – far from it. But what does the *Times* mean by being discreet? I suppose it means that I did not always do as the *Times* thought I should have done. This may be so. But where is all the evidence of indiscretion on my part? Let me hear them, and I shall be able to reply.

When I was first appointed Commissioner, I had all the criminal work to superintend – notably the dynamite crimes. Since 1885, when the Tower outrage was detected by me, there has not been a single dynamite case – and every attempt at outrage of this description was prevented and nipped in the bud – I do not suppose that indiscretion can be charged against me on that score.

Now Monro comes to deal with the period leading up to his resignation in August 1888 and his subsequent appointment to an unspecified post at the Home Office. It is here that we would expect to find out something about his feelings about the events of that autumn. But there is nothing. One wonders if in this case discretion had indeed proven the better of valour, as it is impossible to believe that someone in his position did not have anything to say about these cataclysmic events which so damaged the public image of the police force he cared so much about.

We put this very point to his grandson, James, who did not remember his grandfather saying anything more on the subject than: 'Jack The Ripper should have been caught.' This is a tantalizing and deceptively straightforward recollection in itself – and, when considered alongside Christopher Monro's stated opinion that his grandfather had his own views on the identity of Jack the Ripper, again makes one wonder how much the old detective knew but wouldn't say. Nevertheless, thanks to what the Commissioner does tell us, we begin to see what life was like behind closed Whitehall doors where discretion was everything:

While I was Asst. Commissioner, I had to fight against the machinations of Mr Jenkinson. I had to do this under four different Secretaries of State, and all of them supported me against Mr J. The last Secretary of State dismissed Mr Jenkinson, and much against my will, put me into his post of Chief of the Secret Department. I do not suppose that any of these Secretaries of State could have thought me wanting in discretion.

Similarly while Asst. Commissioner, the Commissioner, Sir C. Warren made life so intolerable that I resigned. What the Home Secretary thought of the merits of the matters at issue between us may be gathered from the fact that he retained me as Chief of the

Secret Department, where all things of discretion were indispensable. My full vindication came when Sir C. Warren resigned. I was recommended by the Home Office authorities to apply for the Commissionership, and I distinctly refused to do anything of the kind. In spite of this refusal my name was the only name sent up to the Queen as recommended for the Commissionership, and I was appointed to that post. Such an appointment surely would not have been conferred in this very exceptional manner on a man who was wanting in discretion! And I was still continued in the post of Chief of the Secret Department, although I asked to be relieved of the duties, and declined to take any salary for performing them.

So now we knew what Monro was doing at the Home Office. As the Central News Agency had correctly deduced, Monro had filled the position previously occupied by the now Sir Edward Jenkinson, KCB, who had risen to his largely undefined role as 'spy-master general' through the Indian Civil Service.

On the formation of Gladstone's Government in 1882 he had become private secretary to Lord Spencer at Dublin Castle, where he was soon to take command of the recently formed anti-Fenian detective force. Not unlike Monro, his experiences in India throughout the 1857 Mutiny had, it was hoped, made him ideally suited to deal with the increasing threat from the Fenian Brotherhood of Irish emigrants in the United States, who were now embarking on their latest and most destructive campaign of terror.

As the head of the CID Monro too was preoccupied with the Fenian threat, but, as we were now to discover, his department was vulnerable to the machinations of powerful men within the Civil Service who considered themselves above and unaccountable to Scotland Yard and the CID. And this in itself introduced an entirely new dimension to the puzzle we had been trying to solve. Though we were initially disappointed by the contents of Monro's memoirs, we could see that there had been far more opportunity for covert activity within Whitehall than would have been possible beneath Scotland Yard's leaky umbrella.

In his somewhat incomplete memoirs, Monro constantly refers to the mischievous attempts by this secret department to do police work in London. Although he and Matthews finally succeeded in removing this thorn in their flesh it is perfectly clear than an organization already existed within Whitehall which saw itself not only as an intelligence gathering agency but as an independent and covert detective force. The exploits of agencies like the CIA and the KGB have become common currency in the fact and fiction of our age. The history of the British secret service can be traced back as far as Tudor times, and Victorian Whitehall's 'secret department' would one day grow up to be MI5, which in turn would father MI6 and other yet more secret and nameless guardians of the *status quo*; while Monro's counter to the more subversive elements in Victorian society was now to be known as the Special Branch of the CID, which was to be given total responsibility for political crime.

In the years leading up to 1888, apart from the Irish threat fears had been growing in government circles about the increasing civil discontent being demonstrated by certain working-class factions, and the emergence of their new champion – socialism. Charles Warren's appointment had been made with the anticipated nature of police work very much in mind, as had James Monro's appointment in 1884 when his considerable experience in dealing with political crime in India was to prove invaluable in his new post at Scotland Yard. Monro had been at Scotland Yard only a few months when simultaneous attempts were made by Fenian conspirators to blow up the Tower of London and the House of Commons. Monro went straight to the Tower and ordered the outer gates to be closed before the visitors could leave. Among those detained was a man named Cunningham, who was afterwards tried, together with an accomplice arrested some days later; both were convicted and given prison sentences.

Shortly before Monro's appointment explosions had occurred at the Local Government Board in Whitehall, the offices of *The Times* and several railway stations. Part of Scotland Yard itself was soon to be dynamited, but this was the last successful act of terrorism under Monro's administration, although many plots were discovered or nipped in the bud – including an attempt to blow up Westminster Abbey on the occasion of Queen Victoria's Jubilee in 1887.

This was a testament indeed to Monro's fine detective work, but it was also in this area that he was to come into contention with Edward Jenkinson, whose activities represented only too clearly the kind of obstacles so often placed before the investigating officers of the Metropolitan Police at the whim of a powerful civil servant. Monro had become aware that, instead of simply collecting information on Fenian matters and making it over to the Metropolitan Police, Jenkinson and his agents had been working directly with the Irish police, effectively thwarting Scotland Yard in its attempts to protect London from Irish subversives. Jenkinson was finally ordered to remove the Irish police from London, but, as Monro was then to discover in a most providential manner, his adversary was still not prepared to cease his undercover detective work.

A man calling himself Connolly had applied to Scotland Yard for a licence to become an omnibus conductor, but when asked to give details of his present employer he refused – except to say that his name was Dawson. Monro, only too aware of potential Irish involvement with Jenkinson, had Connolly brought before him and soon persuaded him to come clean if he wanted to leave Scotland Yard. Connolly then became much more communicative: he gave his and Dawson's addresses, and told Monro that his own job was to watch public houses. This meant, he said, that he had to watch certain men who went to public houses, and follow them, reporting to Dawson. He added that Dawson had several men besides himself employed in the same way, and that he had been told that they were to say nothing about the matter to Scotland Yard. Asked about the men he had watched and reported on, he gave the names of several Fenian suspects in London who were well known to Scotland Yard; a number were even then under observation by the CID. Dawson's rooms and luggage were searched without his knowledge, and in his travelling bag was discovered a list of names as well as some other papers which showed that Dawson had an alias: Llewellyn Hunter. Monro immediately recognized the name as that of a man who was one of Jenkinson's spies. The men on Hunter's list were found and brought to Scotland Yard. Monro informed Warren of the situation, and shortly afterwards a conference was held at the Home Office, attended by Jenkinson, Sir Charles Warren, and Hugh Childers, the Home Secretary.

In the meantime the CID had been investigating Hunter and had discovered that he had recently committed bigamy. Monro was determined to bring him to account, but before he could be arrested he absconded to the Continent, and there could be little doubt who had tipped him off. The only three men outside the CID who knew of Hunter's imminent arrest were Warren, Childers and Jenkinson.

In modern Britain such a scandalous state of affairs could never develop between a civil police authority and one of the more covert instruments of law and order – for the simple reason that procedures and demarcations are clearly established and understood. But during Childers's time as Home Secretary it was a different matter. With the certain knowledge of other public servants, Jenkinson had successfully established a regular school of private detectives for – according to Monro – 'the express purpose of thwarting the action of Scotland Yard'. And it was not until Childers had been succeeded by Henry Matthews as Home Secretary that Monro made up his mind that he could no longer tolerate such a 'mischievous system'.

By no means certain that his threat of resignation would do any good (he had already begun looking for lodgings in Scotland in preparation for his departure from the Metropolitan Police), Monro communicated his objections to Matthews. But as it turned out it was Jenkinson – not Monro – who finally resigned in January 1887, having long complained of the 'stupidity of some so-called detectives' and of the 'greatest jealousy' between himself and his Irish staff.

At first sight all this might seem to have little to do with the horrors in the East End, but it has to be remembered that Jack's subversive activities were politically as explosive as any terrorist bomb. Even before the murders Sir Charles Warren had become almost paranoid about the possibility of a socialist uprising, and he was by no means alone in his anxiety. Bernard Shaw's letter to the *Star* only served to remind a nervous government about the potential side-effects of Jack's campaign of terror, and some newspapers had even picked up on the possibility of a more direct political motive.

Having examined the likelihood of the murderer being either a medical man or a slaughterman, the *Police Chronicle and Guardian* of 6 October 1888 chose to quote from the *Birmingham Daily Post*, which had commented on the fact that 'a vast exodus of persons skilled in secret murder has taken place lately from foreign countries, whose destination has been London', continuing:

> The theory of these murders being attributable to these foreign immigrants is now gaining acceptance. . . . This theory is accompanied with another which touches the question of motive. In the view of some extremists, in political causes all things are deemed lawful, however lawless they may be in other matters, he says that the great cataclysm which was to have commenced even before 1848 is expected to be accomplished in 1889, and in proof of this general expectancy, he [the *Daily Post* reporter] quotes an important letter from an East End curate which appeared some time ago in the *Daily Telegraph*, in which he foretold the rising 'not of a thousand cooped up in a square as hitherto, but of a million men all bent on avenging past neglect.'

Such predictions, however naively expressed, were sending shivers down the backbone of the Victorian Establishment. The existence of foreign anarchist groups in London was no journalistic invention. The capital, and specifically the East End, had become the natural destination for all shades of political outlaw, assassin and agent, either fleeing the turmoil of revolutionary Europe or hoping to create the necessary climate for the violent overthrow of Victoria's elected Government.

Now Jack the Ripper was helping to focus the attention of the world on the poverty and filth in Her Majesty's back yard and her secret service had just as much reason to take an interest in its affairs as anyone else. Elizabeth Stride's murder had taken place in the shadow of an international working men's club, the very kind of establishment that was attracting the attention of Whitehall's secret department and the Special Branch of the CID regardless of Jack's activities. This point was to become increasingly important in the light of an article which appeared in *The People's Journal* on Saturday, 27 September 1919, which not only illustrates the overlapping interests of various law enforcement agencies on the streets of Whitechapel but also gives us one of the potentially most important descriptions of Jack the Ripper ever recorded.

Written by 'A Scotland Yard man' in memory of Detective Stephen White, who had died ten days previously, the writer explains that White was one of the officers who had had to spend weary nights in different disguises loitering about the narrow courts and evil-smelling alleys of Whitechapel looking for Jack the Ripper. But before quoting from one of White's reports of his nightly vigils he also explains:

> The East End is easily the most dangerous place in the London area for the police officer, and White had more than his fair share of the danger. Anarchists were unusually active in London in the 'eighties' and it was the duty of White to visit their dens and to be able to lay hands on some of the most dangerous men in Europe. The Fenians and their successors, the Dynamitards, also flourished in this time, and they also found refuge in the East End, where their plots were hatched by night and day. In addition there were the ordinary criminal classes to be watched, and on top of that the activities of the miscreant known as 'Jack the Ripper' engaged the attention of the East End police during the decade under review.

Undoubtedly Home Office agents would have been just as active in the East End as police detectives, and would have been in many ways far more able to conceal the identity of Jack the Ripper from the public had there been sufficient reason to do so. The three rooms at Scotland Yard where the understaffed, underpaid and overworked officers of the CID were so often kept in the dark were not a likely repository for potentially sensitive intelligence. H Division could continue wearing out their boot leather by walking up countless blind alleys in Whitechapel, totally unaware that important information could all the time be resting in some filing cabinet in Whitehall.

The discovery of a private memo written on 22 September 1888 by Henry Matthews to his Private Secretary, Evelyn Ruggles-Brise, was further to confirm our belief that the Home Office, not the CID, was in the driving seat where the Whitechapel murders were concerned. It read: 'Stimulate the police about Whitechapel murders. Monro might be willing to give a hint to the CID people if necessary.' This memo is telling in two ways. Firstly it confirms the identity of a potentially important individual who was responsible for liaison between the Home Office and the CID, and secondly it could infer that Matthews and Ruggles-Brise might know something the CID didn't. The memo could be entirely innocent, but its tone is curious.

Coincidentally, Evelyn Ruggles-Brise had been a contemporary of Montague John Druitt's at Oxford University, and both men had played cricket against each other in the traditional two-day match between Winchester and Eton in June 1876, with Winchester playing host to their visitors overnight. Was it possible that the two men had also known each other in later life? If Montague John Druitt was also Jack the Ripper, we could at least see how first suspicions about him might well have found their way via a back door in Whitehall to the men who could have been their friends and acquaintances. These were the very men who were best placed to deal with the situation as they saw fit, and only if they thought necessary would the CID be given a hint.

Is this where a cover-up begins? In all fairness, the answer to that is probably not. For one thing Montague John Druitt, for all his superficial respectability, would not have been important enough in his own right to precipitate such a course of action, even if he were guilty; and the memo also meant that the Home Office would have been on to him as early as 22 September. On the other hand, there would be only one more occasion (the night of the double event) on which the Ripper would strike before going to ground throughout October. Detective White's report stated:

For five nights we had been watching a certain alley just behind the Whitechapel Road. It could only be entered from where we had two men posted in hiding, and persons entering the alley were under observation by the two men. It was a bitter cold night when I arrived at the scene to take the report of the two men in hiding. I was turning away when I saw a man coming out of the alley. He was walking quickly but noiselessly, apparently wearing rubber shoes, which were rather rare in those days. I stood aside to let the man pass, and as he came under the wall lamp I got a good look at him.

He was about five feet ten inches in height, and was dressed rather shabbily, though it was obvious that the material of his clothes was good. Evidently a man who had seen better days, I thought, but men who have seen better days are common enough down East, and that of itself was not sufficient to justify me in stopping him. His face was long and thin, nostrils rather delicate, and his hair was jet black. His complexion was inclined to be sallow, and altogether the man was foreign in appearance. The most striking thing about him, however, was the extraordinary brilliance of his eyes. They looked like two very luminous glow worms coming through the darkness. The man was slightly bent at the shoulders, though he was obviously quite young – about 33 at the most – and gave one the idea of having been a student or professional man. His hands were snow white, and the fingers long and tapering.

As he passed me at the lamp I had an uneasy feeling that there was something more than usually sinister about him, and I was strongly moved to find some pretext for detaining him; but the more I thought it over, the more I was forced to the conclusion that it was not in keeping with British police methods that I should do so. My only excuse for interfering with the passage of this man would have been his association with the man we were looking for, and I had no grounds for connecting him with the murder. It is true I had a sort of intuition that the man was not quite right. Still, if one acted on intuition in the police force, there would be more frequent outcries about interference with the liberty of the subject, and at that time the police were criticised enough to make it undesirable to take risks.

The man stumbled a few feet away from me, and I made that an excuse for engaging him in conversation. He turned sharply at the sound of my voice, and scowled at me in surly fashion, but he said 'Goodnight' and agreed with me that it was cold.

His voice was a surprise to me. It was soft and musical, with just a tinge of melancholy in it, and it was the voice of a man of culture – a voice altogether out of keeping with the squalid surroundings of the East End.

As he turned away, one of the police officers came out of the house he had been in, and walked a few paces into the darkness of the alley. 'Hello! what is this?' he cried, and then he called in startled tones for me to come along.

In the East End we are used to shocking sights but the sight I saw made the blood in my veins turn to ice. At the end of the cul-de-sac huddled against the wall, there was the body of a woman, and a pool of blood was streaming along the gutter from her body. It was clearly another of those terrible murders. I remembered the man I had seen, and I started after him as fast as I could run, but he was lost to sight in the dark labyrinth of East End mean streets.

Notwithstanding George Hutchinson's experience, this was the most remarkable encounter yet with a likely Ripper – not least because White was able to get a better impression of his suspect by actually talking to him.

Importantly, in common with so many other descriptions the man was said to have had a foreign appearance, and yet White makes no reference to him having an accent. On the contrary, it was a voice 'altogether out of keeping with the squalid surroundings of the East End'. He was clearly not an East European Jew who had seen better days (a common enough sight in Whitechapel), but rather a man of culture, a 'student or professional man'. In other words, the above description not only lends further support to the already established notion that Jack the Ripper was a respectable young man of about thirty and of medium height, with a somewhat foreign appearance, but – as Donald Rumbelow points out – it also paints an uncanny portrait of Montague John Druitt.

On the night of the double event Jack the Ripper had pushed his luck to the limit. Whoever he was, he had come within a hair's breadth of being caught, and if Stephen White's report also referred to this same occasion then we can see why Jack had no alternative but to lie low for a while: he had given the authorities their best clue yet. Unfortunately, none of the known facts surrounding any murders that occurred in the East End between 1887 and 1895 accurately fit White's report, but by a process of elimination it is possible to say that it had to relate to the discovery in Mitre Square and nowhere else.

To begin with, the very fact that so much police activity was being devoted to catching this one individual indicates an operation that must have taken place at the height of the Ripper's reign of terror. Furthermore, White talks of the night as being bitterly cold. This automatically rules out the first murders, which occurred in August and early September, as it does the night of Alice Mackenzie's murder in July the following year. Mary Jane Kelly's murder took place in November, but indoors, and it was not discovered until eleven o'clock the next morning. The Mitre Square murder was committed at approximately 1.45 on the morning of 30 September, and on that particular day the temperature in London had suddenly fallen by a dramatic sixteen degrees Fahrenheit to just above freezing. Snow had fallen in the North of England, and a week later hard frost in Hyde Park would considerably hamper Sir Charles Warren's bloodhound trials. Despite the fact that Mitre Square was not a cul-de-sac, there could be no doubt that White had managed to get a good look at a man leaving the scene of the crime seconds before Catherine Eddowes's body would be discovered. And once that had been established, a clearer picture of what actually happened that night begins to emerge.

White had been a police officer whose duties were predominantly concerned with the detection of terrorism, as the article in *The People's Journal* clearly indicates. In other words, he would have been an officer of Monro's newly formed Special Branch, which had inherited the responsibilities of Jenkinson's old department in investigating political crime; like the old 'secret department', it was directly accountable not to Scotland Yard but to the Home Secretary.

The two men who reported to White on the night of Catherine Eddowes's murder had been keeping an eye on an area which had been under observation for the past five days. Obviously neither Scotland Yard nor the Home Office knew where or when Jack was going to strike next, and even though there was considerable police activity in Whitechapel at this time it is ludicrous to suppose that every alley and courtyard was being permanently watched by Monro's Special Branch officers in the hope of catching Jack literally red-handed. White's colleagues were keeping their eyes on specific targets – either politically suspect individuals or one of their known meeting places – possibly the Imperial Club in nearby Duke Street.

When City PC Watkins raised the alarm, White, as a Special Branch officer, would have had to take a back seat. He had been involved in a covert operation and he was on somebody else's patch when Jack the Ripper murdered another woman under their very noses. Under the circumstances it was not surprising that Sergeant White's significant encounter was never publicly disclosed at the time, and even when it was reported some thirty years later by a Scotland Yard man the details were sufficiently blurred to make it extremely difficult to identify the specific occasion.

White was never called to give evidence at Catherine Eddowes's inquest – again not surprising – but there can also be little doubt that this particular incident did happen, and that it gave the authorities the best description yet of Jack the Ripper. *The People's Journal* states that it was White's description that gave Robert Anderson his conviction that the murderer was a Jewish medical student. In his Scotland Yard notes, Sir Melville Macnaghten, whose 'well formed' head had been described as being 'crammed full of official secrets', was to say: 'No one ever saw the Whitechapel murderer.' But in his private papers this is expanded to include the important observation: '. . . unless possibly it was the City PC who was on a beat near Mitre Square'. Edward Watkins was the City policeman patrolling that particular beat on the night of the murder, and he saw nothing, leaving only one possible alternative to explain Sir Melville's comments. He was referring to the evidence of Stephen White, whose presence as a Special Branch officer on City police territory would have proved something of an embarrassment at the time, and whose public testimony would have alerted the suspects to the fact that they were being watched.

However, whilst it would have been impossible for the authorities to admit White's presence in the City of London, since that would require an explanation, further evidence that the incident did take place comes out at Elizabeth Stride's inquest. *The Times* reports that special precautions had been taken by the City police with a view to the detection of the criminal or criminals, with several plain clothes constables being ordered into the district, and it also states:

> At about the time when the Mitre-Square murder was being committed two of the extra men who had been put on duty were in Windsor Street, a thoroughfare about 300 yards off, engaged, pursuant to their instructions, in watching certain houses, it being thought possible that the premises might be resorted to at some time by the murderer. Five minutes after the discovery of the murder in Mitre Square, the two officers referred to heard of it, and the neighbourhood was at once searched by them, unfortunately without result.

Stephen White's description would have gone a considerable way towards destroying the innate resistance of many of his superiors to believing that an ostensibly respectable professional man could possibly commit such awful crimes. From Jack the Ripper's point of view, his best-kept secret was in danger of being blown.

If Druitt was the culprit, he may well have been under suspicion as early as September – not by the police but by his old school and university friends, who may not have been inclined to take the information they had on him as seriously as they should. Up to now his social standing would have helped him to conceal his truly psychopathic nature, and his reign of terror would have begun at a time when the CID and the Home Office were in some disarray. Monro had recently resigned; Warren wanted to; and Anderson had gone on holiday to Switzerland, which again raises the question as to why James Monro does not once refer to these dramatic months in his memoirs. Did Matthews never find it necessary to communicate anything to the man who was now head of the secret department and would soon be Chief Commissioner, or is Monro simply being what he tells us he had to be throughout his long and distinguished career – discreet?

At first glance it would appear highly unlikely that a man of Monro's moral convictions would ever have allowed himself to become involved in any sort of cover-up, and yet in many ways he was the only high-ranking police officer in a privileged enough position to be able to co-ordinate such a plot, particularly if it involved political considerations and the ultimate sanction of the Home Office. Much depended on when, how and by whom such a conspiracy was initiated. If someone like Druitt were the Ripper, then a full scale cover-up would seem unnecessary, although we could understand how the final explosion of blood lust in November may well have given him away to the authorities, who had up to now failed to act against a quietly respectable barrister and schoolteacher who had managed to conceal his true nature for so long.

Again, this would mark Mary Jane Kelly's murder as particularly significant. And certainly, if there was any sense of expediency within the CID at this time James Monro would have known about it. As a new broom he would have taken control of his old department just in time to sweep the debris of the past three months under the carpet.

IX

James Monro had a unique relationship with the Metropolitan Police and the Home Office before, during and after the murders, and he was also a close friend of Sir Melville Macnaghten, who had been responsible for including Montague John Druitt as a suspect. Monro and Macnaghten had known each other through their association with the Bengal Police, and were fast becoming lifelong friends. When Sir Melville returned from India in 1888 Monro immediately asked him to become his Assistant Chief Constable. According to Sir Melville, flattering though the proposal was he was not in a position to accept it at that moment, as family work and private interests claimed his whole attention.

But the truth of the matter was that Monro, who for some time had been fighting tooth and nail with Warren over the numerical strength of the CID, was determined to increase the size of his department, just as Warren was equally determined to keep its wings clipped. After considerable argument he grudgingly acceded to Monro's request for an Assistant Chief Constable to be appointed. Monro recommended Macnaghten, and Warren formally endorsed the recommendation to the Home Secretary. But before the appointment could be made Warren withdrew his recommendation, on the grounds that circumstances had come to his knowledge which made it undesirable that the gentleman in question should be appointed.

It takes very little effort to understand what these circumstances were. Warren realized, just in time, what the outcome of having an old friend of Monro's in the same department was likely to be. One cuckoo in the nest was bad enough, but two would have been intolerable.

In December 1888 Monro became Chief Commissioner, and in June the following year Macnaghten was recommended for the second time for the post of Assistant Chief Constable. This time the offer was 'gladly answered in the affirmative'. Melville Macnaghten became a detective officer in the Metropolitan Police, with Robert Anderson as his superior. Reflecting on his time with the CID, Sir Melville was to say in his autobiography:

> I have had many dinners – and always pleasant ones, with the officers of the Criminal Investigation Department. Some have been of a public, and some of a private, nature. Two evenings stand out in special prominence. One was in November 1891, on the occasion of the approaching return to India of Mr James Monro, who had resigned the Chief Commissionership of Metropolitan Police the year before. Mr Monro had previously been the Assistant Commissioner in charge of the Criminal Investigation Department, and I doubt whether any of the gentlemen who filled his position before or after his time ever gained more completely the affection and confidence of their officers. In him and in his judgement they believed, and knew that he would be a strong rock of defence to them in times of storm and stress. I have no intention of ripping up healed sores, or of detailing the reasons which induced Mr Monro to resign a post for which, alike by nature and by training, he was admirably fitted.

It was inconceivable that Macnaghten would not have discussed the Whitechapel murders with Monro, and at the very least shared the same privileged knowledge. Indeed, it was more than likely that Macnaghten's 'private' information would have come directly from Monro in the first place.

Already we could see how someone like Montague John Druitt has to be taken seriously if Macnaghten genuinely favoured him as a suspect, even though his inclusion would seem to diminish the possiblity of a cover-up for the simple reason that a failed barrister and schoolteacher could surely never have warranted the covert protection of a man like Monro, who put his private convictions and his public duty above all else. But it was also becoming transparently clear to us from the evidence presenting itself that James Monro had other problems on his hands apart from his well-aired quarrel with Charles Warren.

The public face of Victorian England frowned sternly on certain types of behaviour, but unforeseeable events still threatened the careers and reputations of eminent and loyal servants whilst fanning the flames of discontent and even revolution. In the 1880s men like Sir Charles Warren and the Prime Minister, Lord Salisbury, knew that any breach in the integrity of Crown or Government could be the touchstone for disaster.

The exposure of a homosexual brothel at No. 19 Cleveland Street in July 1889 had resulted in the arrest of two unfortunate 'rent boys' and the subsequent trial of Ernest Parke, editor of *The North London Press*, for criminal libel against Henry Fitzroy, Earl of Euston, whom he had named as one of the frequenters of the brothel. The reality was, however, that a massive cover-up had been initiated to protect the bigger fish, including the Prince of Wales's Assistant Equerry, Lord Arthur Somerset, and the heir presumptive to the throne, Prince Albert Victor. Parke himself was getting too close to the truth and had to be silenced, and thanks to the efforts of men like a solicitor named Edward Henslowe Bedford the courageous editor was quickly set up. Upon his indictment, the whole affair became *sub judice*, effectively removing the threat of any further criticism, and even though Lord Euston was almost certainly both homosexual and a patron of No. 19, Parke was found guilty and received a sentence of one year's imprisonment.

Whilst Parke was paying the price for his integrity, the zealous Inspector Abberline who the previous year had tracked the Ripper in vain, was continuing to pursue his latest quarry regardless. Unfortunately for him and for Commissioner James Monro, who was just as determined to see the matter through, the silent machinery of the Establishment had already been put into motion. But at least it was clear, from the way that the officers of the CID endeavoured to secure as many arrests as possible, that they were not easily intimidated by the continuing expediency of their political masters, nor were they interested in protecting the wealthy and high-born from arrest and trial. A file was sent to the Director of Public Prosecutions, and there it remained. In the circumstances there was little the police could do, although they must have been aware what was going on.

In this respect it is important that James Monro's private memoirs make no reference to the Cleveland Street affair, any more than they do about the Whitechapel murders, even though he certainly would have had a lot to say about this most blatant miscarriage of justice. He had to know more about both investigations than he was prepared to say. Undoubtedly the dilemma of trying to equate his firm Christian faith and principles with the extreme discretion which was often necessary made the execution of his public duty no easy matter for this conscientious Scot. His memoirs constantly refer to this discretion in a way which indicates a deeply felt need to explain and justify his actions – possibly even his guilt. In trying to put the record straight he refers not to the two most sensitive investigations of his administration but to a relatively unimportant raid on a West End gambling club. The incident nevertheless gives some relevant insight into his problems:

> Such clubs existed not only in the East, but in the West End, and no doubt it was only just that the same justice should be doled out to aristocratic as well as to plebeian gamblers. A notorious club of this description was The Field Club. Gambling went on here to an unlimited extent, and many young fellows of noble family were being ruined. Lady Dudley entreated that something sould be done to stop it, to save her son: Lord Bateman, with tears in his eyes implored me to interfere, as he had been compelled to mortgage some of his estates to pay off his son's gambling debts. But not one of those who complained would give me the slightest assistance in the way of giving me information on which I could issue a warrent to raid the club. However, in the end I got the information, and raided the Club, capturing various noblemen, amongst them Lord Dudley, all engaged in gambling. This was surely nothing but the performance of a public and police duty. But the relatives of the noblemen implicated, and society generally, considered this indiscreet! What they wanted was to get the club stopped, without their friends coming to any grief! and the Conservative papers never, I believe forgave me for this indiscretion!

Two months after receiving James Monro's memoirs we finally made contact with the man who had been responsible for the enigmatic correspondence which had been published in the *Radio Times* some twelve years earlier. In a letter to James Monro's grandson, Christopher, we inquired about his opinion that his grandfather 'had his own views on the identity of the "Ripper"' and that he had bequeathed these notes on the affair to his eldest son. We informed him that we were now in possession of at least some, if not all, of his grandfather's private papers, which contained not the slightest mention of the Whitechapel murders. Had he seen his grandfather's written opinion on the subject? Or was it possibly an inherited impression that the Commissioner had committed his thoughts to paper that prompted his letter to the BBC? He replied:

Perhaps my letter to the *Radio Times* served no useful end; you will be aware that a Dr Warren, who may be dead now, had written in angry mood about the slightest allusions to his grandfather in a Barlow & Watt programme on the subject. (One vicious character in that programme, John Saul, had links with the Cleveland Street scandal a year later.) Most writers on the subject stress my grandfather's bad relations with Warren before the crisis of August 1888, and his independent conduct of the CID. Well, there is truth in that, but James Monro was a man who knew the meaning of discipline and would never have gone athwart a superior who was really worthy of respect. . . .

Now to the point: Whatever my grandfather knew, deduced or conjectured, he apparently set down in a highly private memoranda which at his death in 1920 passed intact to his eldest son. My uncle Charles Monro died in his early sixties about 1929, and a year or two before that he had a conversation with my father (1874–1958) which the latter related to me in India ten years later. The gist of this was that James Monro's theory [about Jack the Ripper] was a very hot potato, that it had been kept secret even from his wife/widow, who survived until 1931, and that he was very doubtful whether or not to destroy the papers. He did not reveal the identity of the suspect(s?) to my father, who told me that he had made no attempt to ascertain them, and had just said 'Burn the stuff, Charlie, burn it and try to forget it!'

He went on to remind us that these recollections went back nearly fifty years, and that not even his father had actually seen the papers, or could swear that they had ever existed, and we took his point. But this in itself only helped to convince us that Christopher Monro's recollections were essentially honest. And the fact that he supports the idea of James Monro having very definite ideas on the identity of Jack the Ripper only served to confirm what we already believed to be the truth. The difficulty for us was to decide whether James Monro had actually been involved with an organized conspiracy to pervert the course of justice, or whether he had merely been aware of certain expediencies surrounding the Whitechapel murder investigations and was now, by choosing to say nothing, simply being discreet. One thing was certain – if anyone in Scotland Yard was in a position to keep the lid firmly on the Whitechapel murder investigations both during and after the events, it was James Monro.

It was a conclusion that had obviously crossed his grandson's mind as well, which led him to the following consideration:

Quite simply, if James Monro had come upon evidence which struck at plotters in high places, he would have gone to the fountainhead and put all the cards down. He was not scared of eminent names, as Lord 'Podge' Somerset and Sir Dighton Probyn found out a year afterwards [Cleveland Street scandal], and though there was a religious cleavage between him and Matthews they understood each other and got on well until the great row about pensions.

Again, for all the reasons already mentioned we found ourselves in accord with Christopher Monro, who goes on to say:

> I doubt whether his suspicions focused on anyone more eminent than Druitt, who was by then dead, and he was enough of a man of his times not to want to make a dead professional person's guilt public. He may have kept the secret in reserve in case any innocent party, dead or alive, was later publicly accused. I think any grandson would have resented being burdened with preserving it.

This was an intriguing possibility. Monro and Macnaghten were close friends. Whatever grounds Sir Melville had for incriminating Druitt – whose name he had surreptitiously slipped into the closed file on the Whitechapel murders in 1894 – would quite probably have emanated from James Monro in the first place. He had been far closer to the heart of the investigation than had his subordinate, who had not become a detective officer until six months after the murder of Mary Jane Kelly – which in itself indicates that Macnaghten's 'private' information needed to have come from someone more closely connected with the case. We believed that man had to be James Monro, but if his knowledge about the affair was such a hot potato how could it involve a seemingly insignificant schoolteacher and failed barrister like Montague John Druitt? And, by the same token, we also couldn't forget that there was another suspect whose bloody hands would have made it essential that the truth should never be known, whatever happened.

The inclusion in the Ripper saga of Queen Victoria's grandson, Prince Albert Victor Christian Edward, known as Eddy, was the result of Dr Thomas Stowell's sensational claim made three years earlier than Stephen Knight's. Both theories were entirely contradictory, and yet they contained compatible elements. The explanation, of course, is that since Joseph Sickert had not begun to tell the story of his mother's royal bastardy until after these earlier revelations, the transparent fiction of the Knight/Sickert solution now allowed elements of Stowell's theory to be deliberately and conveniently grafted on to theirs in just the same way that elements of the earlier BBC/masonic theory had also been absorbed.

Stowell's article appeared in the magazine *The Criminologist* in November 1970. According to Colin Wilson, the eighty-five-year-old patriot and staunch royalist used as his source material the private papers of Sir William Gull, although in the original article only a diary is mentioned, which Dr Stowell was told about but apparently not shown. Needless to say, these documents have never been examined and are now presumably missing or destroyed, and we are therefore left with Dr Stowell's interpretation of them as a basis for his supposition that Jack the Ripper was none other than the Duke of Clarence.

According to the author, Clarence had died not in the influenza epidemic of 1892, as was widely believed, but in a private mental home near Sandringham, and from 'softening of the brain' due to syphilis. As Donald Rumbelow points out, though, this information could not have derived from the private papers of Sir William Gull, who died in 1890 at the age of seventy-three, two years *before* Clarence. Stowell also makes reference to the raid on the homosexual brothel at No. 19 Cleveland Street, to which Prince Albert Victor had been a frequent visitor along with his father's Assistant Equerry, Lord Arthur Somerset.

Again Stowell's and Knight's theories have found common ground. Here it is used only as evidence of Eddy's homosexuality, but in Knight's (Sickert's) story Cleveland Street is of paramount importance. It is here that Walter Sickert is supposed to have shared a studio at No. 15 with Annie Elizabeth Crook, the pretty shop assistant living at No. 6 and working at the confectionery shop at No. 22.

Stowell tries, rather naïvely, to conceal the name of his suspect by using the initial 'S' instead of his title. But unfortunately for him, enough information is given away to leave the Ripper fraternity in no doubts about the accused's actual indentity. Furthermore, Stowell had discussed his theory with other people, including Colin Wilson in 1960, who were left in no doubt about the suspect's identity. The ensuing public sensation that his astonishing revelation caused was undoubtedly more than Stowell had bargained for. And it has even been suggested that his death, just a few days after the article's publication, was hastened by the anxiety.

Certainly his son, understandably distressed by the whole affair and no doubt to some extent blaming these revelations and the attention they received for hastening his father's demise, destroyed his papers. A letter from Dr Stowell published in *The Times* on 9 November (the day after his death) also clearly shows the

111

consternation and dilemma he felt in having implicated the Prince so publicly. The letter read:

Sir

I have at no time associated His Royal Highness, the late Duke of Clarence, with the Whitechapel murderer or suggested that the murderer was of Royal Blood. It remains my opinion that he was a scion of a noble family. The particulars given in *The Times* of November 4, of the activities of His Royal Highness in no way conflict with my views as to the identity of Jack The Ripper.

Yours faithfully,

A Loyalist and a Royalist

But it was too late. Try as he did to deny the deduced identity of his suspect, it was perfectly clear that he was referring to Clarence. Amongst other equally obvious clues, he mentions his suspect's nickname – Collar and Cuffs (given him because of the high starched collars he wore in order to conceal his 'swan-like' neck and his liking for showing more than the usual length of shirt cuff). Stowell even makes reference to a photograph of his suspect, which is easily identified as one of the most well known of the Prince.

The article of 4 November to which Stowell refers appeared in *The Times* Diary under the heading 'Court Circular clears Clarence':

Buckingham Palace is not officially reacting to the mischievous calumny that Albert Victor, The Duke of Clarence and Avondale and Earl of Athlone, was also Jack The Ripper. The idea that Edward VII's eldest son and, but for his early death of pneumonia aged 28, heir to the throne, should have bestially murdered five or six women of 'unfortunate' class in the East End is regarded as too ridiculous for comment.

Nevertheless a loyalist on the staff at Buckingham Palace has engaged in some amateur detective work and come up with evidence on the Duke's behalf. Two women were murdered on September 30th, 1888, in Berners Street and Mitre Square, and the murders were fully reported in *The Times* the following day.

The Times of October 1 also carried a court circular from Balmoral stating: Prince Henry of Battenberg, attended by Colonel Clerk, joined Prince Albert Victor of Wales (The Duke of Clarence as he was to be) at Glen Muick in a drive which Mr Mackenzie had for black game.

Further, but less surely, he believes that the Duke was at Sandringham celebrating his father's 47th birthday, on the occasion of the last murder of Maria Jeannette Kelly, in Miller's Court, Spitalfields, on November 9, 1888. The court circular simply says that the then Prince of Wales celebrated his birthday with his family; but diary entries and other notes in the archives at Buckingham Palace suggest that the Duke was in fact at Sandringham during the early days of November until November 11.

Speculation that the Duke of Clarence might have been Jack The Ripper springs from an article by Thomas Stowell, a senior surgeon, in *The Criminologist*. Stowell says he has kept to himself for 50 years evidence about the identity of the killer which points to a man of noble family and, in some particulars, to the Duke. Stowell refuses to reveal who he thinks it was, but seemed to accept tacitly that it was the Duke on the BBC news programme, *24 Hours*, on Monday night.

The Prince of Wales's Engagement Diary at the Royal Archives, Windsor, records on Thursday, 1 November 1888: 'Pr. Eddy arrives fr. York', and there is a letter written by Eddy from Sandringham to a friend, dated 9 November, in which he comments: 'We have a large party staying here now and had three nice days shooting although it had turned very cold with a cutting East wind.'

All this evidence considerably weakens the case against Clarence and is weakened further with the knowledge that the Prince continued in public life after the murders until his untimely death in 1892. In March 1889 he opened the Working Lads' Institute at Bethnal Green, and in May he opened a new dock at Belfast where he was 'received with great enthusiasm by the populace'. In October 1889 he accompanied his father to a royal wedding in Athens and afterwards departed, via Egypt, for a tour of the southern provinces of India, arriving in Bombay on 10 November 1889. Returning to England in May 1890, he was created Earl of Athlone and Duke of Clarence and Avondale on the occasion of his grandmother's seventy-first birthday – and in June he took his seat in the House of Lords. Early in December 1891 the Duke became officially engaged to his cousin, the Princess Victoria Mary (May) of Teck.

As Colin Wilson points out, it is hardly likely that the man known by his own Royal Family to have been Jack the Ripper would have been allowed to become engaged to the Princess – later to become Queen Mary. It appears to us just as perverse for Queen Victoria to have bestowed the title of Duke of Clarence and Avondale on the man whom she knew to be Jack the Ripper!

In 1972, two years after the publication of *The Criminologist* article, Michael Harrison's biography *Clarence* was published. Inspired by Stowell's article, he lent a new interpretation to this largely discredited theory. According to Harrison, the Ripper was not the Duke but his tutor and lover at Cambridge – James Kenneth Stephen.

At first sight, it has to be said, Harrison's plausible tale appears to have found the truth behind the incorrect assumptions of another. For whilst we could understand that Stowell had got it wrong, it was more difficult to believe that he had totally fabricated his hypothesis. Whether he had in fact seen Gull's private papers or diary, or whether he had merely discussed them with Gull's daughter, Lady Caroline Acland, we shall probably never know. The latter possibility at least explained how Stowell might have jumped to the wrong conclusions. But at least there was now a common factor in his theory – Harrison's and later Stephen Knight's as well. It was not only the Duke of Clarence, but Sir William Gull himself.

If we are to believe Dr Stowell, Sir William had surreptitiously entered the arena as early as 1931, when the *Daily Express* ran a series of three articles telling how clairvoyant Robert James Lees had tracked down Jack the Ripper to the house of a highly respectable physician. According to Stowell, Caroline Acland had told him that her mother, Lady Gull, was greatly annoyed one night by an unannounced visit from a police officer, accompanied by a man who called himself a medium, and she was irritated when they asked her a number of questions which seemed to her impertinent. She answered them with non-committal replies such as 'I do not know', 'I cannot tell you that' and 'I am afraid I cannot answer that question'. Later Sir William himself came down and, in answer to the questions, said he had occasionally suffered from 'lapses of memory since he had a slight stroke in 1887'; he said that he once had discovered blood on his shirt.

In Stowell's mind Sir William is incriminated because his patient (Clarence) was Jack the Ripper. The blood on his shirt was probably due to Gull's examination of his patient after one of the murders. In Harrison's mind, Stowell had merely got the wrong patient. But by 1976 Joseph Sickert's testimony would pin the atrocities fairly and squarely on the seventy-one-year-old shoulders of this eminent man, who by now had already suffered two strokes.

As we have already said, Harrison's suspect – James Kenneth Stephen – looks on the face of it an extremely likely candidate.

But, alas, it was only on the surface. For Stephen Knight and Joseph Sickert, the suspect whom Stowell called merely 'S' was a fictitious Albert Sickert. This was because Prince Albert Victor had apparently been introduced to Walter's circle of acquaintances as the artist's younger brother. In Harrison's mind, 'S' stands for Stephen – the Prince's tutor at Cambridge, James Kenneth Stephen. Again, the subject of Clarence's possible homosexuality is raised and a relationship between him and Stephen intimated as if established fact. Harrison's motive rests entirely on the possibility that the murders were committed by Stephen after his Prince had spurned his affections. This could be a motive, of course, if both the relationship between the two were established (which it is not) and the depth of passion in Stephen's heart were ascertainable (which it is not).

At least Harrison is on firmer ground when he examines the psychological stability of this particular branch of the Stephen family. J.K.'s father, Sir James Fitzjames Stephen, was forced to resign from the bench in April 1891 because of an increasingly debilitating brain disease, and ten months later his son would also die in an asylum for the insane. The present Sir James Stephen, now in his late seventies, whom we met at his home in Dorset, has also suffered. His entry in *Debrett's* even registers his long years of certified insanity. Disenfranchised from 1945 until 1960, he was discharged from hospital in 1972.

Without prying deeper than is necessary here, there is no need to make any assumptions regarding the nature of the afflictions that have beset this unfortunate family. What is readily ascertainable is that before his decline J. K. Stephen was a man of exceptional intellectual ability. His family and friends felt sure that he was destined for high office – Prime Minister or Lord Chancellor.

The line between genius and insanity is often a very fine one, and the Stephen family have had their share of both. Virginia Woolf and Vanessa Bell were cousins of J. K. Stephen. They both had brilliant intellects, but of course Virginia Woolf committed suicide. Rumours of suicide had surrounded J.K.'s death, which was actually attributed to a mania lasting two and a half months, the persistent refusal of food for twenty days, and exhaustion. All the indications point to a man who was – to all intent and purposes – a manic depressive. Sir James told us that he had suffered from schizophrenia, whereas his uncle J. K. Stephen had suffered from cyclothemia, a condition characterized by periodic swings of mood between excitement and depression, activity and inactivity.

In his book Harrison quotes several instances from Quentin Bell's biography of Virginia Woolf which further demonstrate the nature of his condition:

> One day he [J. K. Stephen] rushed upstairs to the nursery at 22 Hyde Park Gate, drew the blade from a sword stick and plunged it into the bread. On another occasion he carried Virginia [Woolf] and her mother off to his room in De Vere Gardens; Virginia was to pose for him. He had decided that he was a painter – a painter of genius. He was in a state of high euphoria and painted away like a man possessed, as indeed he was. He would drive up in a hansom cab to Hyde Park Gate – a hansom in which he had been driving about all day in a state of insane excitement. On another occasion he appeared at breakfast and announced, as though it were an amusing incident, that the doctors had told him that he would either die or go completely mad.

J. K. Stephen had been a man of exceptional ability and force of intellect. He was famous for his brilliant addresses to the Cambridge Union, he was 'a man with a natural bent towards dainty and exquisite language in prose and verse', and he was a leading figure in one of the most exclusive Cambridge societies – The Apostles. Six years before his death, however, Stephen had met with a serious accident to the head, as his uncle, Leslie Stephen, was later to recall in 1895:

> At the end of 1886 he had an accident, the effects of which were far more serious than appeared at the time. He was staying at Felixstowe, and while looking at an engine employed in pumping water he received a terrible blow upon the head. He returned to his work before long, but it was noticed that for sometime he seemed to have lost his usual ease in composition. He was supposed, however, to have recovered completely from the effects of the blow.

The point is: where is Harrison's evidence to show that J. K. Stephen may have developed homicidal tendencies? The unfortunate accident in 1886 had precipitated a weakness that was eventually to spiral a brilliant man into even more debilitating moods of elation and depression, but that does not mean that he had been transformed into a psychotic personality whose only release could be found on the streets of Whitechapel. Harrison's main thrust, however, comes in suggesting that J. K. Stephen was also a misogynist. Certainly some of his attitudes would find little sympathy from modern liberal thinkers, but they demonstrate as much an unguarded chauvinism towards his own sex as any misogynistic tendencies, and reveal, if anything, that he was an arrant snob above everything else. In one poem his blatant snobbery, sense of superiority and general intolerance towards his own sex is just as obvious. Writing about an incident which occurred whilst he was sitting in a railway carriage at Malines in Belgium, in which a fellow passenger (a Belgian) accidentally trod on his toe, he finished his tirade thus:

> Oh mays't thou suffer tortures without end:
> May fiends with glowing pincers rend thy brain,
> And beetles batten on thy blackened face!

Harrison finds this more frightening than some of Stephen's more obviously misogynistic verses – though it is surely just as possible to perceive something else – a sense of humour, however black.

For Donald Rumbelow, the weightiest argument against Harrison's elaborate conjecturing is that nowhere does the author make a point-by-point comparison of Stephen and Stowell's 'S' to see if they were the same person. He had done this with Clarence. Had he done it with Stephen he would have seen at once that they could not be one and the same man.

Even without further investigation it is obvious that the case against Stephen, like so many other hypotheses, is weakened by the pure force of common sense and logic. Furthermore, it seemed to us that, as with Clarence, the fact that J. K. Stephen continued in public life (albeit intermittently and inefficiently) until 1891 must be the single most relevant factor in assessing the likelihood of guilt. After all, both Stowell and Harrison establish the need for a conspiracy in order to protect the Royal Family and the Establishment from a damaging scandal. It is therefore inherent in their respective argument that the initiators of such a cover-up would care more about defending the *status quo* than the life or well-being of the unfortunate individual who, by committing the most heinous of crimes, had threatened its very existence.

The fact that each atrocity was more horrific than the previous one clearly demonstrates the continuing decline of Jack the Ripper's state of mind. Considering the Victorians' well-established attitude to and ignorance about serious mental disorder, there can be little doubt that Jack the Ripper, whoever he was, would eventually give himself away. After this point he would not have been allowed his freedom and the opportunity of implicating the Queen herself, let alone Sir William Gull, as accessories. But it is Harrison himself

117

who gives us a clear indication of his own motives for incriminating J. K. Stephen.

In 1972 he appeared on the BBC Television programme *Late Night Line-Up*, and part of his conversation was transcribed in *The Listener* on 17 August. It appeared that Harrison had been preparing his biography of the Duke of Clarence when Stowell's article, naming Clarence as the Ripper, appeared in *The Criminologist*. 'I didn't agree,' says Harrison. 'But I couldn't leave the reader high and dry, so what I did was find somebody who I thought was a likely candidate – So I had to look for a man very near to the Duke who was a homicidal maniac.' What could be clearer? Here was a man quite openly playing the game of Hunt the Ripper by the time-honoured rules laid down by successive generations of participants. There was no real case against Stephen – only the need to distract attention from someone else's.

X

If there was any veracity in the three existing conspiracy theories it lay somewhere between the lines of their imaginative accounts and not actually in them – as well hidden from our inquisitive gaze as from the blinkered commitment of their advocates. But the possibility of a cover-up remained as viable as ever despite Messrs Stowell, Knight and Harrison's respective candidates' lack of credentials. In all three instances, by incriminating Prince Eddy the authors had at least supplied us with a sufficiently powerful motive to accept that a cover-up would have been necessary in the first place.

In contrast, the inclusion of Montague John Druitt as a suspect owed nothing to the devious machinations of faceless conspirators, but everything to the opinion of the eminent Sir Melville Macnaghten. In this respect Druitt is at least a genuine suspect. By 1973 the portrait of this shadowy barrister was as complete as it was ever likely to be, thanks to Farson, Cullen and the efforts of Irving Rosenwater, who in January of that year wrote an article in *The Cricketer* about Montague's involvement with the sport. The sum total is a fascinating insight into a man who was born on 15 August 1857 into one of the most respected and respectable families of Wimborne in Dorset. His father, William, had been the town's leading surgeon until 1876, when he was compelled through failing health to retire from practice. To all intents and purposes it would seem that Montague had been endowed with enough intellectual ability and good breeding to ensure a successful, happy life in upper middle-class Victorian England. At the age of thirteen he was to win a scholarship to Winchester College, where, apart from an obvious dearth of talent as an actor in the school production of *Twelfth Night* – a critic in the college magazine wrote of his Toby Belch that it was 'better imagined than described' – he excelled in school debates and was a good sportsman. He was the school fives champion and played cricket for the first eleven. In his final year he had the honour of being elected Prefect of the Chapel, and in 1876 he won another scholarship, to New College, Oxford.

When he arrived at the university his sporting activities were as many and varied as ever. He played for the New College Eleven, where in the Freshmen's match of 1877 he took five wickets for thirty in the second innings. He also played rugger for the college and was the university fives champion in 1877. But Oxford in many ways marked a turning point in the life of this bright scholar. Taking a second class honours degree in classical moderations, he managed only a third class honours in classics when he graduated in 1880. From now on he would never fulfil the promise of his earlier years. Two years were to pass before he enrolled at the Inns of Court, which encourages Donald Rumbelow to surmise whether he may have been undecided about his future career – law or medicine. Certainly his formative years would have been spent surrounded by men of both professions. His father, uncle and cousin Lionel were all surgeons, but the medical roots of the Druitts go far deeper. There had been surgeons in the family since the eighteenth century, and whatever the reason for the delay in settling on a career it is entirely reasonable that Montague might have at least toyed with the idea of following in the family tradition. As it was, his lack of success as a barrister was to find him teaching at a private school in Blackheath prior to his death in December 1888.

The school, at No. 9 Eliot Place, Blackheath, was run by the tall, imposing figure of George Valentine. Like Montague he was a keen sportsman, and with probably only Druitt plus one other assistant master to care for the educational needs of his pupils it would be reasonable to assume that Montague would have had some responsibility for games. The school even boasted a small swimming bath which had been inherited from an earlier establishment whose fame as a nursery for the great public schools had been known far and wide. By the late 1880s, however, the fortune of this and many other crammers was on the wane, and for Druitt too the future was not bright.

He had been called to the bar on 29 April 1885, but, then as now, entry into this most exclusive of professions was an expensive affair. In Montague's case the only way was by borrowing against the £500 legacy his father had already set aside for him. On 27 September of that year his father died of a heart attack, leaving an estate worth £16,579 4s 5d. This was divided among Montague's three sisters, with a farm at Child Okeford passing to Montague's elder brother, William. His mother, Ann, was to benefit from all rents, income and other articles of consumption. It was hardly the most conventional of wills, and made little provision for Montague and his two younger brothers. To all intents and purposes he had been left to fend for himself.

Following his father's death, Montague took chambers at No. 9 Kings Bench Walk, but in the three years left to him he didn't receive a single brief. Was he prepared for this? Who knows? The failure rate was high for any would-be barristers without sufficient private income, but Montague might well have expected more support from the family estate. As it turned out he was now trapped in a privileged and highly competitive world but lacked sufficient talent or means of support to ensure his success. His temporary position at the school, which he had taken up as early as February 1881, and possibly before, had acquired a depressing permanence.

Throughout the summer of 1888, as Irving Rosenwater discovered, Montague was able to turn out to play for Blackheath against, among others, the Incogs, Royal Artillery, MCC and the Band of Brothers; and on 21 July he played against Beckenham on Blackheath's home pitch at the Rectory Field. But all was not well. Earlier that month his mother had gone insane and had been committed to a private asylum in Chiswick where she would eventually die in two and a half years' time. The discovery of Montague's body in the river at Chiswick in December 1888, together with the further discovery of a note in which he had stated that 'Since Friday I felt I was going to be like mother, and the best thing for me was to die', pointed to the fact that he had visited his mother at the asylum before ultimately taking his own life.

The question that has to be answered, of course, is: does any of this point to Druitt being Jack the Ripper? The answer is no, if taken in isolation. But we have to remember that Macnaghten refers to Druitt as being allegedly 'sexually insane', and whatever else we think of Sir Melville's utterances we must allow that his private information had to be not only explicit enough for him to be able to make such a statement, but substantial enough for Montague John Druitt to be regarded as a homicidal maniac worthy of inclusion as a suspect in the first place.

Unfortunately Farson's *Jack the Ripper*, published a full seven years after Cullen's book, is reduced to mentioning missing dossiers and a lost publication in Australia in the hope of strengthening the case against his candidate any further, and even his attempt to connect Druitt with the East End had been easily discredited. Farson had discovered from the medical register for 1879 that Dr Lionel Druitt, Montague's cousin, had kept a surgery at No. 140 The Minories, on the Whitechapel/City border, which at least suggested that Montague may have visited him here and had a convenient bolt-hole available to him in 1888. However, as Donald Rumbelow had discovered, Lionel had assisted at Dr Thomas Thyne's practice at this address for less than a year before moving to Strathmore Gardens, Kensington, in 1880. This meant that even if Montague – who was still at Oxford at this time – had visited his cousin in Whitechapel, it could only have been for the briefest of periods.

Our research supports this conclusion and also reveals that in 1878 Lionel had been assistant house surgeon in an Edinburgh poorhouse, before leaving in 1879 to replace Dr Thyne's ailing colleague Dr Joseph Taylor, soon to die from a self-administered overdose of morphine. By 1880 Lionel is at Strathmore Gardens, and by 1882 Dr Thyne has also left The Minories for his new practice in Twickenham. The East End surgery was passed on to a Dr John Cotman.

Clearly Montague's link with the East End – if there was one – was still unestablished, and in fact even the relationship between him and his cousin turns out to be far more tenuous than Farson would like it to be in order for him to argue convincingly that Lionel would probably have looked after his younger cousin in London. Far from the two boys being brought up within twelve miles of each other in Dorset, as Farson makes out, Lionel had been born in London and brought up at the family home at No. 39a Curzon Street, Mayfair.

In 1886 Lionel finally departs for Australia, where he plays an even more important part in Farson's drama thanks to a missing letter from a Mr Knowles. The author explains that the letter was one of those taken with his other material when his file was stolen. This letter tells of a document entitled 'The East End Murderer – I knew him', written by a Lionel Druitt, Drewett or Drewery, and printed privately in 1890 by a Mr Fell of Dandenong; the correspondent had read it whilst in Australia. Too late does Farson realize the import of this letter, for it is only after the file and the letter are stolen that he comes across Macnaghten's notes and the name Druitt.

One can only sympathize with Mr Farson if he is telling the truth. But it has to be said, particularly since our experiences to date had only served to nurture a growing scepticism, that it looked much more likely that the letter from Mr Knowles and its contents were a mere fabrication, a desperate attempt to strengthen the case against Montague John Druitt by an advocate who perhaps felt he had not received sufficient recognition for his original lucky find, and whose efforts to close the case forever had been thwarted by a singular lack of incriminating evidence. Now he shared the stage with other advocates of his champion – each likely to discover those vital pieces of jigsaw that would finally put us in the picture.

The fact that Christabel Aberconway's typewritten version of her father's notes differs in essential details from the verifiable Scotland Yard ones is unfortunate, and futhermore it must be remembered that they are themselves a copy of missing handwritten originals. For anyone wanting to diminish the case against Druitt it is all too easy to suggest that, at best, an inaccurate copy has been made, or, at worst, a deliberate fabrication has taken place in order to strengthen the case against him. But, having said that, we also have to say that there is a certain amount of independent evidence which points to the contrary.

Major Arthur Griffiths's book *Mysteries of Police and Crime* was published in 1898. Major Griffiths was not only a distinguished crime historian and author but also one of Her Majesty's Inspectors of Prisons. His observations regarding the possible identity of Jack the Ripper are so close to Sir Melville's 'private' notes that there can be little doubt that he is quoting either directly from Macnaghten or from the same source as Macnaghten when he says:

> The second possible criminal was a Russian doctor, also insane, who had been in the habit of carrying about surgical knives and instruments in his pockets: his antecedents were of the very worst and at the time of the Whitechapel murders he was hiding, or, at least, his whereabouts were never exactly known.
>
> The third person was of the same type, *but the suspicion in his case was the stronger* [authors' italics] and there was every reason to believe that his own friends entertained grave doubts about him. He was also a doctor in the prime of his life, was believed to be insane, or on the borderline of insanity, and he disappeared immediately after the last murder, that in Miller's Court on the 9th of November, 1888.
>
> On the last day of that year, seven weeks later, his body was found

floating in the Thames and was said to have been in the water a month. The theory in this case was that after his last exploit, which was the most fiendish of all, his brain gave way and he became furiously insane and committed suicide.

Cullen and Farson's names are so closely linked with the Druitt theory that one could be forgiven for thinking that the two men were colleagues or even close friends. This, however, is not the case. In fact there was every reason to expect that Farson would have been less than ecstatic to learn that another author had not only begun his own investigation into Druitt but was able to publish the full name of his man a full seven years earlier. When Farson's book was eventually published it added nothing to Cullen's established facts surrounding the suspect, and was hard pressed to take the case against Druitt any further. In other words, Tom Cullen's *Autumn of Terror*, researched quite independently, very much takes the wind out of Farson's sails. Considering the circumstances, there was absolutely no advantage to be gained in colluding with Cullen – quite the opposite.

On 7 October 1972 Philip Loftus reviewed Farson's book in the *Guardian* and, as Donald Rumbelow tells us, Mr Loftus's own indirect association with the Macnaghten family allowed him to throw some light on the problem of the two sets of notes:

His own interest in Druitt had started several years earlier – in fact in 1950 when he was staying with a friend, Gerald Melville Donner, who happened to be also the grandson of Sir Melville Macnaghten. Donner owned a Jack the Ripper letter, which Loftus thought was a copy, written in red ink, framed and hanging on the wall.

'Copy be damned,' Donner said, 'that's the original.' As proof that he owned some original documents he pulled out Sir Melville Macnaghten's private notes which Loftus described as being 'in Sir Melville's handwriting on official paper, rather untidy and in the nature of rough jottings'. Loftus thought that they mentioned three suspects: a Polish tanner or cobbler; a man who went around stabbing young girls in the bottom; and a 41-year-old doctor, Mr M. J. Druitt.

Donner died in 1968 and the notes then seemed to have disappeared. Loftus wrote to his family inquiring their whereabouts, but the family told him that they did not know. He also wrote to Lady Aberconway – who was Donner's aunt and Sir Melville's other daughter, asking her the same questions. She explained, 'My elder sister, ten years older than myself, took all my father's papers when my mother died – which is why Gerald has them: I have never seen them. But in my father's book *Days of my Years* he talks of "Jack The Ripper" . . . that is all the information I can give.'

The notes that are still in her possession, which Farson and Cullen both quoted from, are *typewritten copies*. Farson says 'she was kind enough to give me her father's notes which she had copied out soon after his death.' Tom Cullen also told me, in conversation, that the notes he had seen were typewritten.

Objectively, everything pointed to the fact that copies of Macnaghten's notes would seem to have been made at some time after Sir Melville's death, and that the originals had probably remained with Lady Aberconway's elder sister, Julia Donner. Only those Ripper enthusiasts who wished to diminish the case against Druitt would seriously want to consider the possibility that Macnaghten's private notes had not existed at one time. But until further verification of them was forthcoming the veracity or otherwise of Farson and Cullen's source material with regard to the actual content of these notes, which supposedly confirmed Sir Melville's convictions, would remain a subject of debate.

If only typewritten copies had been available for scrutiny no more need have been said, but now our own investigations into these elusive papers was to confirm the existence of two handwritten pages alongside the typed pages that had formed the basis of both Farson's and Cullen's earlier assertions.

These two pages are identical word for word with Farson and Cullen's typewritten version, and to begin with at least our expectations were raised. Did we have in our possession the original notes written by Sir Melville himself? Comparing them with a photocopy of the Scotland Yard notes, it was possible to see distinct similarities between the two; some words were virtually identical. The obvious thing to do was to have the handwriting of both versions analysed, but there were enough indications to suggest, despite the similarity of style, that these had in fact been written by Lady Aberconway and not her father. Her son believed it more likely, and as the handwritten pages were numbered 6a and 6b and accompained seven typewritten sheets it seemed almost certain that these were Christabel Aberconway's copies which she had personally made some time after her elder sister Julia had taken charge of the originals following their mother's death in January 1929. We decided therefore to try to date the paper, as this would test the veracity of the copy and therefore the authenticity of its contents.

A simple test under ultra-violet light determined two things. Firstly, the paper could not have been manufactured as early as

1894, when Sir Melville wrote his notes, as the paper contained an optical whitener – a chemical whitening agent which fluoresces under ultra-violet light. Such additives are widely used today in washing powders, fabrics and paper, but they were not manufactured until the 1930s. Secondly the paper we were now examining had the faintest reddish glow, which meant that there was only residual fluorescence, whereas paper manufactured in the 1960s, 1950s or even 1940s shone with a much brighter blue glow.

There could be no doubt that the notes we had before us had been written in the early thirties and were a faithful reproduction of Sir Melville's rough jottings which had formed the basis of his final draft deposited with the Scotland Yard notes. Since they were written at a time when public knowledge of Druitt's inclusion as a suspect could have caused his family considerable shame and embarrassment, although Lady Aberconway allowed a third party (probably her secretary) to type out most of her father's first draft she preferred to copy the two highly confidential pages herself. By 1959 the need for discretion had somewhat abated, and this time she must have allowed a secretary to copy all the notes, which were then given to Dan Farson. As for the originals, our researches indicate that they almost certainly travelled with Gerald Donner to India, where he died in November 1968. In the past several members of his family have tried to discover whether they still exist, but to no avail; the chances are that they are lost forever. But there could be no doubt now that Macnaghten did harbour a growing conviction that Montague John Druitt and Jack the Ripper were one and the same.

Nineteen years later his opinion remained unchanged. On the occasion of his retirement in June 1913 he gave an interview to the *Morning Post* in which he remarked:

> I have two great regrets in my life – one is that I was not allowed to play in the match against Harrow, having been turned out of the Eleven before the match, and the other that I joined the CID six months after the Whitechapel murderer committed suicide and I never had a go at him.

The following year he stated in his autobiography:

> I incline to the belief that the individual who held up London in terror resided with his own people; that he absented himself from home at certain times, and that he committed suicide on or about the 10th November 1888, after he had knocked out a Commissioner of Police and very nearly settled the hash of one of Her Majesty's principal Secretaries of State.

All the time we must remember that Sir Melville's beliefs are based on 'private' information which must have been passed on to him by the one man who wasn't saying anything – and who may not even have told his old friend the whole truth. According to Christopher Monro, this theory was such a hot potato that James Monro would not even share his secret with his own wife. Whatever it was, however, the one assumption that we can reasonably make is that if Monro did have strong feelings on the matter – and we believe he must have – it almost certainly would have revolved around Montague John Druitt.

According to the statement of Watkin Wynn Williams, the grandson of Chief Commissioner General Sir Charles Warren, 'I cannot recall that my grandfather ever stated in writing his personal views on the identity of Jack The Ripper. . . . My impression is that he believed the murderer to be a sex maniac who committed suicide after the Miller's Court murder – possibly the young doctor whose body was found in the Thames on December 31st, 1888.'

Sir Basil Thomson, Assistant Commissioner of the Metropolitan Police from 1913 to 1919, says in *The Story of Scotland Yard*, published in 1935, 'The belief of the CID officers at the time was that they [the murders] were the work of an insane Russian doctor and that this man escaped arrest by committing suicide at the end of 1888.' He is wrong about his nationality, obviously confusing Druitt with Macnaghten's other possible suspect, Michael Ostrog. But if Thomson did not actually know Druitt's name, then he had obviously been influenced by the common belief that the man dragged from the Thames was a doctor; therefore the most relevant piece of information contained in his statement is still the reference to a suicide. According to Macnaghten both Ostrog and Kosminski were detained in lunatic asylums, and only Druitt's body had been found in the Thames on 31 December 1888.

Sir John FitzGerald Moylan, Assistant Under-Secretary at the Home Office from 1940 to 1945, was able to write: 'The murderer, it is now certain, escaped justice by committing suicide at the end of 1888.' Again he is echoing Thomson when he talks of the suspect escaping justice, and again there can be no doubt but that he is referring to Druitt. Both men, however, are surely inferring something else. In implying that the suspect escaped arrest by committing suicide they are suggesting that the police were at least on to their man prior to his death and that had he survived he would have been apprehended. As James Monro knowingly told his grandson: 'He should have been caught.'

XI

One of the dangers we had encountered in the year that had passed since our Whitechapel walk was the continual inclusion by other writers of material that could not be supported; and yet we had learnt, by virtue of our own research, that it was an element in the puzzle that could hardly be avoided. Christopher Monro's opinion that his grandfather had definite views on the identity of the Ripper is a case in point. If taken at face value such a declaration could profoundly affect our appraisal of the mystery, and ultimately our conclusion.

So too, when we turn our attentions to Montague John Druitt, we are asked by Dan Farson to believe in the existence of a privately printed article in Australia called 'The East End Murderer – I Knew Him', by Lionel Druitt, Montague's cousin. If ever there was a real possibility of presenting positive evidence of Montague John Druitt's guilt, this was surely it. But once again we discover that – like so many pieces of the jigsaw – the letter to Farson from a Mr Knowles, informing him of the existence of this document, is now missing together with the rest of Farson's research file. No Mr Knowles ever comes to Farson's aid, and the file with its supposedly invaluable contents is never seen again. At least where Christopher Monro's testimony was concerned there was enough independent evidence to suggest that his grandfather had to have had very strong views on the matter, which makes his grandson's testimony look that much more tenable.

As far as 'The East End Murderer – I Knew Him' was concerned, the very possibility that such a document existed excited us as only dedicated amateurs can be excited. Constrained as we were in South London, we found the idea of the secret Victorian past of an Australian settlement called Dandenong just as remote and inaccessible as any lost city or hidden treasure, and just as enticing. If a document had been written which explained Montague Druitt's involvement in the mystery, then it would be a very important piece of evidence indeed. It might even prove to be the missing link in a chain of hitherto unrelated events, which would lead to our eventual understanding of this century-old enigma. But the problem to begin with was how we could finance our investigations; the question of whether it was wise even to consider such an endeavour never crossed our minds.

The Australian Connection intrigued us, and we wanted to believe that 'The East End Murderer – I Knew Him' had existed, regardless of whether its discovery would support or weaken the case against Druitt. Where, though, did the facts end and the fiction begin? If the document still existed, we believed that it should be possible to trace it – but how, when others including Colin Wilson and the BBC had tried and failed?

Our first step was obviously to contact Dan Farson. But some considerable time was to pass before we finally met for a drink at his London club. Alas, it was not a happy occasion. The ice had hardly begun to melt in our gin and tonics before our host concluded that we were either mad, or incorrigible rogues, or both. Why did we want to meet him? Why were we asking such searching questions? Were we questioning the veracity of his book? And what did we have to tell him? The answer to that one was easy – nothing. It was an impossible situation. Not for the first time we recognized the naïvety of our approach.

If Dan Farson had possessed any further information of any value he would almost certainly have used it himself or would be planning to do so. Under the circumstances it might well have looked to him as though we were questioning the validity of what he had already contributed, and in many ways we were – that was our prerogative. But it was ingenuous of us to expect Farson to aid us in our endeavours. To cap it all, we had not given enough consideration to the fact that a good many years had passed since he had written his book. To us it was as fresh in our minds as if it had been written yesterday; for Dan Farson the course had been run long ago.

We had hoped to find an ally in our quest, but it was not to be. We would have to begin at the beginning by ourselves. Names, addresses, dates and statements would have to be collated from scratch, with the slender information supplied in Farson's book as the starting point. Initially we tried to establish the existence of Mr A. Knowles, the gentleman who had supposedly sent the author the letter referring to the Australian document. Farson makes a plea in the original 1972 publication of his book for anyone who had known Mr Knowles (who was in his eighties when Farson heard from him in 1959, and was probably dead by now) to come forward, but to no avail.

A year later, when Farson's book was reissued in paperback, some further information was supplied by a Mr Edhouse of Kentish Town. Among other things, a search at Somerset House had revealed the death of an Arthur Knowles of Hackney in June 1959, aged eighty-four. 'His death', says Farson, 'now explains why I never heard from him again.'

We were able to ascertain that this Mr Knowles, who had died at St Joseph's Hospice, Hackney, had in fact lived in Blackheath, and eventually we managed to trace a long-standing neighbour who had known the old man very well. There was no doubt in the neighbour's mind that, in all the years he had known him and all the long conversations they had had, this Arthus Knowles had never mentioned anything to do with Jack the Ripper or once been to Australia.

At this point we could well have decided to call it a day. But the author had also mentioned a second correspondent, a certain Maurice Gould of Bexleyheath, who quite independently had written to tell Farson that he had been in Australia between 1925 and 1932 when he met two people who claimed they knew the identity of Jack the Ripper. This in itself is meaningless but according to Gould their information had come from a Mr W. G. Fell. Gould remembered that one of the men was a freelance journalist called Edward MacNamara who 'knew this Mr Fell of Dandenong who died in 1935', and that Fell had housed a man called Druitt who left him papers proving the Ripper's identity. The other man was called McCarrity or McGarrity, and was sixty when Gould had met him in 1930. Farson credits Gould with saying: 'I lost track of him in a little place called, I think, Koo-Wee-Rup, near Lang Lang, where Fell, also an Englishman, at times looked after him.' Obviously if we could find Gould, and if he could clarify the reality of those far-off days in Australia, and confirm Farson's version of events, we would be better placed to assess the author's veracity and the likelihood that something at one time existed in Australia that might still be worth looking for.

In the meantime we tried to glean what we could from the pages of Farson's book. In 1961 he tells us he visited Australia to make a television series, and took the opportunity to drive out to the Dandenong Ranges in the company of an Australian reporter, Alan Dower, in search of evidence. The trip was disappointing. 'But,' says Farson, 'at least the places existed. We found Koo-Wee-Rup . . . and at Lang Lang I saw the end in sight when I heard of a storekeeper called Fell – but when I met him he said he was no relation to the Fell who printed the document.' In a town called Drouin Farson met a woman called Miss Stevens who remembered Dr Lionel Druitt. But that was it. No trace of the vital document.

None of this is too surprising except that none of these places is in the Dandenong Ranges. Drouin, where Lionel Druitt practised in 1903, lies sixty miles south-east of the ranges themselves, and the same distance from the town of Dandenong. So too with Koo-Wee-Rup and Lang Lang, which lie south-west of Drouin, close to the coast and even further from the mountains.

Farson's belief in the importance of the Dandenong Ranges had been encouraged by some other correspondence from Australia in 1961. This time the letter had been signed 'G.W.B.', by a man who believed that he was related to Jack the Ripper. In later correspondence the man was to mention that a close lady friend of his lived in the Dandenong Ranges which must have further encouraged Farson to believe that his decision to search for 'The East End Murderer' in the area was correct. By the time Farson comes to write his book, some ten years later, his Australian evidence has become a kind of composite of all the Australian information received over the years. This he had utilized as best he could, playing his own hunches as much as anything else and employing a certain amount of journalistic licence in order to make some cohesive sense of it all for the benefit of his readers.

In a curious way this in itself lends credibility to his account of the 'Mr Knowles letter' and its subsequent loss. It may not have contained as much information as Farson had wanted to believe, but clearly all the subsequent information he had received from other sources – from Gould, even G.W.B. – had convinced him of the existence of something in Australia which was potentially valuable, and that somehow the name Dandenong was particularly significant. How much easier it would have been for a disreputable author to have plucked a more convenient placename from a map of

Victoria. 'Nilma' for instance, or 'Longwarry', two settlements within a few miles of Drouin and Lionel Druitt; or why not Drouin itself? But Dandenong – over sixty miles away? Mr Farson would have wanted to come back from Australia with more than that; instead he is reduced to trying to establish a relationship between Lionel Druitt and Dandenong as best he can.

By now we had telephoned all the Goulds in south-east London and Kent but to no avail. A search of the death indexes from 1959 onwards also failed to reveal the relevant Maurice Gould, so there was still a chance that he was still alive and well and living – where?

In the meantime, while we were still cogitating about the unfortunate encounter we had had with the one man who probably knew the answer, we came across a small advertisement in an international genealogical directory, placed by an amateur genealogist in Sydney, requesting assistance in seeking information about the Druitt family of Wimborne Minster, and it was for us an extraordinary piece of luck. Our limited resources had made it impossible for us to pursue Farson's Australian connection to any depth, but now the possibility existed that we had, quite fortuitously, discovered someone who was more than likely directly connected with a branch of the Australian Druitts, and who, by virtue of her own interest in the family's history, was ideally situated to further clarify Lionel's involvement, if any, with the Whitechapel murders and the existence or otherwise of 'The East End Murderer . . .'

Needless to say, our first correspondence with the lady concerned was somewhat guarded. We expressed our interest with the Druitt line without specifically mentioning why, merely stating that our own project touched on the Druitt family and that we were interested in Lionel. We received an immediate reply, informing us that our Australian correspondent was researching her late mother's pedigree (the Mayo family), and through marriage this also involved the Druitt family of Wimborne. It was a genuine project, totally unconnected with Montague's involvement with the Whitechapel murders, and indeed it was even possible that the lady concerned was unaware of Montague's inclusion as a suspect. But it was also obvious that no advantage was to be gained by subterfuge. We were, after all, in a position to offer mutual advantage in any collaboration and were just as prepared as ever to accept Montague's innocence as well as his possible guilt.

So our link with Australia was born, and in the next few months our knowledge of Lionel's movements and of those of the

Australian Druitts in general was to expand considerably. The existence or otherwise of 'The East End Murderer', however, remained unestablished. We knew that Dr Lionel Druitt had arrived at Cooma in New South Wales by August 1886, and that he stayed with his uncle, Archdeacon Thomas Druitt. He practised in various country places before moving to Wagga Wagga where he married on 2 April 1888. On 20 October 1889 his first daughter, Susan Katherine, was born. On 1 August 1890 he registered with the Medical Board Victoria and began practising in St Arnaud. In May 1891 he registered as a medical practitioner in Tasmania, and in the same month his second daughter, Isabella, was born in Swansea, Tasmania, where he continued to practise until 1896.

Then, a listing in an Australian directory revealed for the first time that between 1897 and 1898 Lionel had been living and practising in Oakleigh, a thriving industrial suburb of Melbourne. His address: Dandenong Road. The significance of this seemed to be obvious. Dan Farson had been looking in the wrong place. In 1903 Lionel Druitt had been practising medicine in the small town of Drouin as Farson already knew. But this was sixty miles from Dandenong and all Farson's efforts to trace a W. G. Fell anywhere in the area were, alas, to no avail. But this was not surprising. Six years earlier, Lionel Druitt – unknown to Farson – had been living in Dandenong Road in the suburb of Oakleigh. Was it possible that the shadowy Mr Fell also originated from here? If so, there was a chance, however small, that he could still be traced and a relationship between him and Lionel established beyond reasonable doubt.

This was still a long way from finding 'The East End Murderer', of course, but for us the major significance in all this was that Farson could not have plucked the word 'Dandenong' from mid-air. Unfortunately his visit to Australia prompted him to look for W. G. Fell, somewhere in the Dandenong Ranges. But almost certainly whether the original information emanated from a Mr Knowles or from Mr Gould, or from both, Dandenong had been of major significance together with the names Fell, and Druitt or Drewett. Unfortunately 1890 was particularly significant as this was the year when 'The East End Murderer' had supposedly been privately printed, but Lionel Druitt had not arrived in the Dandenong Road until 1897, which made it unlikely that he would have had any connection with a Mr Fell of Dandenong seven years earlier. In 1890 he had been practising in St Arnaud, Victoria, as confirmed by an announcement in the local paper, the *St Arnaud Mercury* on

23 July 1890: 'Dr Lionel Druitt, MD Edin., MRCS Eng., LRCP Lond., will commence practice in St Arnaud on the 1st August 1890.' On 30 July he had consulting rooms at Bilton's Hotel in St Arnaud, and between 8 August of that year and 24 March 1891 he was to be found at his own residence in McMahon Street. By 1899 he had again moved, this time to Koroit, where his third daughter, Dorothy Edith, was born in February of that year. From here he moved to Drouin in 1903, and in 1907 he packed up his bags for the last time and settled in Mentone, where he died on 7 January 1908.

At this point we did not believe that Farson had necessarily been pulling the wool over our eyes, but without being able to talk to him constructively it was impossible to ascertain what avenues he himself had gone down in an attempt to discover where, if anywhere, Lionel Druitt may have met a W. G. Fell. Thanks to the tireless efforts of our invaluable Australian colleague, our knowledge of Lionel Druitt and of many of his descendants was as complete as it was ever likely to be. As for Mr Fell, our by now somewhat desperate investigations had even included writing to every Fell in the Melbourne telephone directory in the hope that some present-day descendant might hold the key to the mystery. We also contacted several historical societies, including the one at Kooweerup.

The nearest we had managed to place anyone called Fell in the vicinity of Dandenong, or Dandenong Road, was a Mrs Cecilia Fell, who was the licensee of the Bridge Hotel, Dandenong, in 1904. In 1905 this lady was at the Royal Hotel, Melbourne, and although the thought crossed our minds that Maurice Gould's recollection of a man called Druitt being 'looked after' by a Mr Fell could possibly have meant a connection with a commercial landlord or a hotel manager, we realized that we were merely clutching at straws. In 1904 Lionel Druitt was practising in Drouin, over sixty miles from Dandenong.

Establishing the existence of 'The East End Murderer' or proving that this pamphlet did not exist would have given us the satisfaction of knowing that we had discovered the truth, whether the new evidence strengthened the case against Montague John Druitt or not. Either way, our conviction that there was a truth to be uncovered, and that it revolved around the names Druitt, Drewett or Drewery, and the settlement of Dandenong, was now proving extremely frustrating as there was little more we could do to enable us to reach a satisfactory conclusion one way or the other. Only one glimmer of hope remained. At long last we had managed to track down in the Home Counties a Maurice Gould, who turned out to be the man we had been looking for over the past months.

Now in his seventies, he could only vaguely remember the events of sixty years earlier when he was a young man of eighteen in Australia. But he did remember that he had spoken to a man called Edward MacNamara in a famous Melbourne pub called Young's – the old man recalled with some affection the large portrait of a reclining nude above the bar. He remembered his conversation with MacNamara turning into a discussion about the Deeming Case which concerned an English emigrant who had been executed in Australia on 23 May 1892. Eventually they began talking about Jack the Ripper, at which point MacNamara produced from his pocket two or three handwritten sheets which Gould thought had been a 'confession' by the Ripper himself.

These could not have been a 'privately printed' document, as Farson had imagined, and in no way did Gould's story support the evidence of Mr Knowles's letter. But Gould did confirm that Dandenong was somehow relevant, as was the name Druitt or Drewett. As for W. G. Fell, the years had taken their toll and at such a distance it seemed just as likely to our informant that the name could have been Kell, or Bell, or any other like surname. But it was all rather academic. The penny had begun to drop.

Frederick Bailey Deeming murdered his first wife and four children and buried their bodies under the kitchen floor before emigrating to Australia with his second wife in 1891. Within weeks of arriving in Australia Deeming had already proposed to his third prospective victim and the body of his second wife had been discovered behind the bedroom fireplace of their Melbourne house. In prison he was supposed to have confessed to being Jack the Ripper, which has readily been dismissed by many commentators on the grounds that he was in jail at the time of the murders.

In fact, even if he had confessed to anything – which his solicitor was later to dispute vehemently – it was to the 'last two Ripper crimes'. That is to say, he confessed to the last two murders which occurred in the years preceding Deeming's arrest in Australia, which at this time were still widely thought to be the work of Jack the Ripper. They were the murder of an unidentified woman whose torso was discovered under the railway arches in Pinchin Street, Whitechapel, on 10 September 1889, and the murder of Frances Coles on 13 February 1891 – the date on which Deeming had been in Hull Prison for fraud. Even if we allow for the possibility that he actually meant one of these confessed murders to include Alice Mackenzie's in July 1889, it is fairly certain that Deeming had not arrived in England from South Africa until August. Nevertheless the public spectacle of his arrest, trial and subsequent execution was made all the more exciting as a result of this confession, and for some time he was regarded as such a serious candidate for the Whitechapel atrocities that the Australian police sent his death mask to Scotland Yard, where it still smiles benignly from its perch in the Black Museum.

The significant factor in all this was that shortly after arriving in Melbourne Deeming had assumed an alias. He was known as Mr Drewen! Furthermore, before his arrest he had rented a house in the small Melbourne suburb of Windsor, through which ran the main Dandenong Road, and his third fiancee and next prospective victim was a Miss Rounce*fell*, which may have influenced Maurice Gould's 'vague recollections' about such a name. In fact there was another Fell connection with Maurice Gould, as we were about to discover, but at last we were beginning to see the light. Whatever Gould had been shown by MacNamara had related to Frederick Deeming, or Drewen – not to Lionel or Montague Druitt – and he had been shown some handwritten documents, not a printed publication with the cliché title of 'The East End Murderer – I knew him!'

Something else which had been bothering us now began to make sense. In Farson's book Gould says that the journalist who originally showed him the 'confession' had wanted £500 for his valuable merchandise. All along it had been hard for us to accept that the unsupportable confession of an unknown English schoolteacher/barrister would have been so highly prized. But the confession of Deeming – Australia's own Ripper – would have been an entirely different matter. Maurice Gould's evidence had been misinterpreted by Dan Farson, encouraging him to believe that whatever information had been included in the letter from Knowles somehow referred to the same document that Gould had seen. Clearly this was not the case, unless of course Knowles had also seen something which referred to Drewen/Deeming. But if this had been so, he wouldn't have mentioned a document which had been printed in 1890 (Deeming was not to be arrested until 1892), and this still meant that whatever Knowles had seen in Australia was as much of a mystery as ever. The more we thought about it, the more convinced we were that if 'The East End Murderer' had ever existed, it had to have been a printed publication and almost certainly one intended for a fairly wide circulation – the very title contained more than its fair share of journalese. So we decided to cast our net even wider.

Our Australian colleague had done everything in her power to establish a link between Druitt and a W. G. Fell, as well as managing to investigate a considerable number of other avenues including most of the collateral branches of the Druitt family in Australia. All her attempts to track down the elusive document through the major newspaper repositories in Melbourne, Victoria and Canberra had also proved a waste of time, and although many of the Fells we had written to had been kind enough to reply to our inquiries, the harvest only served to confirm our suspicions that there had never been a connection between Lionel Druitt, W. G. Fell and a document called 'The East End Murderer'. The inescapable conclusion was that we had been on a wild goose chase from the very beginning, and most depressing of all was the fact that we still didn't fully understand the genesis of Farson's claim and the relevance of Knowles's letter.

Then, quite unexpectedly, we received a reply to our initial inquiries from the Kooweerup Historical Society. Historical researcher John Ruffels, of Bondi, explained that he had been drawn to the search for the Dandenong document when he read the paperback edition of Farson's book in 1973. He had never had more than a casual interest in Jack the Ripper, but he had found 'the possibility of discovering a mysterious pamphlet which might well hold the key to this hundred-year-old conundrum a tantalizing prospect'. We knew the feeling well!

Mr Ruffels, with the invaluable help of the Dandenong and Kooweerup Historical Societies, and fellow historians David Mickle of Dandenong and Jeffrey Burton of East Bentleigh had seemingly covered all the same ground that we had – and more – but there was still no sign of the elusive evidence. As he explained,

No clue turned up to lead us to the Dandenong document and the only mention of Jack The Ripper in a country newspaper whilst Dr Druitt was in the town occurred in the *St Arnaud Mercury*, in a supplement dated 29th November 1890. The article was along the lines of a 'Jack The Ripper was my lodger' type story, by an East End landlady.

Having had no luck with approaching the search from the Druitt angle, Mr Ruffels and his colleagues turned their attentions to the 'Mr Fell of Dandenong', and contacted the storekeeper at Lang

Lang whom Farson had met on his visit in 1961. This was the man who had told Farson that he was no relation to the Fell who had printed the document. However, what he presumably had not told Farson was that his own initials were W.G. and, most important of all, Maurice Gould had not only known him but had actually worked for him in 1930!

Inevitably, Mr Ruffels and his colleagues had arrived at the same conclusion that we had. But it also seemed to us that our Australian acquaintances had missed something. In his book Farson refers to the missing publication as a 'privately printed document' – in other words an entity in itself, as opposed to a small article in the columns of a newspaper. Alan Dower, the Australian journalist who accompanied him on his visit to the Dandenong Ranges, was to refer to the same document in the *Melbourne Truth*, in May 1961, as an 'ageing, printed pamphlet'. Because of its apparent insignificance John Ruffels had discovered all this without even realizing it. The supplement he had come across in the *St Arnaud Mercury* of 29 November 1890 was in essence 'The East End Murderer'.

The W. G. Fell, Dandenong and Drewen connections were no more than the hazy recollections of Maurice Gould from a night some sixty years before, when as a young man of eighteen he had found himself discussing Frederick Deeming and Jack the Ripper while he was working for a W. G. Fell. And the *St Arnaud Mercury* publication was an unsupportable piece of tittle-tattle about an East End landlady who had housed Jack the Ripper, a story which once again raised his spectre following the particularly brutal murder of a woman in Hampstead in October 1890, but it had appeared as a supplement – or, if you prefer, a pamphlet – in St Arnaud in the very same year that Dr Lionel Druitt arrived to set up practice. It was an inconsequential piece of nonsense, but there had always been a chance that Dan Farson's conclusive evidence would prove to be no more.

XII

All the theories we had considered so far, including the case against Macnaghten's drowned barrister, had readily revealed their inherent weaknesses. Some were transparent contrivances hardly worth a mention, let alone an exhaustive examination, and few retained their plausibility once a committed attempt was made to verify their specific claims. Only two theories emerged totally unscathed. They were depressing alternatives which constantly reminded us that our search for a killer long dead could be – and maybe always had been – a waste of time. They were, firstly, that Jack the Ripper was a truly anonymous lunatic who had died with his terrible secret shared only with his maker; and, secondly, that whilst there may have been some person or persons unknown who had once known the truth, the passage of time since the murders would now have put the solution finally beyond our reach.

Perhaps it was time to call it a day. We were expending more and more energy in trying to verify the word of others, amid the realization that there was nothing more to be gleaned from the facts surrounding the case. These scant and often contradictory fragments of information had long been wrung dry of any further meaning. Was Jack the Ripper left- or right-handed? Did he possess any surgical knowledge? Which, if any, of his correspondence was genuine? How many women did he murder? These are but a handful of the questions that have been argued for and against from the beginning, and for all our efforts there was little more that we could add.

We could strongly support the widely held view that the

murderer killed only five women, and did not believe it was necessary for him to have had any great surgical skill. There were some indications that he may have strangled his victims first, but we have no idea whether he was left- or right-handed – or ambidextrous for that matter – as the answer to this question rests simply on whether the assailant attacked his victims from the front or from behind. Even if we could be sure, the knowledge would hardly bring us significantly nearer to catching the killer. As for the short list of plausible suspects, Druitt alone had seemed worthy of further investigation.

It wasn't so much that the case against him stood up to much, but rather the fact that it wouldn't lie down. For one thing, other writers were inadvertently strengthening his claim when they hoped for the contrary. According to Knight, Walter Sickert believed Druitt to have been a scapegoat, when clearly he had been anything but. If it were not for Macnaghten's notes coming to light in 1959, Montague Druitt's name could conceivably have remained secret until 1992, when Macnaghten's private notes would become public domain. But if Knight is to be believed at all, Walter Sickert knew of Druitt's involvement decades before the case for and against this drowned barrister would surface.

In Donald McCormick's 1970 revised edition of *The Identity of Jack the Ripper* he says he traced a London doctor whose father was at Oxford with Druitt. In the doctor's own words:

My father always told me that the story about Druitt being the Ripper arose through the barrister being blackmailed by someone who threatened to denounce him as Jack the Ripper to the school at which he worked. Whether this was a heartless hoax or a cruel method of extorting money from a man who was just recovering from a nervous breakdown was not clear. There was nothing seriously wrong with Druitt, but he suffered from insomnia and blackouts and these threats preyed on his mind and paved the way to a further breakdown. He may under severe stress have given a muddled account of the threats to his mother. My father, who was an experienced doctor, was quite convinced he could not have been the Ripper and that the gold found on his body was originally intended to pay off the blackmailer. He certainly confided in his mother about the whole affair and she presumably told the police when he was reported missing some time during December 1888. Anyhow, my father was emphatic that Druitt was living at Bournemouth when the first two Ripper crimes were committed.

Even if the doctor's name were known and some proof offered to support his testimony, we would still have to ask some pertinent questions. If his information was correct, for instance, how could Druitt's family or Macnaghten ever consider Montague a serious suspect? If he was living at Bournemouth at the time of the first murders, he had a cast iron alibi. Secondly, there is no evidence to suggest that Druitt ever had a nervous breakdown or suffered from blackouts. What we do know is that he was an active sportsman up to and including the period of the murders, and that he had a trained legal mind. If anyone was capable of dealing with a spurious blackmail threat, he was – and apart from anything else it would surely be ludicrous to threaten a man with blackmail if he had nothing to hide.

McCormick states that this doctor also knew Walter Sickert. According to the doctor, at some time Walter Sickert met Sir Melville Macnaghten at the Garrick Club in London and told him his student lodger story. The name of the student was supposed to be something like Druitt, Drewett or even Hewitt. Sir Melville was convinced it must have been Druitt because he knew of his suicide and the fact that he had a widowed mother living in Bournemouth.

He then goes on to suggest that this is where Macnaghten's 'private information' emanates, and therefore explains the inclusion of Druitt as a suspect. But this is nonsense. Walter Sickert's story was hardly private information. From all accounts it was a frequently repeated anecdote, eventually finding itself perpetuated in print by Osbert Sitwell. And whilst we could readily accept that Sickert might well have kept the name of the student secret to all but his closest friends, not once does his story display any knowledge that the student's family believed him to have been the murderer, or that he was sexually insane. On the contrary he was a 'gentle, quiet, ailing youth . . . a delicate consumptive young man'. Furthermore, it is Macnaghten himself who irrevocably crushes any possibility that Sickert's yarn could have influenced him sufficiently to incriminate Druitt. He says in his autobiography, 'I do not think that there was anything of religious mania about the real Simon Pure, nor do I believe that he had ever been detained in an asylum, *nor lived in lodgings* [authors' italics].'

But the fact was that Montague John Druitt's widowed mother had lived at the family home in Wimborne, Dorset, just ten miles from Bournemouth; and that Willim Harvey Druitt, who came to London to look for his missing brother, had been contacted at Bournemouth following the discovery of Montague's body. It is

Bournemouth to which Macnaghten refers when he talks of the drowned barrister in his notes. McCormick's supposition does not fit the bill, and yet the probable truth had been staring us in the face all the time.

Allowing for the possibility that Walter Sickert and Macnaghten could have met at the Garrick Club, and the fact that Sickert's story includes information about 'a widowed mother living in Bournemouth', which so closely applied to Ann Druitt, the conclusion is inescapable: not that Sickert informed Macnaghten of this fact, but the other way around. Sir Melville confided to Sickert some details of the man he suspected of being Jack the Ripper, enabling Sickert to embellish his tale further.

Much of Donald McCormick's source material for his Pedachenko theory is derived from the lost three-volume *Chronicles of Crime*, an unpublished work by Dr Thomas Dutton, who died in November 1935 very much a recluse. Once again the reader is faced with the unpleasant possibility that the author's evidence may be contrived. From bitter experience we knew how much effort was needed to try to verify somebody's uncorroborated statements – only to fail or, worse, discover that a contributor had deliberately fabricated information in order to strengthen his particular case.

The Pedachenko, Ostrog, Konovalov or Kosminski – possibly all the same man – theories are the offspring of the 'Russian secret agent' school of Ripperology. And whilst we could see that such a pedigree allowed for maximum conjecture with minimum supportable evidence – the Russian secret service, even less than the CID, doesn't advertise or give interviews! – we could not ignore the fact that McCormick's hypothesis once more raised the possibility that some covert agency was responsible for the intrigue. Earlier we showed how the Home Office and its agents were keeping an eye on known political subversives in relation to these crimes, and we could also see that if there were sufficient reason to keep the results of their investigations from the public they were in a position to do so without Scotland Yard's knowledge.

Ultimately, McCormick's complicated theory falls down because there is simply no way of checking any of the 'evidence', and one is left with the impression that the author has been playing a hunch. Reasonably enough, the testimony of his London doctor does not turn up in his book published in 1959, for the simple reason that Druitt's name had not then been revealed. But, importantly, this makes a story that was included in the first publication of particular significance. According to McCormick, a rumour had spread shortly after the Mary Jane Kelly murder that the Ripper had either been put in an asylum or had died. McCormick goes on to say: 'This story was never published for the simple reason that there was nothing to substantiate it.' He then quotes from a statement made by Albert Bachert, one of the founder members of the Whitechapel Vigilance Committee, concerning the rumour that Jack the Ripper had drowned in the Thames:

I was given this information in confidence about March, 1889. I had complained to the police that there seemed to be too much complacency in the force simply because there had been no further murders for some months.

I was then asked if I would agree to be sworn to secrecy on the understanding I was given certain information. Foolishly, I agreed. It was then suggested to me that the Vigilance Committee and its patrols might be disbanded as the police were quite certain that the Ripper was dead.

I protested that, as I had been sworn to secrecy, I really ought to be given more information than this. 'It isn't necessary for you to know anymore,' I was told. 'The man in question is dead. He was fished out of the Thames two months ago and it would only cause pain to relatives if we said any more than that.'

Again I protested that I had been sworn to secrecy all for nothing, that I was really no wiser than before. 'If there are no more murders I shall respect this confidence, but if there are any more I shall consider I am absolved from my pledge of secrecy.'

The police then got very tough. They told me a pledge was a solemn matter, that anyone who put out stories that the Ripper was still alive might be proceeded against for causing a public mischief. However, they agreed that if there were any other murders which the police were satisfied could be Ripper murders, that was another matter.

I never believed the yarn, though I kept my pledge until after the McKenzie murder in 1891. Maybe some police officers kidded themselves that this was the truth, though I have my doubts about that. Dectective-Inspector Abberline told me years later that he was quite certain that the story was untrue and that the Ripper remained alive and uncaught.

The reference to 'the McKenzie murder in 1891' is unfortunate. Alice McKenzie was killed on 17 July 1889, and it was Frances Coles who was murdered in February 1891. Nevertheless, for an author who would later want to discredit the Druitt theory the information contained in this story, far from being helpful, is patently debilitating, which in itself encourages the belief that there may be some truth in it. Indeed, further investigation reveals that the Vigilance Committee was run down throughout 1889 and 1890, until events in 1891 forced Albert Bachert to reconsider the position.

On the day before the inquest of Frances Coles was due to open Bachert told the *Pall Mall Gazette*: 'I have been called upon to serve on the jury tomorrow afternoon, and it is my intention to inquire into this case. If evidence is brought forward which can prove that it has been committed by the *late* [authors' italics] Whitechapel fiend, I shall at once re-form the Vigilance Committee, and appeal to the public for aid.' That one word 'late' proves beyond a shadow of doubt that Albert Bachert knew that Jack the Ripper was supposed to be dead at a time when this would have been privileged information. None of the newspapers at the time had ever commented on the possibility, for the simple reason that the rumour had not yet been generated. Besides, few people at the time would have believed it. When it did finally come out, it was almost certainly because of Albert Bachert himself.

His reference to the most recent crime having been committed by the 'late Whitechapel fiend' was tinged with sarcasm, and was most likely designed to give fair warning to the authorities that he was no longer prepared to accept that Jack the Ripper had drowned in the Thames. This would also mean that he was about to break his pledge of secrecy, as his informants would have been only too aware. They were not prepared to tolerate that, as subsequent events would show.

The next day Mr Wynne E. Baxter opened his inquiry into the death of Frances Coles. When the names of the jury men were called, only eight answered. Albert Bachert had originally been called as a substitute, and now he stepped forward to offer his services in the place of a Mr Fielder. However – no doubt to his surprise – the coroner declined to let him serve.

Bachert: Why?
Coroner: Because I decline.
Bachert: You decline simply because I happen to be chairman of the Vigilance Committee, and you think I shall fully investigate this matter. I have a right to be on the jury.
Coroner: I have decided you are not to serve on this jury.
Bachert: Yes, because you know I shall enquire into this case.
Coroner: You have already been told I shall decline to accept you.
Bachert: (Walking to the back of the court). – You will hear more of this.

Baxter had no justification for his actions and could offer no reply to Bachert's question. But in the final analysis there could be only one explanation. Albert Bachert was obviously convinced – wrongly – that the murder of Frances Coles could have been another 'Ripper event'. He had been told as early as March 1889 that Jack the Ripper was dead, and he had promised to keep silent unless there was another murder probably by the same hand. His informants accepted this for the simple reason that they themselves had been told that the business was all over. But they had not reckoned on the power of the legend that had already been created. With almost every subsequent unsolved homicide the cry would once again be raised that Jack had struck again. Now, two years after Bachert had been given his inside information, steps were still being taken to curb his zealous pursuit of the truth – which in itself only further demonstrates just how classified this original information was intended to be.

In the revised edition of his book in 1970, Donald McCormick's main objection to Druitt being identified in Bachert's statement as the drowned Ripper is that this man is constantly referred to as a doctor, or a young medical student, even by Sir Melville; in fact Druitt was a barrister. But even McCormick points out that there are no records of any doctors having committed suicide in late 1888 or early 1889. Furthermore, Bachert's statement makes no reference to the profession of the deceased – weakening the argument rather than strengthening it.

The fact remains that Druitt, and Druitt only, was Macnaghten's prime suspect for the Whitechapel murders, and Druitt was pulled from the Thames in the weeks following Kelly's murder. But the question of why he should be thought of as a doctor is an important one, and we felt it needed to be answered.

Edwin Thomas Woodhall, writing in the mid-1930s, admits when talking of his own particular search for Jack the Ripper that his main difficulty had been the minimal assistance from those connected with these crimes. Whenever possible he made notes, and writes: 'Although of no use for many years, I am glad I kept them, for now they have proved invaluable in the telling of this story.'

They became invaluable for Woodhall some time after the publication in 1914 of Macnaghten's autobiography, in which he makes reference to the 'knocking out of a Commissioner of Police, and settling the hash of a Secretary of State'. This 'high-flown style' of Macnaghten's, as Alexander Kelly describes it, was, it seems, now responsible for Woodhall's revelations, which resulted in the author adding two and two together and making five. Macnaghten is speaking not literally but metaphorically. The Commissioner of Police he is referring to is undoubtedly Sir Charles Warren, who was to all intents and purposes knocked out of office by Jack the Ripper. He was forced to resign largely as a result of his inept handling of the case. Henry Matthews had also been under extreme pressure throughout the autumn of 1888, and was fortunate to survive.

According to Woodhall, during the period of the murders certain individuals had taken to scaring women out of their wits by jumping out at them and frightening them half to death. During this time many complaints came in from Spitalfields and the Stepney area about a tall man with a frightful face who kept doing this sort of thing. White-eyes, as the man had become to be called, had evaded all attempts to capture him; then one night he jumped out on two women when a constable was just round the corner. The policeman gave chase and seized him, but the man struggled so fiercely that a running fight took place all along the street. After about twenty minutes two more officers arrived, but instead of easing up the struggle started afresh, with renewed violence on the part of the resisting prisoner. With the superhuman strength of a madman the man kept throwing off his would-be captors until, with aid from members of the public, he was at last brought to the ground and held there.

At the police station it became obvious that the man was insane, but he could quickly revert from a violent human animal to a mild, polite human being. His face was entirely coloured black with burnt cork; and, starting at the forehead, the eyes, nose, moustache and mouth were painted white. This gave the impression in the dark of some weird-looking skull or death mask. On account of his strange statements, but more likely to prevent him doing further violence, White-eyes was at once placed in the police cells, with the ultimate idea of removing him to an asylum.

Woodhall goes on to say that this never happened. Much to the surprise of the East End police the man was taken to Old Palace Yard, Whitehall, at the request of two highly placed officials. However they had no chance to question their suspect. No sooner was he left alone with them in a room there than he leaped at a desk, snatched up a big ebony ruler and savagely assaulted both officials. Then, before he could be restrained, he darted out of the room, past two constables and bounded out of the building.

Apparently three weeks later his body was recovered from the Thames by the river police near Hungerford Bridge. A paddle boat tied to Waterloo Pier had been shifted, causing the black swollen body to come to the surface, for it had lodged under the wheel. The black burnt cork and white paint on the already decomposing features were hideously evident. Who he was and where he came from were a complete mystery. White-eyes's brief notoriety was over, and would have remained so if it had not been for Edwin Woodhall's intervention.

Woodhall is essentially correct about one element of his story. A strange-faced man was indeed arrested on the night of 11 November 1888, and the event was duly reported in *The Times* the following day:

> Great excitement was caused shortly before 10 o'clock last night by the arrest of a man with a blackened face who publicly proclaimed himself to be 'Jack The Ripper'. This was at the corner of Wentworth Street, Commercial Street, near the scene of the latest crime. Two young men, one a discharged soldier, immediately seized him, and the great crowd, which always on a Sunday night parades this neighbourhood, raised a cry of 'lynch him.' Sticks were raised, the man was furiously attacked, and but for the timely arrival of the police he would have been seriously injured. The police took him to Leman Street station, when the prisoner proved himself to be a very remarkable person. He refused to give any name, but asserted that he was a doctor at St George's Hospital. He is about 35 years of age, 5ft 7in. in height, of dark complexion, with a dark moustache, and was wearing spectacles. He wore no waistcoat, but had an ordinary jersey vest beneath his coat. In his pocket he had a double peaked, light check cap, and at the time of his arrest was bareheaded. It took four constables and four other persons to take him to the station and protect him from the infuriated crowd. He is detained in custody, and it seems that the police attach importance to the arrest, as his appearance answers to the police description of the man who is wanted.

There are enough discrepancies between this report and Woodhall's version of events to suppose that he has indulged in a game of Chinese Whispers – ill reporting and misinterpreting information passed on from various sources. Unfortunately he has also committed himself to a seemingly unlikely hypothesis, based on this one article, without being aware that both the *Star* and the *Daily News* carried a report of the same incident but in a somewhat different version from *The Times*. The *Star* and *Daily News* reported:

> About ten o'clock last night the idle and inquisitive crowd, who since the ghastly discovery was made have infested Dorset Street and

its immediate neighbourhood, had their attention attracted to the extraordinary behaviour of a man who for some short time before had been officiously making inquiries and generally conducting himself in an unusual manner. Over a pair of good trousers he wore a jersey in place of a coat, and his face was most palpably artificially blacked. His manner led to considerable remark and at last a cry was raised that he was 'Jack The Ripper'. . . . Fortunately for him, there were a large number of policemen about, both in uniform and plain clothes, by whom he was surrounded on the first alarm being given. He at first resisted capture, but, happily for himself, soon realised his position and consented to go quietly to Leman Street police station. . . . As it was, he was very roughly handled and considerably bruised by the time he reached the police-station, where he gave his name, and address, which are withheld by the police authorities. He stated that he was a medical man, and that he had disguised himself in the absurd manner above described in order to endeavour by what he thought were detective means to discover and apprehend the perpetrator of the Whitechapel horrors. He also gave particulars of himself as enabled the police to quickly substantiate their accuracy, and to discharge him after a short detention in the cells.

The obvious discrepancies between all three versions do little to encourage faith in Woodhall's integrity, and his account of the eventual escape of the prisoner borders on the fantastic. Apart from anything else, would such a dangerous lunatic be allowed such freedom of movement and opportunity of escape considering the difficulty with which he had been apprehended in the first place? And even if he had escaped, the ensuing chase, with police running through the street blowing their whistles, attracting the attention of an anxious public only too willing to involve itself in such pursuits, would have been a worthy follow-up to that first article in *The Times*. What did appear in *The Times* on the following day was a report which began: 'During yesterday several arrests were made, but after a short examination *in all cases* [authors' italics] the persons were set at liberty, as it was felt certain they had no connection with the crime.'

Woodhall's fiction would appear as far from the truth as anyone could hope to get. Yet there were elements in his account that deserved further consideration, not least because although he seemed to have overstepped the mark it was important to understand what his real motive was, and how he came to commit his particular incident to print.

In attempting to find out the identity of Jack the Ripper, he believed he had to look for a man who had been dragged from the

Thames towards the end of 1888 – a young doctor or medical student. But why pick on the arrest of a black-faced doctor as being at all significant? Was the author simply trying to pull the wool over his readers' eyes – or had he tried to make some sense of the unrelated snippets of information that he had received in the past?

The fact that there were two contradictory reports of the same incident was not incompatible with Woodhall's assertion that the man had reverted from a 'wild animal' to a 'polite human being'. The *Times* article had appeared on the morning of 12 November, the day after the incident, and there is no reason why it should not have been essentially correct. The *Star* and *Daily News* articles did not appear until the evening of the 12th and the morning of the 13th respectively, and in all probability these accounts would have echoed an official police statement on the matter. Had the police deliberately played down the incident in order to say that all those arrested had been released, when in fact the black-faced man had been passed on to a higher authority, as Woodhall asserts?

Once again we found ourselves in the land of unsupportable testimony; not necessarily the valley of deceit, but an extremely fertile plain where small white flowers of truth hide amongst choking weeds and where Old Father Time stands sharpening his scythe. How much of Woodhall's story was pure fantasy, and how much was based on inside gossip, we would certainly never know for sure; but we still couldn't entirely dismiss his colourful account.

As Woodhall himself wrote, he was not so much an author turned detective as a detective turned author. He had joined the Metropolitan Police in 1907, and during the next thirteen years was to graduate through the CID to the Special Branch and eventually to the secret service department, before retiring in 1919. Much of his future writing would contain information gleaned from these valuable years, however inaccurately the knowledge would be reassembled, and his White-eyes story was no exception. Despite its implausibility, it contained facets which were obviously relevant and potentially valuable. For instance, it is a fact that in cases of prolonged contact with water dead human skin turns black within about half an hour after recovery. As a postcript to his story, Woodhall recalls talking to an old pensioned police sergeant of the H or Whitechapel division who had taken part in the investigation of the crimes. The old man handed him a faded, yellow-looking cardboard picture which the author immediately recognized was a police mortuary photograph. 'With a nauseating feeling of sickness,' says Woodhall, 'I studied it in silence for a few seconds and handed it back.'

If the old policeman was to be believed, Woodhall knew he had looked at the blackened remains of Jack the Ripper, a man whose body had been dragged from the Thames a few weeks after Mary Jane Kelly's murder. That man would have been Montague John Druitt. By the time Woodhall came to try and identify the suspect in 1937, the notion that the body in the Thames had been that of a young student or doctor was firmly established. From Woodhall's point of view it was a question of find the right doctor and you've found Jack the Ripper.

Unfortunately Druitt was not a doctor, but Rumbelow, in trying to make some sense of the conundrum, suggests that he may well have embarked on a medical career before turning to the law. In a letter in the Scotland Yard file reference is made to some inquiries about three insane medical students, two of whom had been traced and interviewed, and Rumbelow questions whether Druitt could have been one of these.

It was a perfectly reasonable suggestion and it would at least explain the subsequent confusion. But in fact all three suspects were known to have studied at the London Hospital, whereas a search of the registers there does not reveal Druitt's name. However, it was the third of these students who actually held the key to the enigma of Druitt's mistaken profession.

Before November 1888 initial inquiries had been made by Inspector Abberline concerning the whereabouts of these medical students, and later Warren reported to the Home Office that two of the young men had been traced and that the third, John Sanders, had apparently gone abroad. This, however, did not entirely satisfy the Home Secretary, who continued to press Warren for the date of the third student's departure and whether any further inquiries had been made. Abberline again reported to his Commissioner that searching inquiries had been made at the student's last known address in Aberdeen Place, St John's Wood. The only information was that a lady named Sanders had resided with her son at No. 22, but had gone abroad two years earlier.

Whether this second reply satisfied the Home Secretary we cannot say but it seems doubtful. Warren had not been able to give a satisfactory answer to either of the Home Secretary's questions because there was no way of knowing whether John Sanders really had gone abroad. More importantly he would have had no way of knowing if the elusive student had returned, and so presumably he would have had to keep him on the 'wanted' list just in case. This brings us back to the events of 11 November and the arrest of the strange black-faced doctor. Importantly, the *Times* report of the incident finishes by saying that this obviously unbalanced individual was 'detained in custody, and it seems that the police attach importance to the arrest, as his appearance answers to the police description of the man who is wanted'.

John Sanders was wanted at the time; he had become a medical student at the London Hospital, Whitechapel, on 22 April 1879, and he had been placed in an asylum some time after 1882. Furthermore, information about him had reached the Home Office only days before the black-faced doctor was arrested on the streets of Whitechapel. If John Sanders and White-eyes had turned out to be one and the same, it would not be at all surprising to discover that the Home Office had taken a personal interest in his arrest, which again brings us to Woodhall's hypothesis. After the arrest of White-eyes, Woodhall says that 'much to the surprise of the East End police the man was taken to Old Palace Yard, Whitehall, at the request of two highly placed officials'.

In March 1903 Inspector Abberline was asked his opinion of an article in a well-known Sunday newspaper in which it was made out that the author of the Whitechapel crimes had been a young medical student who was found in the Thames in December 1888. The retired detective said, 'Yes, I know all about that story. But what does it amount to? Simply this. Soon after the last murder in Whitechapel the body of a young doctor was found in the Thames, but there is absolutely nothing beyond the fact that he was found at that time to incriminate him. A report was made to the Home Office about the matter. . . .' The very fact that someone in Abberline's position accepted that the body in the Thames had been that of a young doctor proves that the CID were not fully aware of all the relevant facts concerning this particular suspect at the time – an important deduction later confirmed by Sir Melville Macnaghten in his autobiography.

Albert Bachert's evidence and the circumstances surrounding the Frances Coles inquest strongly support the proposition that nameless and faceless people were determined to keep the real identity of the drowned man secret. Now that Bachert had betrayed his trust there was a very good chance that all their efforts would turn out to be in vain. It would only be a matter of time before somebody would correctly identify Druitt as the man who had drowned in the Thames in December 1888 and start asking questions. Fortunately, however, a decoy had readily presented itself in the shape of John Sanders, alias White-eyes.

As explained earlier, it was extremely unlikely that this suspect actually escaped custody. However it must be remembered that other people besides Woodhall would have needed him to escape in order to promote the idea that the body in the Thames was that of the same young doctor who had screamed his guilt on the streets of Whitechapel before being arrested, later escaping, and finally throwing himself in the river.

With this notion firmly established, there was very little danger that the unfortunate death of a respectable barrister would ever be associated with the atrocities in Whitechapel, and whether Scotland Yard accepted that Jack the Ripper was dead or not was beside the point. The important thing was that any inquiry into the death of an un-named doctor would lead nowhere and the real Jack the Ripper would remain as anonymous in death as he had been in life.

XIII

For all our determination, we realized that we were in danger of falling into the trap that all along we had so conscientiously tried to avoid. We found ourselves beginning to accept that Montague John Druitt could have been Jack the Ripper when the evidence against him was far from conclusive. But although our Australian connection had turned out to be a red herring, much of our research had led us to the conclusion that, whoever had been responsible for that autumn of terror, Montague John Druitt had for some reason or other precipitated the need to keep his identity a secret.

Whether this had meant a full-scale cover-up we could not be sure, and there was much to indicate that Scotland Yard would not necessarily have been involved. Men doing the donkey work in the lower ranks of the CID would not have been party to the kind of information available to a few select men in Whitehall had someone as eminent as Prince Albert Victor, or even his Cambridge mentor J. K. Stephen, been involved with the sordid business. All we had to go on were fragments of circumstantial evidence, and the fact that Druitt's name does, after all, appear in the private notes of an eminent police officer.

Perhaps Montague John Druitt was not so much of an outsider as we may at first have imagined. At the very least we could accept that his guilt would have been a crippling embarrassment to his class at a time when socialists lurked under every Establishment bed. His public trial might have uncovered something far more damaging, something which would make it imperative that he should never stand trial.

If we truly accepted anything at all, however, it was simply that many other investigators had got close to the truth without enough evidence at their disposal to jump to the right conclusion. Even where it could be shown that a particular hypothesis was way off beam, we felt it usually contained a grain of truth. Woodhall's story is a good example. The ex-detective was barking up the wrong tree in many respects, and yet his contribution at least allowed us eventually to understand how Druitt's identity could remain secret for so long.

Once again we were drawn back to Macnaghten's drowned barrister and a particularly weighty question. If Druitt was the Ripper, why was someone so desperate to keep his name a secret? We had found nothing that supported Druitt's innocence and plenty to indicate that others beside Sir Melville considered him a strong suspect. Other writers had inadvertently strengthened the case against him when they had hoped to do the opposite, and some had managed to contrive their own theories around a germ of truth which led us nowhere. Yet nobody had managed convincingly to dismiss the only genuine suspect in the frame.

On Wednesday, 2 January 1889, the *County of Middlesex Independent* carried this report of Montague John Druitt's death:

FOUND IN THE RIVER: The body of a well dressed man was discovered on Monday in the river off Thorneycroft's torpedo works, by a waterman named Winslow. The police were communicated with and the deceased was conveyed to the mortuary. The body, which is that of a man about 40 years of age, has been in the water about a month. From certain papers found on the body friends at Bournemouth have been telegraphed to. An inquest will be held today.

It was not until 5 January that Druitt's death was reported in the *Southern Guardian*:

SAD DEATH OF A LOCAL BARRISTER: An inquiry was on Wednesday held by Dr Diplock, at Chiswick, respecting the death of Montague John Druitt, 31 years of age, who was found drowned in the Thames. The deceased was identified by his brother, a solicitor residing at Bournemouth, who stated that the deceased was a barrister-at-law, but had recently been an assistant at a school in Blackheath. The deceased left a letter, addressed to Mr Valentine, of the school, in which he alluded to suicide. Evidence having been given as to discovering deceased in the Thames – upon his body were found a cheque for £50 and £16 in gold – the Jury returned a verdict of 'suicide whilst of unsound mind'.

The deceased gentleman was well known and much respected in the neighbourhood. He was a barrister of bright talent, he had a promising future before him, and his untimely end is deeply deplored. The funeral took place in Wimborne cemetery on Thursday afternoon, and the body was followed to the grave by the deceased's relatives and a few friends.

So Druitt's funeral in Wimborne had been attended by a mere handful of relatives and friends. And although we could understand that in the latter days of his life he might well have become estranged from the companions of his college days, one might have expected more for this unfortunate barrister and schoolmaster. Throughout the summer of 1888 he had regularly played cricket for at least two very respectable clubs, and he had been playing for the Morden Cricket Club in Blackheath since 1881. In 1884 he became its secretary, and in 1885, when the Morden Club merged with the Blackheath Cricket, Football and Lawn Tennis Club, Druitt became its first honorary secretary and treasurer. Here we begin to glimpse Druitt's considerable social standing. His fellow directors were well-known sporting and public men like Rowland Hill, one of England's most renowned rugby footballers; Aubrey Spurling, another fine sportsman, whose family was one of the most influential in Blackheath; and Dr Lennard Stokes, another internationally distinguished sportsman and captain of the England rugby team; and R. H. Poland, a weathly fur broker.

On 19 November 1888 Druitt proposed that 'an acre of land be taken behind the Grand Stand at a similar proportion of rent to that paid for the present land', and clearly he was still managing to fulfil his social responsibilities at this late date, as the minutes of the Blackheath club testify. But the outward signs of normality hid an increasingly disturbed personality whose frustration and growing sense of failure were hastening his final descent into madness.

On 31 December the minutes record that the honorary secretary and treasurer, 'having gone abroad', should be 'removed from the post'. And on 7 February 1889 a final entry records that 'the Directors had heard with much regret of the death of Mr M. J. Druitt who had zealously and faithfully fullfilled the duties of Hon. Sec. of the company for three and a half years'.

It was a suitably restrained tribute for a man who had been so ignominiously dismissed from his teaching post nine weeks earlier, and one wonders how much his fellow directors actually knew of the unfortunate circumstances surrounding his departure. Certainly his colleagues at 9 Eliot Place – the headmaster, George

Valentine, and assistant master, Frederick Henry Lacey – were both involved with the Blackheath sporting fraternity, and both men had proposed Druitt for the Blackheath Hockey Club.

A man described as on the verge of sexual insanity implies, as Colin Wilson points out, that he is sane in other departments; in Druitt's case this was probably not too far from the truth. As a typical Victorian euphemism, however, the expression almost certainly means that Montague John Druitt's derangement, as understood by Sir Melville Macnaghten, was of a homosexual nature. Heterosexual deviations within a relationship were hardly likely to come to the attention of the police, and if a mentally disturbed heterosexual's behaviour was to manifest itself in violence then the offence would almost certainly have been dealt with as such, and would never have been regarded by Victorian society in the same light as the 'sin that dare not speak its name'.

The law saw a wife's body as little more than a convenience for her husband, whilst any woman foolish enough to squander her maidenhood outside marriage could expect little sympathy, and those who took to the streets deserved everything they got – though even the most ardent retributionist would have drawn a line somewhat earlier than Jack the Ripper. Where homosexuality was concerned, a deviant immediately placed himself on the edge of 'sexual lunacy'. The very notion appalled and disgusted the public face of Victorian hypocrisy, and the slightest hint of a homosexual tendency in a man identified him as being, at the very least, 'queer'.

Druitt's sudden dismissal from the boys' school in Eliot Place had to be related in some way to his state of mind at the time, and therefore related to the nature of his 'insanity'. For at least seven years this Oxford graduate had sublimated his more sinister desires and had carried on an outwardly normal existence. Then, in July, his mother entered an asylum and something snapped inside him. (Remember Walter Sickert's actual contribution to the Ripper legend, when the strange young lodger is taken back to Bournemouth by his devoted mother.) As the weeks went by he found it harder and harder to function within the acceptable confines of social behaviour. He did something at the school which left Mr Valentine no choice but to dismiss him on the spot. Within a matter of days, he would be dead.

Druitt's homosexuality would have influenced his circle of acquaintances at the Inner Temple too. The need for secrecy meant that all Victorian homosexuals who hoped to pursue a career within the Establishment would have to pick their friends and confidants very carefully indeed. For someone like Druitt, the very fact that he had not succeeded in his chosen calling would have meant an extra burden. How long could he hope to go on enjoying the company of men who were now beginning to reap the fruits of their education, talent and class? He was headed in another direction altogether.

For three years he had kept on his chambers at No. 9 Kings Bench Walk, and for three years before that he had been a student in one of the most exclusive professions. This residential enclave of the judicial heritage epitomizes the tradition and continuity of the English legal system. In the 1880s it was at the very heart of a way of life that was far removed from the ignorance and filth in the streets of Whitechapel. The common doorways of the East End tenements led to abject poverty and despair. The portals of Kings Bench Walk ushered the visitor into a world of privilege and power; its granite stairs and black oak boards guided the caller to the sanctuaries of great and ambitious men where judges and advocates worked, met, ate and slept. It was a place for weighty discourse and vintage port, for dedication and companionship, and it was here that Montague John Druitt would have had every hope of forming lasting relationships with some of his neighbours and colleagues.

It is when we begin to look at this distinguished peer group that a picture begins to emerge. And it is Stephen Knight whom we have to thank for pointing us in the right direction. Knight recognizes very early that Druitt cannot easily be removed from the suspect list. His credentials for being there are better than most; but removed he must be if the Sickert/Knight theory is to gather speed. Walter Sickert is very early attributed with having said that Druitt 'was a scapegoat'. We need not concern ourselves too much with the fact that Joseph Sickert has once again plucked out from Walter Sickert's intimately remembered account a name which would have meant nothing at the time the story was told. (It would be at least another twenty years before Druitt's name would become relevant and therefore memorable.) But Knight cannot ignore the fact that other writers had tenuously linked Druitt with Clarence. Michael Harrison had found that Prince Albert Victor's tutor, Canon John Neale Dalton, had been educated at Druitt's school in Blackheath (although there may be confusion here with Blackheath Proprietory School, of which Dalton was a distinguished old boy). Thomas Toughill had established that Druitt's younger brother, Edward, had been in the same regiment as the artist Frank Miles, and Frank Miles's brother was the Prince's equerry.

157

Most significant of all was the unavoidable fact that Harry Lushington Stephen, the brother of J. K. Stephen (Harrison's favoured candidate for Jack the Ripper and Prince Albert Victor's possible lover at Cambridge), had chambers at No. 3 Kings Bench Walk, just three doors away from Druitt at No. 9. J.K. himself was at Lincoln's Inn, while Herbert Stephen, J.K.'s other brother, was immediately opposite Kings Bench Walk, at No. 4 Paper Buildings.

The more Knight looks at Druitt the more he realizes that he is surrounded by people who were, or who have become associated with, the Whitechapel murders. At No. 9 Kings Bench Walk itself, on the floor below Druitt, was fellow Wykehamist Reginald Brodie Dyke Acland, the brother of Sir William Gull's son-in-law. Also here was the solicitor Edward Henslowe Bedford, who one year after the Ripper murders would be deeply involved in covering up the Cleveland Street scandal in which certain aristocratic and influential homosexuals, including Clarence, were narrowly to avoid public shame and ruin.

Not for the first time we could see how someone had touched on the truth but was unable, or unwilling, to accept the implications of its discovery. The Sickert/Knight theory is a cleverly constructed fantasy, with much of Joseph Sickert's original story being skilfully moulded to accept some of the incontrovertible facts standing in its way. Druitt is a case in point. His importance as a suspect cannot be denied, and by the same token the evidence which now presented itself could not be ignored. But – and this cannot be stressed too strongly – he never was, nor ever could have been, a scapegoat.

Almost every serving police officer had his own ideas about the identity of the Ripper, and if anybody was being framed it was the young medical student/doctor who had conveniently been mistaken for Montague at the bottom of the Thames. Robert Anderson's conviction that the murderer was a Polish Jew – which has already been shown to be unsupportable – had also helped to obscure the truth. Now the intrigue surrounding Macnaghten's favoured suspect lay in the fact that no evidence or official police file on him existed, and that every indication suggested that an attempt had been made to keep him out of the limelight – and no wonder.

If Montague John Druitt were involved with an influential clique of homosexuals which included the heir presumptive to the throne of England, the Victorian Establishment would have had every reason to make sure that he should not stand trial for the most disgusting series of murders ever perpetrated. Kosminski, Ostrog, Pedachenko or any one of a hundred low-class foreigners would have been more suitable as a scapegoat than he. Druitt's publicly asserted guilt would by association have damaged the standing of his ambitious friends and colleagues – by the very nature of his breeding and profession.

So far the case against Druitt has always been established purely and simply on evidence which in no way implied an association with Prince Albert Victor or his circle of friends. On the other hand a great many people have suspected that more was known about the identity of Jack the Ripper than was being admitted, and this in turn gave rise to a spate of 'conspiracy' theories, implied and specific. If Druitt knew Eddy or any one of his close friends – particularly if this association implied a homosexual liaison – then many unrelated fragments in the Ripper legend would at long last fall into place and the case against Druitt would surely be proven beyond all reasonable doubt.

Stowell's inclusion of the Prince as a suspect had to be based on misinterpreted information which originally emanated from Sir William Gull. Knight points out that the Stephens were patients of Sir William, and as we know there was an indirect link between Druitt and Gull through Reginald Brodie Dyke Acland. Could Gull have come to know of Druitt's association with Eddy, or with J. K. Stephen? If so, it is quite possible that the Prince could indeed have fallen under suspicion, for both Clarence and Druitt were remarkably alike in physical appearance. The two photographs commonly used to demonstrate this likeness are startling enough, but the later photograph of Druitt (reproduced in this book for the first time) clearly shows him sporting a moustache which would have made the resemblance even more dramatic. If Druitt had been mistaken for the Prince on just one occasion, his nocturnal wanderings through the back streets of Whitechapel may well have led Sir William to jump to the wrong conclusion, at least for a time.

All this was supposition, of course, and not worth a brass farthing unless we could show that Druitt moved in the same circles as his illustrious neighbours, at the hub of which was Prince Albert Victor. The common bond between the Prince and the intelligentsia who now inhabited the Inns of Court had been Cambridge. It was here, in October 1883, that this diffident and unremarkable scholar was sent to Trinity College to complete his formal education under the prodigiously talented wing of James Kenneth Stephen. His influence on the vulnerable Eddy, which had begun when preparing him for university life at Sandringham, was to be considerable. Under the general supervision of Canon Dalton the young social climber gathered around his charge men like his younger brother, Harry Lushington Stephen; Henry Francis Wilson (Harry); Harry Chester Goodhart; Arthur Hugh Clough; James Duff; Arthur Hamilton Smith; Henry Babington Smith; and Henry John Cust. There were others, notably the Hon. Patrick Bowes Lyon, Joseph Robson Tanner and James William Clark. But the first group were of particular importance for a reason which was not readily apparent.

In 1820 the Cambridge Conversazione Society had been founded, ostensibly as a debating society, by twelve earnest Christian scholars. Its original purpose was to give its members the opportunity to discuss in private the difficulties and doubts inherent in having to present the Gospels and a united Christian philosophy to a wider audience. Soon the members of the Society were to become recognized as the Apostles. Though it was an unremarkable union of like-minded students to begin with, its semi-secret nature allowed for a freer exchange of views between its members than would have been generally acceptable in a more open forum. In a short space of time, however, the group was to evolve into a more sophisticated, semi-mystical organization. It became more arcane, more élite and more sinister. In the next sixty years the nature and influence of the group would change and increase dramatically. It was now centred on Trinity College, and the underlying homosexuality which for some time had been an increasingly influential factor within the society would by the end of the nineteenth century totally engulf this esoteric clique.

Had Eddy's mother, Princess Alexandra, and his overtly heterosexual father, the Prince of Wales, had any idea what the predominant influence on their impressionable heir was to be in the two years he was at Cambridge, they no doubt would have sent him to Oxford, or on another trip around the world in the safe company of his younger and brighter brother George. As it was, the impressionable Prince was to be surrounded by brilliant young men whose ideology (whether manifested physically, or as a platonic ideal) was one of the Apostolic traditions of the age. It was that the love of man for man was greater than that of man for woman, a philosophy known to the Apostles as 'the Higher Sodomy'.

In the rarefied atmosphere of Trinity, such a proposition might at one time have been interpreted as nothing more than intellectual gymnastics, a flexing of the cerebral muscles of these young Greek gods. The analogy is apt: the Apostles saw themselves as neo-Greek in outlook. But such sentiments were not confined to debate, and manifested themselves in more obvious expressions of a homosexual and misogynistic kind.

Oscar Browning, who was 'among the high priests of this sexual cult in the late 1850s', and in whose rooms at King's College the Prince often spent his Sunday evenings, was to continue to exert his influence and overt homosexuality on Apostolic thinking, just as the more sinister Richard Monckton Milnes had since the 1830s. A man 'of many fine tastes and some coarse ones', according to the *Dictionary of National Biography*, he was still corresponding with fellow Apostles – men like Harry Wilson – as late as 1884.

In his book *Clarence*, Harrison, in trying to establish J. K. Stephen as the Ripper, demonstrates his suspect's overt misogyny which is present in much of his poetry. Earlier we showed where the case against Stephen falls down, but once again it can be seen how close Mr Harrison was to the truth. J. K. Stephen resigned from the society in 1882 and became what was known as an Angel, someone who was no longer obliged to attend meetings but who remained a member for life, free to attend meetings whenever he wished. The sentiments expressed in the two poems below, if not whole-heartedly shared would have found many a sympathetic recipient in fellow 'Greeks'. Stephen was not a man alone but a brilliant high flier at the centre of a highly privileged group of academics and aesthetes whose destinies – as they knew only too well – were to influence, govern and judge their fellow men throughout Victoria's Empire. As we judge the writer, we must also adjudicate the influence of the intimate brotherhood who drank from the same well, to say nothing of questioning the bias of the editorial staff of *Granta* and the *Cambridge Review* who were prepared to publish it.

A Thought

If all the harm that women have done
Were put in a bundle and rolled into one,
Earth would not hold it,
The sky could not enfold it,
It could not be lighted nor warmed by the sun;
Such masses of evil
Would puzzle the devil
And keep him in fuel while Time's wheels run.

> But if all the harm that's been done by men
> Were doubled and doubled and doubled again,
> And melted and fused into vapour and then
> Were squared and raised to the power ten,
> There wouldn't be nearly enough, not near,
> To keep a small girl for the tenth of a year.

More deplorable yet are the sentiments contained in another poem called 'In the Backs':

> As I was strolling in the Backs,
> I met a woman whom I did not like.
> I did not like the way the woman walked:
> Loose-hipped, big-boned, disjointed, angular . . .
> . . . I do not want to see that girl again:
> I did not like her: and I should not mind
> If she were done away with, killed, or ploughed.

J. K. Stephen was cast very much in the mould in which Montague John Druitt may well have once seen himself when the future looked bright and assured. We need only remember Druitt's love of debate at Winchester and later at Oxford, and the fact that both men chose a legal career, to begin to see how compatible the two might have been had Montague's earlier promise been sustained. Like so many of Eddy's chosen companions at Cambridge, Druitt was good at games: a champion at fives, and a keen cricketer and rugby player. He was not – as some have made out – an insecure neurotic. Both his and Stephen's life would be marred by dreadful catastrophe. But, for a time at least, they and others like them took advantage of the blind eye conveniently turned to their elevated status by society – the same unenlightenend society which made it necessary in the first place for homosexuals to seek out the company of others in secret. In due course many would become important figures within the Establishment – high-ranking civil servants, judges and diplomats, whose influence would ensure the continued duplicity necessary for their fellows to thrive in their chosen careers whilst paying lip service to the rigid social *mores* of the age.

We cannot be sure whether any of the Apostles were actually familiar with the interior of the brothel at No. 19 Cleveland Street, but Prince Albert Victor certainly was – in the Department of Public Prosecutions file on alleged patrons he was referred to as

162

'P.A.V.'. So did his father's equerry and superintendent of the stables, Lord Arthur Somerset, and many other wealthy and influential men. The important point was that many homosexuals – including Apostles – were able to secure Establishment appointments regardless of their sexual predilections. For most of the time the process would promote men of integrity, intellect and often genius into positions of considerable influence and trust, which for the most part they undoubtedly deserved. They were men for whom their sexuality, hetero or homo, would have played little or no part in influencing their decisions in the execution of their duties. But it is just as clear that the privileges afforded to men in positions of power and influence included the means to extinguish almost any threat or smother any potential scandal before it could do any real harm. It was the price to be paid for the duplicity of Victorian morality. The homosexual dominance within the Apostles, and the constant need to protect its members – and the Establishment they hoped to serve – from its own values, simply made the possibility of scandal that much more likely and the need for secrecy that much more necessary.

When a humble Post Office delivery boy, Charles Swinscow, was questioned by PC Luke Hanks about the large amounts of cash he had been spending, it was assumed that the situation might have had something to do with some recent unsolved thefts. But the fifteen-year-old Swinscow confessed to having been made an offer by another delivery boy, Henry Newlove, to go to No. 19 Cleveland Street to participate in homosexual activities with certain wealthy men, including Lord Arthur Somerset. During questioning Newlove broke down and gave Inspector Abberline the name of a man called George Veck, supposedly a clerk in Holy Orders but in fact another Post Office worker. Veck was eventually arrested, and he and Newlove were both charged with 'having committed unnatural offences with male persons and with having induced others to do the same'. Both men pleaded guilty and were sentenced to prison, Veck to four months and eighteen-year-old Newlove to nine months. Ernest Parke was not slow to point out in the columns of his North London newspaper that, only a year earlier, a clergyman facing a similar charge to Veck's had been sentenced to no less than life imprisonment.

The implication would not have been missed by Monro. Veck's and Newlove's silence had been bought, and in return for not implicating the 'names' involved they had both received relatively light sentences. Monro and Abberline had at least tried to do their

163

duty as best they could. But, yet again, well oiled wheels had turned and skilful operators were demonstrating how effectively they could deal with any unpleasant eruptions on the self-righteous face of upper-class democracy.

The brothel keeper Charles Hammond had been allowed to move out all his furniture from Cleveland Street and leave for France four days *after* the authorities had been told about the brothel, and Lord Arthur Somerset was also allowed to escape. At the same time, every effort was being made by nameless servants of Whitehall masters to intimidate and silence any potentially dangerous witnesses. In this case the Treasury Department, working independently of Scotland Yard, was using its own agents to subvert the course of justice, just as Jenkinson had been able in previous years to thwart the efforts of the CID from within the Home Office. Solicitor Arthur Newton had been employed by certain parties to pay off the rent boys concerned and get them out of the way, planning to ship them off to Australia with a complete set of clothing, £20 in their pockets and a promised income of £1 a week for the next three years.

With the case against Parke successfully concluded, the cover-up was able to accomplish its most important task – to protect the future Duke of Clarence and heir to the throne of England from being publicly associated with his fellow homosexuals. Imagine how much easier it would have been to conceal the identity of Jack the Ripper from an ignorant public. Whereas the Cleveland Street scandal had been generated from without by the unfortunate arrest of insignificant male prostitutes, the discovery that Jack the Ripper was one of the chosen few would have made it an entirely internal affair. There would be no need to initiate a huge conspiracy. The only requirement would be the co-operation of certain influential men to help remove the culprit from the stage quietly and quickly, without the knowledge of Scotland Yard and without a sensational trial. All that was needed was to make sure that Jack the Ripper could never be associated with the Prince or with any of the young men of the ruling class who shared his friendship and who were set to inherit the earth.

If there had been a growing suspicion within the circle of royal acquaintance that one of their number was Jack the Ripper, it stands to reason that this 'private' information would be carried via the Establishment grapevine to Whitehall. It would not travel to Inspectors Abberline, Swanson or Moore, with their feet planted firmly on the cobbled streets of Whitechapel; it would be passed to the Oxbridge associates and peers of Clarence or J. K. Stephen who held positions of enormous influence and power, and who would have had every reason – and means – to keep their dreadful discovery a secret. Any assumption that intelligence gathered in this manner would automatically be passed on to the CID – considering what we had gleaned from James Monro – is naïve.

If the truth could be found at the bottom of the Thames, as Sir Melville suspected, and our supposition was correct thus far, we could not escape the possibility we now faced: Druitt's death might not have been suicide. If certain people excluding Scotland Yard had discovered that he was Jack the Ripper, only one course of action would have been open to those who wished to ensure that this one man's guilt did not destroy the future of others.

For us, and for the case against Druitt, this was where the buck stopped. There was no doubt in our minds that if we could be sure that Druitt knew Clarence, J. K. Stephen, Harry Wilson or any of the other Apostles, and if there was anything to show that he might not have taken his own life, the weight of evidence against him would be profound. So many pieces in the jigsaw would fall into place, not only revealing the identity of Jack the Ripper but explaining for the first time why his century-old ghost has refused to lie down. With Druitt out of the way, the Royal House of Windsor and the Victorian Establishment would have been able to breathe a sigh of relief, and the esoteric Cambridge clique in whose care the impressionable Prince Albert Victor had been placed in 1883 would continue to grow in strength and influence.

Significantly, this secret brotherhood still exists today. Its members, even though they may wish to deny it, are as ever an élite within an élite. Their ranks have included men like Tennyson, Bertrand Russell, Lytton Strachey, Roger Fry and John Maynard Keynes; and more recently Lord Annan, Peter Shore, Dr Jonathan Miller and many more less well-known intellects whose influence on our society continues to be enormous. In one respect, however, the nature of the Apostles has changed dramatically in recent years. In 1970 women were introduced for the first time, and even before this date the need to take advantage of the society's inherent secrecy as a screen for its members' homosexuality had become less and less necessary. The major cause of most of the society's ills in the past could no longer be a potent force in an increasingly liberated age; but it was obviously not always the case.

In the 1930s this same group, with the same undercurrent of homosexuality, engendered the most notorious spy ring of modern times. Both Guy Burgess and Anthony Blunt were homosexual Apostles. In 1951 Burgess and a Cambridge associate, Donald Maclean, defected to the Soviet Union. In 1963 another Cambridge man, Kim Philby, followed suit, and in 1964 Anthony Blunt confessed to having recruited all three agents. Yet again the Establishment sought to protect their own. Sir Anthony Blunt continued in his exalted post as Keeper of the Queen's Pictures and was given immunity from arrest. It was not until 1979 that the truth was at last made known to a stunned public. Blunt was forced to resign, but it soon became apparent that the Establishment was even now protecting the identity of the fifth member of his treacherous cell.

In his book *The Cambridge Apostles* Richard Deacon does much to put the more unsavoury activities of the society into perspective. He is at pains to point out that not every Apostle in the 1930s became a Russian agent, even though certain commentators had pounced on a controversial declaration by the novelist E. M Forster, who became an Apostle in 1901, as evidence of the subversive influence within the society. Forster had said, 'If I had to choose between betraying my country and betraying my friend, I hope that I should have the guts to betray my country.' But rather than supporting the notion that the Cambridge Apostles as a whole were a subversive or anti-patriotic cell, Richard Deacon sees Forster's statement as 'evidence of how the homosexual mafia can operate and how from the earliest times it has tended to be a crypto-protection society in that the bond of friendship has been used to cover up all manner of questionable activities and sometimes even to protect members from being prosecuted'. The author even goes on to say, 'This was truer in the 1880s and 1890s than in more recent years', which would prove something of an understatement if our conjectures were at all well founded.

The ultimate irony here is that Deacon, of all people, should be unwittingly contributing to our case. For it turns out that Richard Deacon is the pseudonym of author Donald McCormick who, over a quarter of a century earlier, had written *The Identity of Jack the Ripper*, in which the perpetrator turns out to be none other than Russian secret agent Alexander Pedachenko. Not for the first time the author appears to be close to the heart of the matter without realizing it, as so many others have also been. Albert Bachert's story, as related by him in 1959, refers to Druitt's body and no one else's being dragged from the Thames. Now the likelihood was that McCormick's 'homosexual mafia' had actually been involved with putting him there in the first place!

XIV

James Edmund Vincent's fawning memoir of the Duke of Clarence, published in 1893, a year after his subject's premature death' makes the following comment:

> One of the charms of life at Cambridge . . . is to be found in the modest dinner parties which bring men, whether princes or commoners, into closer intimacy. It was by means of them, principally, that Prince Albert Victor's circle of acquaintance was enlarged. There lies under the writer's eye the rough diary of an undergraduate, who will probably prefer to remain unnamed, which gives us the skeleton outline of some of these happy parties, deciphered as best may be, but with some difficulty, owing to the habit indulged in by the diarist of distinguishing men by initials written not in capital letters. For example, here is an entry:
> '*Nov. 2.* – dine with hrh, jekstudd, hcgoodhart, ronald, etc., to cust's later.'

The undergraduate who would 'probably prefer to remain unnamed' was none other than Harry Wilson, and the only reason Vincent chooses to keep him anonymous here is to give the impression that the Duke mixed in a wider social circle than was in fact the case. The biographer has no qualms about quoting Wilson's letter and poems at length, and referring to him by name when he wants to illustrate the affection Wilson felt for the Prince, but it does not suit his purposes to let his readers know that Clarence was surrounded by the same élite clique for his whole two years at Cambridge. The other undergraduates at this particular 'happy party', whom Vincent is implying were a 'typical' and random

168

sample, included Sir John Edward Kynaston Studd, who became Lord Mayor of London, and Lord Ronald Sutherland Gower, who was as extrovertly 'gay' as any Victorian homosexual dared be. 'hcgoodhart' is fellow Apostle Harry Chester Goodhart, as was their late-night host-to-be Henry Cust. Even the 'etc' in Wilson's list implies the same old faces.

H. L. Stephen wrote of Wilson, 'He was my most intimate friend at Rugby and Cambridge, and that during the fifty-seven subsequent years that friendship has never been clouded or diminished . . . if the Duke of Clarence had not died in 1892, Harry would have been his private secretary.' Wilson's relationship with the Prince had continued after Eddy had left Cambridge and been commissioned a lieutenant in the 10th Hussars, although it was obviously becoming more and more difficult for the young Albert Victor to escape his ever-increasing public duties. In February 1888 he replied to a letter from Henry Wilson:

> Dear Harry,
>
> . . . I was very glad to hear from you again, and it is good of you to think of asking me to come to your place to see the boat-race from. I should be delighted to do so, for it would be very nice to meet some of our old Cambridge friends again whom I have not seen for some time. But the question is whether I shall be in town then or not at the end of March, for if I am not I fear I shall be detained at York then by my duties with my regiment. But I had better let you know again for certain a little later on, if that would be the same to you. . . .

Distanced for a time at least, Wilson was encouraged on more than one occasion to write to his Prince in verse:

> *Upon my soul there lies a load*
> *Of song, not sin – the promised ode.*
> *By day these unproductive brains*
> *Are cudgelled for befitting strains;*
> *And when at eve I seek my bed*
> *Slumber deserts my weary head,*
> *What time I turn and toss about,*
> *And try to 'beat' my 'music out.'*
> *So now, Prince Edward, deign to take*
> *These verses, fashioned for your sake*
> *To wish you health and happiness,*
> *A shadow never growing less,*
> *Fine larks by day, sweet sleep at night,*
> *And undiminished appetite. . . .*

. . . Our company is most select,
But that, of course, you would expect;
Goodhart was here for half a day,
Then found it slow and rushed away;
Inches of unregarded dust
Lie on the chairs of Harry Cust.
We don't know what's become of Clough;
Benson's at Lambeth; only Duff,
And I, and half a dozen more,
Remain to vote our life a bore. . . . .

. . . And finally a word we send
To our Philosopher and Friend;
They say he's coming in July –
We hope 'tis true, for, verily,
We miss our mine of curious knowledge,
And, when we get him back in College,
We mean to drop a pinch of salt on
The tail of Mr J. N. Dalton.

But 'Halt! Genug!' I hear you say,
I've done, and wish my Prince good-day.

The difficulties of keeping in touch were to continue, but, as Vincent says, 'The next letter is interesting as showing the strenuous efforts which Prince Albert Victor made to keep up his intimacy with his friends and the regret which he felt at losing sight of some of them':

My Dear Harry,

I was very glad to hear from you again, as it is a very long time since we met. I am afraid it is the natural result after leaving college, as one sees so little of one's old friends. It has struck me that, as I am going up to town tomorrow afternoon on some business – would you care to come and dine with me at the Club, as I shall not be returning here till after dinner? Will you telegraph to the Marlborough Club as soon as you receive this, and at which place I propose we should dine.

By 1892, the year in which Clarence died, the relationship between the Prince and Wilson had obviously matured. J. K. Stephen's unfortunate death a year earlier now meant that Wilson was the closest of all the Prince's college associates. Following the Prince's funeral at Windsor on 20 January 1892 Wilson wrote to his father to describe the occasion: 'The invitation sent to me was for the choir of St George's chapel, a special privilege extended only to some hundred persons, whose positions in the country, or personal relations with the Duke, entitled them to such a distinction.' And later, following the ceremony, when Wilson had found himself standing next to Harry Goodhart:

> . . . he and I returned to town together talking sadly of the happy old days at Trinity, not without a thought for poor Jim Stephen, who would certainly have been with us if fate had not stricken him too, though in a different way. Goodhart and I and Harry Cust (who knew the Prince better than any other Trinity man – except perhaps John Baring) were, so far as I know, the only Cambridge friends invited to the inner parts of the chapel, although there were others in the nave – and I need not say we were proud of the honour done us.

Before ending, Wilson touches on the matter of his promising future as hinted at by H. L. Stephen:

> There is no occasion for me to dwell upon the loss I have personally sustained by the death of one who has always shewn himself a kind and considerate friend. He had given me repeated proofs of his desire to help me and there is little doubt that his intentions would in some form or other have taken practical shape, to use his own words 'at no distant date.' Now that he is gone, however, I prefer to think of him without any reference to any possible advantage that I might have secured from an acquaintance, either immediately, or in years to come. As Goodhart said to me yesterday (and he knew the Prince as intimately as anyone in the country outside the circle of his own relations) 'One has no recollection of him that is not pleasant, for he was incapable of an unkindly word or deed.'

Not only was Harry Wilson a close friend of the Duke, but he was also an Apostle and a barrister; in fact he was one of several Apostles who had chambers at the Inns of Court not far from the one man suspected by Sir Melville Macnaghten and others of being responsible for the Whitechapel murders. The Duke's other close friend, J. K. Stephen (also an Apostle), had resided at Lincoln's Inn, while his brother Harry Stephen (another Trinity man and friend of the Prince) had not only shared rooms with Wilson at Rugby and Trinity, but was now residing at No. 3 Kings Bench Walk, close to Druitt. Even Harry Chester Goodhart (another Apostle) – a close friend of the Prince, who was 'almost as well known at Harrow and Winchester as at Eton, at Oxford as at Cambridge' – had played cricket against Druitt in the 1876 Winchester *v*. Eton match, as had Evelyn Ruggles-Brise (Personal Private Secretary to Henry Matthews) and Kynaston Studd (bowled by Druitt for four).

Unfortunately there was no record of whether Wilson's diary had survived since the tame Mr Vincent had referred to it in 1893. And even if it had, and could be located, we would not expect it to reveal anything very significant for the obvious reason that, if our suspicions were correct, Druitt would have become very much *persona non grata* in the crucial year of 1888 and any specific evidence of his association with Eddy or his friends would have been destroyed long before now. In any case, it was far more likely that the diary would cover only that period of Wilson's life spent at Cambridge, in which case he might not yet have met Druitt. Nevertheless, by an extremely circuitous route we did eventually track down this potentially valuable document to Trinty College Library, Cambridge.

The rough shorthand jottings were, as we suspected, concerned with the years 1883 to 1887. Invitations to Sandringham and to Eddy's rooms were duly noted, as were less prestigious social occasions. In the margin on one page, opposite an entry which referred to H. L. Stephen, Wilson wrote, 'I love him, I love him.' But there was no mention of Druitt – nor did we expect there to be.

It was therefore with some relief that, fatigued after several hours of deciphering Mr Wilson's peculiar shorthand, we turned to the names and addresses scribbled on the inside back cover. There was the name J. H. Lonsdale, and the address No. 5 Eliot Cottages, Blackheath. It was another remarkable coincidence. Druitt's school at Blackheath was at No. 9 Eliot Place, less than one hundred yards from the cottages. But the coincidence did not end there. We were soon to discover that John Henry Lonsdale was not only a barrister but that his chambers were at No. 4 Kings Bench Walk, right next door to H. L. Stephen and just five doors from Druitt. Lonsdale and Druitt lived in sight of each other at Blackheath and they were even closer at the Temple. All the indications were that both men would have known each other well, and at the very least they would have had mutual friends.

The opportunity existed for Lonsdale to introduce Druitt to his friend Harry Wilson, but in many respects Druitt would have needed no introduction. He had contributed enough to the game of cricket to have been well known to his fellow Oxbridge devotees, Evelyn Ruggles-Brise and H. C. Goodhart included. As a resident, he would have dined at the Inns of Court more regularly than most,

172

and he would have been drawn into the same cosseted homosexual circle as other men of similar disposition. In 1887 Lonsdale turned his back on his legal career in favour of the Church. His first ministry was at Wimborne Minster – Wimborne was the home town of the Druitts and the very place where Montague's funeral would take place in January 1889.

At some point one has to accept that the very weight of circumstantial evidence pointing to Druitt's involvement with other leading players in the drama is too great for even the most sceptical of investigators to bear. He certainly wasn't anti-social – his love of cricket proves that – just as his choice of career demanded a certain self-confidence and ability to address his fellow men in public. Until those last few months when his life finally fell apart he would have been a man to take full advantage of his social position in his efforts to succeed, as so many of his friends and colleagues were doing around him – and yet his funeral was attended only by members of his family and a few friends.

For many, the society which surrounded life at the Inns was merely an extension of what their lives had been at Oxford or Cambridge, and as we can see in Druitt's case, he was surrounded by ambitious 'angels' and their influential friends, not the least of whom was Prince Albert Edward Victor. Beyond any reasonable doubt, Druitt was a part of this privileged and clandestine league. His bright beginnings at Winchester and Oxford; his all-round abilities as a sportsman; his fondness of debate; his choice of profession; his proximity to Eddie's Cambridge cronies and to Wilson's friend at Blackheath; and even his socially unacceptable sexuality mark him out as someone who may well have been considered for membership of the secret society had he gone to Cambridge instead of Oxford. To use the Apostolic jargon of the time, he would have been an 'embryo'. Had the evidence been equally balanced on both sides we might well have had to consider an open verdict, but the reality of our investigation was that the more we dug the more we knew we were revealing the truth.

On 17 December 1888, at the very time when Montague's body was lying at the bottom of the Thames, the quiet country town of Wimborne was blessed with an unexpected visit from none other than Prince Albert Edward Victor himself. From an article which appeared in the *Southern Guardian* it is apparent that the Prince's decision to join Lord Wimborne's shooting party caught everybody off-guard, and a ball had to be hastily arranged to honour their royal visitor. This is doubly surprising, since the Royal Family were in official mourning for Prince Alexander of Hesse and Eddy's apparent lack of respect did not go unnoticed. But most surprising of all is the astonishing inclusion in the guest list for the ball of Montague John Druitt!

The man whom no one seems to want to call a friend is now specifically invited to accompany his mother to this prestigious occasion, when she is supposed to have been in a lunatic asylum since July and he is meant to have been dead for more than a fortnight! Of course, Lord and Lady Wimborne would not necessarily be aware of either of these two unfortunate circumstances, but as Montague was not even the head of the Druitt household, and had not been living in the county for at least seven years, his specific inclusion on the guest list is startling. Could it be that Eddy's hosts knew of his friendship with Montague and therefore took the opportunity of inviting him personally? Had Lord and Lady Wimborne merely wished the Druitts to be represented they would almost certainly have been obliged to invite Montague's elder brother, William, to accompany his mother. He was now the head of the family, unmarried and still living in Bournemouth.

Ann Druitt's mental illness and her subsequent committal had been of great significance in the last few months of Montague's life. If he was Jack the Ripper, then it would not be unreasonable to assume that his state of mind was somehow very closely linked with that of his mother. Remember his suicide note: 'Since Friday, I felt I was going to be like mother, and the best thing for me to do was to die.' And if we recall Walter Sickert's somewhat fanciful tale of the ailing student which quite likely included elements of factual information supplied by Sir Melville Macnaghten, the young man was taken back to Bournemouth by his devoted mother.

All our efforts to find out much more about the asylum at Chiswick than the scant information already known had been to no avail. All we knew was that the establishment was exclusively populated with disturbed middle-class patients and the occasional aristocrat. The 1881 census reveals nineteen domestic staff and servants, one nurse plus nineteen attendants, and thirty-six inmates which included a baronet's daughter, a dame, a retired colonel, a clergyman and several Oxford undergraduates. As for Ann Druitt, the only other information in our possession had originally been supplied by Stephen Knight, who in his quest to establish

Montague Druitt as a scapegoat had discovered yet another link between the Druitts and the Royal Family:

> After the notorious Mordaunt divorce scandal in which the Prince of Wales was implicated in 1860, Lady Mordaunt was conveniently certified insane and placed in an asylum where she spent the rest of her life. Whether she was really insane is open to doubt, but the fact remained that her incarceration was fortunate for the Prince of Wales. The records of the Lunacy Commission show that only about twelve lunatics in the whole country were of sufficient importance or interest to warrant regular reports. Tracing the records through the years, one fact cannot be missed: two names appear regularly together in that small list of inmates – Lady Mordaunt and Mrs Ann Druitt, Montague's mother.

As a matter of course we made an application at the Public Record Office to see the relevant minutes of the Lunacy Commission in order to verify Knight's statement, and although it would be correct to say that he has exaggerated the importance of and interest in Ann Druitt's case (there are many other names which also occur regularly), her name appears on three separate occasions between June 1889 and April 1890.

None of this was particularly remarkable in itself, except that we saw that Knight had missed something. The register that we were now examining contained the scantiest information about the patients admitted into private asylums each year. Each contained the patient's name, sex, date of admission and discharge, and name of asylum. The incredible reality staring us in the face was to have repercussions which even we could not appreciate fully at the time. On 5 July 1888 the following entry occurs: 'Druitt Anne . . . Brooke.' We suddenly realized that Ann Druitt had not been admitted to the asylum in Chiswick, as everybody had assumed. Dr Thomas Seymour Tuke's establishment was called the Manor House Asylum, and although Montague's mother was eventually to end up here between May 1890 and her death in December that year, she was clearly not there during the relevant period of July to December 1888. This meant that our explanation for Montague's journey, the veracity of his suicide note and the credibility of his ensuing inquest are all brought further into question.

On 2 January Montague's inquest opened at the Lamb Tap in Church Street, Chiswick, with Thomas Diplock as presiding coroner. Unfortunately the official report of the proceedings has not survived, which has meant that we had to rely on the good offices of three newspapers. As the inquest was held in Chiswick, where the body was found, the proceedings were covered most thoroughly by the *Acton, Chiswick and Turnham Green Gazette* on Saturday, 5 January 1889:

Found Drowned.

Shortly after mid-day on Monday, a waterman named Winslade of Chiswick, found the body of a man, well dressed, floating in the Thames off Thorneycroft's. He at once informed a constable, and without delay the body was conveyed on the ambulance to the mortuary. On Wednesday afternoon, Dr Diplock, coroner, held the inquest at the Lamb Tap, when the following evidence was adduced:

William H. Druitt said that he lived at Bournemouth, and that he was a solicitor. The deceased was his brother, who was 31 last birthday. He was a barrister-at-law and an assistant master in a school at Blackheath. He had stayed with witness at Bournemouth for a night towards the end of October. Witness heard from a friend on the 11th of December that deceased had not been heard of at his chambers for more than a week. Witness then went to London to make inquiries, and at Blackheath he found that deceased had got into serious trouble at the school, and had been dismissed. That was on the 30th of December. Witness had deceased's things searched where he resided, and found a paper addressed to him (produced). The Coroner read the letter, which was to this effect: 'Since Friday I felt I was going to be like mother, and the best thing for me was to die.'

Witness, continuing, said deceased had never made any attempt on his life before. His mother became insane in July last. He had no other relative.

Henry Winslade was the next witness. He said he lived at No. 4, Shore Street, Paxton Road and that he was a waterman. About one o'clock on Monday he was on the river in a boat, when he saw the body floating. The tide was at half flood, running up. He brought the body ashore, and gave information to the police.

PC George Moulson 216T said he searched the body, which was fully dressed excepting the hat and collar. He found four large stones in each pocket in the top coat; £2. 10s in gold, 7s in silver, 2d in bronze, two cheques on the London & Provincial Bank (one for £50 and the other for £16), a first-class season pass from Blackheath to London (South Western Railway), a second half return Hammersmith to Charing Cross (dated 1st December), a silver watch, gold chain with a spade guinea attached, a pair of kid gloves and a white handkerchief. There were no papers or letters of any kind. There were no marks of injury to the body, but it was rather decomposed.

A verdict of suicide whilst in an unsound state of mind was returned.

The impression one gets from this account is that, as was always the case, a very real effort has been made to report all the relevant detail of the proceedings, and whilst some editorial discretion must have been employed it is essentially an accurate account of what occurred. It is, for instance, difficult to imagine that the testimony of other material witnesses would have been entirely omitted when comparatively innocuous information like the entire contents of Druitt's pockets is catalogued in full. In other words, it is reasonable to assume that Montague Druitt's inquest was carried out as expeditiously as possible to save his brother the anxiety of a protracted investigation into what was, to all intents and purposes, an obvious suicide. Following William's testimony and the production of the suicide note, Mr Diplock was able to bring his inquiry to a speedy conclusion.

What Mr Diplock did not realize at the time was that William had begun his testimony by perjuring himself. He had said that Montague had no other relatives, when this was clearly not the case. Of course, one might immediately assume this was to protect the family in some way, but, as Dan Farson points out – from what? Not only did the other brothers and sisters know that Montague was dead, but apart from their own private suspicions about him the inquest was merely a formality. In fact William's actions become even more confusing if we do accept such a reason for his deceit. By producing the 'suicide note' he is publicly airing one of the family's skeletons – his mother's insanity. A man prepared to perjure himself for the sake of his kin one minute would hardly be likely to introduce evidence in the next that would reveal his mother's lunacy.

This letter was the most crucial and – apart from possibly the stones in Druitt's pockets – the only evidence that indicated suicide. Without it, the cause of death could not have been established without many more questions having to be asked. Not the least of them would have been: Who was the last person to see Montague John Druitt alive? More crucial yet would have been an attempt by the coroner to establish Druitt's state of mind prior to his disappearance. This would almost certainly mean questioning Mr Valentine in order to ascertain the reason for Druitt's dismissal. His colleagues at the Inner Temple would know something of the unfortunate man, and if Montague did not travel to Chiswick to visit his mother at the only private asylum in the area, whom did he see? What was wrong with Druitt? Why would he want to commit suicide? William thought he knew, as Macnaghten has already told us. He was convinced his brother was Jack the Ripper. The possibility undoubtedly existed that Montague's suicide note could have been a fabrication. William's testimony under oath was clearly suspect, and a closer examination of the evidence as presented to Mr Diplock raises further questions.

The last time William saw his brother was towards the end of October, when he stayed for one night at Bournemouth. Six weeks later, on 11 December, he heard from a friend of Montague's that he had not been seen at his chambers for more than a week. William then went to London and discovered that his brother had been dismissed from the school on 30 November. He then went to the address where Montague resided and discovered a letter addressed to himself.

(Though the newspaper reports says 30 December, clearly this is a misprint. It is obvious from the phrasing of the report that, after hearing from a friend that his brother had not been to his chambers of late, William did not wait for another three weeks. Furthermore, Montague's letter to his brother, written just before his death some time after 1 December, clearly indicates that Friday, 30 November was a particularly significant day. 'Since Friday . . .' had to refer to this date, the day we know he had been dismissed from the school.)

It is almost certain that Montague had been living at No. 9 Eliot Place until his dismissal, but that he would have stayed at his chambers for the night of the 30th. The two cheques found on his body indicate that Mr Valentine had settled his financial obligations with him on the same day that he left the school for good. The London and Provincial Bank had a branch in Blackheath, and the £50 cheque would be the equivalent of a term's salary for a teacher in Druitt's position; the £16 may well have been in lieu of a month's notice. This could have been drawn against Mr Valentine's personal account, rather than a school account, which could explain the existence of two cheques rather than one.

Be that at is may, what is apparent is that under the circumstances it was highly unlikely that Montague would have been allowed to keep his room after being summarily dismissed by Mr Valentine, and even less likely that his personal effects would have remained untouched for two weeks – suicide note and all – before William Druitt would finally discover this vital piece of evidence. This had to have happened at Montague's chambers, but even now the letter is not readily apparent, and would not come to light until William searched his brother's things.

The London evening newspaper the *Echo* adds further confusion, however, by stating that another letter addressed to Mr Valentine was found which alluded to suicide. But apart from two small Dorset papers that later carried this same report, the most comprehensive coverage of the inquest, as quoted above, makes no mention of a second letter – neither does the other local newspaper, *The Richmond and Twickenham Times*. The *Echo* also misreports the contents of Druitt's pockets, which further undermines this particular account, and as Valentine was not called as a witness it seems highly likely that the *Echo* has misinterpreted William Druitt's testimony. Either way, it is only William's evidence that firmly establishes that his brother committed suicide. Yet if we are to accept that a suicide note was left, we also have to accept that Montague John Druitt had premeditated his own demise, and, having penned his last words, he bought a return ticket, took a train from nearby Charing Cross and threw himself in the Thames.

When Inspector Abberline was asked in 1903 what he thought of the rumour that a young medical student who was found in the Thames in December 1888 had been the author of the Whitechapel atrocities, he had replied: 'Yes, I know all about that story. But what does it amount to? Simply this. Soon after the last murder in Whitechapel the body of a young doctor was found in the Thames, but there is absolutely nothing beyond the fact that he was found at that time to incriminate him. A report was made to the Home Office about the matter. . . .'

We can see that Abberline – like so many other people – has been allowed to believe that the drowned suspect was a young doctor, probably the young man called John Sanders whom he had been looking for. But it is important to remember that the death in the river actually refers to Druitt, and even though Abberline energetically stated his opinion, Sir Melville Macnaghten, armed with 'private' information and the growing conviction that the truth at one time *did* lie at the bottom of the Thames, had been able to close the file eleven years earlier.

Again this demonstrates that, although Abberline had been in charge of investigation on an operational level, he had obviously not been a party to all the relevant intelligence. But leaving this aside for the moment, his dismissive statement made to a *Pall Mall Gazette* reporter from his well-beloved garden in Bournemouth is important in itself. To begin with, if we accept Druitt's innocence on what grounds could he ever have fallen under suspicion? A respectable barrister on the verge of a nervous breakdown finally realizes that he is going to end up like his mother, who is already in an asylum, and takes his own life. His inquest is carried out as a matter of course and brought to an expeditious conclusion. According to Abberline, there was nothing to incriminate the drowned man apart from the fact that he was found at 'that time'. But what was 'that time'? It is only with the benefit of hindsight that we can now say that Mary Jane Kelly's murder was the last. There had been a lull in the murders throughout October, and another following Kelly's murder in November; but why suspect an unfortunate man whose body was dragged from the Thames on the last day of December of having anything to do with a series of crimes for which there was no reason to believe had finished yet?

The truth was that Druitt's death could not have been seen as relevant unless it was already suspected – if not known for a certainty – that Mary Jane Kelly's murder was the final act of a man now beyond the reach of earthly justice. Jack the Ripper had gone so far beyond the bounds of rational behaviour by this time that he may well have finally lost his grip of reality. This echoes Macnaghten's feelings that the killer's brain gave way and he committed suicide after his awful glut, and undoubtedly this was the time when Jack could have been most vulnerable.

Could it have been that, instead of finding satisfaction in Mary Jane Kelly's destruction, he was left in a state of impotent frenzy? Each murder had taken him further and further into his own sexual Hell, when each potential climax required a higher degree of violence to satiate his lust. The mayhem in Miller's Court was born of a man in search of a 'fix', an addict who had grown used to the smell and taste of blood, and every indication in that miserable room points to the possibility that he may not have achieved the release he was seeking. There was no way back and there was nowhere to go. He could do no more to the lumps of human flesh strewn about him. For the past three months he had managed to control his cravings, at least as far as being able to function adequately within society was concerned, but slowly, inevitably, his private world was crushing him, and sooner or later someone was bound to find out the truth.

If we accept Macnaghten's opinion on the matter, Druitt's family began to realize the awful truth possibly as early as October, when Montague stayed overnight with his brother in Dorset. This would have been the last time they would see him alive, and, importantly, the date of this last family visit was the last weekend in October, one of the dates when we might reasonably have expected the Ripper to strike again.

In July 1888 his mother had been committed to an asylum, as noted before, and about the same time his own deterioration gathered momentum. Five weeks later the killing started. Soon he would be dismissed from the school where he had been a respected member of staff for the past eight years. At about the same time certain people in authority would also become suspicious of this deranged barrister, but before any real evidence could be amassed against their suspect he disappeared. A month or so later, his body was dragged from the Thames. William lied at the inquest, and no meaningful attempt was made to ascertain his brother's last hours. More had to be known about our dead barrister than anyone was prepared to reveal. And yet his inquest was carried out with the minimum fuss and cross-examination, despite the fact that Abberline stated that his death warranted a report to the Home Office.

Once again the wheel turns full circle and we find ourselves looking to faceless and nameless men for an explanation. Suddenly, other elements of the Ripper legend become relevant – Edwin Woodhall's story, for instance. Up to now we had always agreed with Alexander Kelly, who attributes his tale of a deranged young doctor being interrogated by two officials as a misreading of Macnaghten's *Days of My Years*, which refers to Jack the Ripper committing suicide after he had 'knocked out a Commissioner of Police and very nearly settled the hash of one of Her Majesty's principal Secretaries of State'. This is beyond any shadow of doubt a metaphor describing the ill-fated careers of Sir Charles Warren and Henry Matthews. But in Woodhall's account the author, fully cognizant of what Macnaghten actually said, writes:

> It would appear that the 'painted menace' or 'white-eyed man' was taken to Old Palace yard, Whitehall, from the East End by four wheeled cab, in charge of two constables, and at the request of two highly placed officials – not general service police officers – brought into their presence to be interrogated. Sir Melville describes these two authorities by a grade, and designates them by the titles of an Under Secretary and an Assistant Under Secretary.

None of this can be ascribed to Macnaghten, and the last sentence is such a blatant untruth that one wonders why Woodhall should choose to underline any deceit in this way. It would have been far better not to have mentioned the status of the two officials at all. But the fact is that he does, and once more we are left wondering

181

why. That is, until we realize that if the young doctor whom Abberline had been looking for, and the black-faced doctor who had been arrested and questioned by higher authority, were one and the same – then the story of this man's escape would not have been Woodhall's invention but a necessary device which allowed the real suspect to assume the conveniently escaped prisoner's identity. In other words, the ex-detective had, by virtue of his involvement with Whitehall's secret service department, learnt of the very same story that the Home Office had used to pull the wool over Scotland Yard's eyes half a century earlier. From that point on the mad doctor and the drowned man had been irrevocably linked, and the true identity of the actual suspect had been effectively left to sink beneath the mud of the Thames.

Where then did this leave Druitt? Insignificant schoolteacher and failed barrister who ended up as a prime suspect for the Whitechapel murders for no good reason, or a man whose public trial could have spelt ruin for the privileged élite of his day? If he was Jack the Ripper, why do we not know more about the evidence against him? Why is there no trace of the police report sent to the Home Office regarding his death? Why is there no mention of him in any of the police files? Why is it not until several years later that Sir Melville Macnaghten hears of 'private' information which inclines him to believe in Druitt's guilt? If he was not the killer why was he ever suspected at all? Why did his own family believe him to be guilty? And why were the Whitechapel murder files officially closed without any explanation in 1892, at about the same time that this new information finally arrived at Scotland Yard?

We are told by William Druitt that a suicide note was left for him at his brother's chambers. The note says that Montague realizes he is going mad and is going to kill himself. He then takes a train to Hammersmith – not to visit his mother – and he buys a return ticket! But why Hammersmith? If it was not to visit his mother at nearby Chiswick, are we to assume that he wished to prolong his life just long enough to jump off his favourite bridge?

The hypothesis is ludicrous, and yet if we are to accept William's statement this is what we must believe. At the very least, we can see how imperative was the coroner's need to ascertain the last person to see Montague alive; the fact that he did not even try, when a report about this barrister's death was being prepared for the Home Office, is highly suspicious. Furthermore, the river at Blackfriars was a mere quarter of a mile from Montague's chambers at Kings

Bench Walk. If he had planned his own demise his most likely destination would appear to be the Embankment. Or was it?

Montague Druitt was a keen sportsman. He was one of two masters at a school that boasted its own swimming pool. He came from an educational system where swimming was regarded as a necessary part of a boy's development. He was almost certainly a strong swimmer himself, and it must therefore be regarded as extremely unlikely that given the choice, such a man would kill himself in this way.

William's testimony at the inquest is seriously flawed, not only because he states that there were no other living relatives when in fact there were three sisters and two other brothers, but because there is no way that Druitt's family would continue to believe Montague guilty of the Ripper murders once a suicide note had been found which clearly indicated his innocence. Quite simply, and as others have commented before, if Montague was Jack the Ripper you might have thought he would have suspected that there was something wrong with him long before that first day in December when he decided to pen his last words: 'Since Friday I felt I was going to be like mother. . . .'

In other words, as we know from various sources, Druitt's family believed him to be the murderer, and yet his brother was supposed to possess information which clearly pointed to his innocence. How can this be, unless this vital piece of evidence is fabricated? The implication is clear: Druitt's death was murder rather than suicide. He must have travelled to Hammersmith to meet someone, and he expected to return.

XV

With each step we were able to see more clearly what had been surrounding us all the time. Tom Cullen and Dan Farson must take full credit for promoting Macnaghten's candidate in the first place, even though the case against him was always lightweight. But other writers too had reached out and hit on part of the truth without realizing it.

Dr Stowell had introduced Clarence into the picture, which by necessity inferred a cover-up. Michael Harrison, knowing that the Prince was not the culprit, picked on someone close to him, intuitively sensing that somehow Clarence could still be involved in the affair. Stephen Knight, whilst creating the most sensational piece of fiction, is still forced to accept Druitt's importance in the scheme of things, and even points to his relationship with Eddy and his friends. Donald McCormick had given us Albert Bachert's statement, which points to Druitt's death being of some relevance, and even though the author vainly champions the cause of Dr Alexander Pedachenko his intuition had been absolutely correct. Nameless and faceless men have ultimately been responsible for the legacy we have inherited, but we need not have looked to Russia for an answer any more than the BBC needed to incriminate the Brotherhood of Freemasons in the murders themselves in order to justify an essentially correct hunch.

What no one had given enough consideration to in the past was the nature of British society and the way in which what we call the Establishment functions within it. Even today, the repercussions of Sir Anthony Blunt's spy ring are being felt, and the British

Government's continuing attempts to stop further exposure of its all too naked secret service inevitably raises the question of how many other privileged men the Establishment has protected from prosecution or public scorn.

As we have shown, Montague Druitt was surrounded by the predecessors of Blunt's homosexual clique, whose need for secrecy – more necessary in the 1880s and 1890s than at any other time since – was both their strength and their weakness. For a time the welfare of a future King of England had been placed in their hands, with disastrous results. The discovery that Jack the Ripper was one of their number merely activated the machinery by which the real power in the land – the masters, servants and agents of obscure government departments – protects the *status quo*. Just one year later the same Establishment was called upon to extricate the wayward Eddy and his aristocratic friends from the Cleveland Street scandal, and this time they only just made it.

In the 1880s not even the Metropolitan Police were sufficiently independent or powerful to curb the autocratic excesses of its administrative superiors. James Monro's experiences demonstrate the very real difficulty and frustration he faced in having to equate his public duty with what he calls the 'extreme discretion' expected of him in his sensitive and vulnerable position. The fact that his memoirs do not touch upon the Cleveland Street affair or the Whitechapel murders – undoubtedly the two cases his children and future generations would have been most fascinated to hear about – indicates the considerable amount of discretion this honest Scot was employing, since he had to know more about these two investigations than any other police officer.

It was Monro who dealt with Alice Mackenzie's murder in July 1889. Arriving in Castle Alley to see the body, he very quickly and confidently asserted that this was not another Ripper murder. Why, one wonders, does he not even touch on this incredible series of crimes when he was able to take such an authoritative stance at the time? And we also know from his grandchildren that he may have actually visited the scene of Mary Jane Kelly's murder, even though he had officially retired from the Met. and was working for the Home Office. His grandson, James, recalls him saying, 'It was a terrible sight, even the ceiling was splashed with blood.' James Monro was fully cognizant of all the relevant facts surrounding one of the most notorious series of murders ever perpetrated in Britain, and yet he chose to say nothing about them in his private memoirs.

But in case we are creating any confusion, let us state quite categorically that we do not believe there was any police involvement in directly covering up the identity of Jack the Ripper or that the police had a hand in any way with the suspicious death of Montague John Druitt. James Monro was a remarkably fine detective with an unshakeable Christian faith and a firm sense of duty. So too were most of his dedicated officers who were at the sharp end of the Ripper investigations.

It was men like these who, with a growing sense of professionalism and pride, were to do so much to establish the fine traditions of the British police force which was fast becoming the envy of the world. But it is still impossible to believe that certain officers – James Monro included – did not at some late date become a party to privileged and private information which enabled Macnaghten to close the case. Monro's 'We should have caught him' conceals a wealth of knowledge, as does Assistant Commissioner Basil Thomson's 'This man escaped arrest by committing suicide', or, from the Home Office, Sir John Moylan's 'The murderer, it is now certain, escaped justice by committing suicide at the end of 1888.' Sir Melville Macnaghten says it all: 'The Whitechapel murderer in all probability put an end to himself soon after the Dorset Street affair in November 1888, certain facts pointing to this conclusion were not in the possession of the police till some years after I became a detective officer.'

Knowing what we now did about Druitt we could understand what this information was and where it emanated. It was not from Druitt's family, whom Macnaghten also knew had suspected Montague, but from inside information which had not been available to the police at the time of the murders and which had somehow filtered down to them from a higher authority at a later date.

To someone like Monro, the knowledge that justice had not been seen to be done, and that his police force had not been vindicated for its valiant efforts of the past months, must have caused considerable anguish. But in the end expediency and discretion won the day. The result would have been the same for Jack the Ripper whatever happened, and now there was little that the police could do. The only possible course of action for men like Monro, Anderson and Macnaghten would have been to expose the men who had successfully circumvented the law, and that would have meant putting at risk the very same monarchy and system of government which these eminent policemen were duty bound to serve.

Almost as a last gesture, Sir Melville Macnaghten surreptitiously slipped Jack the Ripper's true name into the closed police file as if to preserve the truth in some small way. Druitt's name was not plucked out of thin air. There had to be a very good reason why it was known to Sir Melville to begin with, just as we can see from the discrepancies between the official and the private notes that the Assistant Commissioner was in a dilemma about what and what not to say. The other two lunatics, both of whom had been detained by the authorities, were merely there to soften the focus on the real suspect.

With each passing generation living memory has faded and died, making the task of any investigator that much more difficult. The plethora of literature on the subject that was available to us at the beginning had often confused the issues as much as elucidated them, a factor which in itself has ensured the uninhibited growth of the versatile and many-faceted legacy we now came to understand. How much more hidden treasure there is for future generations to discover is hard to say. We were confident that any real find would only further support what we already knew to be the truth. We had almost arrived at out destination – for now, at least – and our journey would soon be over. But that would not happen before we had uncovered two more pieces of evidence which were to crystallize our findings once and for all.

We knew that Ann Druitt had not been admitted to the Manor House Asylum in Chiswick until eighteen months after Montague Druitt had been fished from the Thames, and that in July 1888, just five weeks before Ann Nichols's murder, she had been admitted to the Brooke asylum. The question was, where was the Brooke Asylum? The answer: less than two miles north-east of Whitechapel!

Now, at last, the final pieces of the jigsaw were falling into place. Montague's route to the asylum from the school at Blackheath would have taken him directly through Whitechapel. His close bond with his mother, together with the incredibly significant location of her asylum, enables us for the first time to glimpse the kind of motive that undoubtedly drew her increasingly disturbed son deeper and deeper into his own living Hell. When Montague Druitt took that first awful plunge into the murky depths of his own psychosis his instinct was to kill. He was not a sadist in the true sense of the word – he had no desire to torture his victims and prolong their agony. Had this been his way, the quiet alleys and courtyards of the East End would hardly have suited his purpose. He was down on whores and he craved retribution. But he soon discovered that merely extinguishing the dull flames of their miserable existences was not enough. The experience thrilled him and drove him on to plunder the very source of life itself, ripping, tearing and gouging out the sexual organs of his victims, who were all pathetic examples of female humanity whose only solace was the temporary oblivion at the bottom of a mug of gin. They were used to copulating on the pavement or against a wall for the price of another drink, and they were both the recipients and the donors of a disease which was to terrorize the upper and middle classes in a far more profound way than Jack the Ripper's knife ever could.

Without effective treatment, fifteen, twenty or even thirty years after the disease is contracted it begins to attack the cerebral motor functions, causing general paralysis of the brain, lethargy, depression, loss of co-ordination and eventual madness and death. The direct relationship between syphilis and its later manifestation as a brain disease however was not scientifically established until 1913. Earlier it was believed that later insanity was somehow a result of the disease, rather than a new manifestation of the active disease itself. Therefore any cause of death relating to syphilis could reasonably be described as general paralysis of the brain, brain disease or severe melancholia. Ann Druitt's death certificate states 'melancholia' and 'brain disease, 21 months'.

Leonard Matters had recognized the possibility that syphilis could somehow have played a part in Jack the Ripper's story, and had tried to make some sense of his intuition through his largely allegorical Dr Stanley. The same disease had also been influential in Dr Thomas Stowell's theory, which had been based on information supposed to have emanated from Sir William Gull. The point was, could this disease have been the cause of Ann Druitt's decline, and the trigger for her son's latent madness?

Of course this is pure speculation and nothing more, but neither should such a possibility be casually dismissed. Apart from anything else, Ann Druitt's marriage to Wimborne's leading surgeon would have exposed her to a certain amount of 'innocent' risk, as doctors, surgeons, midwives and so on were particularly vulnerable to the disease in the course of their ordinary work. It is neither inconceivable nor outrageous to suggest that a perfectly respectable woman like Ann Druitt could have fallen victim to syphilis.

Supposition or not, something had distorted her son's mind to a degree that led him to slaughter five derelict prostitutes in a deeply significant fashion. Discovering that his own mother's mind and body were in the process of being tortured to extinction as a direct result of this 'whores' curse' could certainly have given a direction to his immature psychosis. His lack of self-esteem was already pointing him in the right direction, and now, with the realization dawning on him that he would soon be alone in the world to face his own growing madness without his mother by his side, he finally stumbled over the edge of the abyss.

The portrait we begin to see of this unfortunate barrister is of a man caught up in a downward spiral. His school and college days had shown great promise, but with the passing years two shadows loomed even larger in his life. Whatever his sexual predilection, it was gathering sinister overtones. Some time before his disappearance his family had become aware of the problem, as Mr Valentine almost certainly had as well. Macnaghten, too, was later to appreciate the nature of Druitt's derangement. On top of this, Druitt had had to face the fact that, according to the standards imposed by the society in which he moved, he was a failure. Yet constantly he rubbed shoulders with the great and successful men of his generation in the cricket pavilion, or at one of the compulsory dinners at the Inns of Court. Many of his contemporaries at Oxford had already achieved high office in Government or made their mark in their chosen profession.

Here again we begin to see in Druitt's psychological footprint the potential for eventual disaster. Writing in the introduction to Donald Rumbelow's book, Colin Wilson – who can in no way be regarded as an ardent 'Druittist', but who has over the years contributed more than most to our understanding of the psychology of murder – asks us to appreciate the kind of sexually abnormal man that could become a multiple killer. To begin with, he presupposes a personality that has been twisted with frustration and resentment and someone whose self-esteem has been badly damaged. By way of example he suggests that a man who leaves school without any particular qualifications and yet is expected to earn his living could be what Shaw calls a 'downstart' – someone whose natural path is down rather than up. He may be forced to accept a lowly position as a public servant or a clerk. As far as Jack the Ripper is concerned, that could have meant a City location, for this would give the opportunity to develop an obsession with Whitechapel.

Again we can see how such a composite picture applies to Druitt, particularly as Colin Wilson also sees the culprit as a man who would have had time on his hands – enough time to nurture resentment into paranoid proportions. He points out how many sex killers – Vacher, Kurten, Heirens, Heath and Ian Brady – had at some time before committing their major crimes been petty criminals who had spent many an idle hour behind bars, just as

189

Montague Druitt had plenty of time to brood in his chambers waiting for clients who never came.

All the time we must remember that 1888 was the year in which Montague Druitt's life fell apart. The loss of self-esteem he must have felt with the passing years was compounded not only by the death of his father and the realization that he was financially adrift in a moneyed society, but by the fact that he was unwanted in his chosen profession. In July 1888 his mother was committed to an asylum, and five weeks later the first murder took place. Three months later the killings would stop as suddenly as they had begun, and no more would be known of Montague John Druitt until a waterman recovered him from the Thames in a state of decomposition soon after midday on Monday, 31 December.

Did he imagine, or had he actually succumbed to, the same disease that was slowly taking his mother away from him? Looking through the grossly distorted mirror before him he may have believed so. 'Since Friday I felt I was going to be like mother. . . .' This was no genuine suicide note, as circumstances surrounding Montague's death clearly indicate, but if anything like it had been written by Montague it might well have been sent to William at the only time that such an obvious cry for help would have had any relevance. It would not have been written toward the end of November, as William had wanted the coroner to believe, but shortly after that first Friday in August when Montague finally began to identify the madness that festered in his own mind with his mother's tragedy. It was the Friday when the sight of her had fired his rabid torment beyond the point of no return. As the eminent psychiatrist Bruce L. Danto has stated:

Many violent and homicidal persons give early warning signs through their behaviour. In my experience, these individuals are psychotic and usually suffering from either a schizophrenic reaction or paranoid type of personality trait disturbance. They are asking for help from others and communicating their need for control. When a homicide occurs, it is because that help and control has not been forthcoming and their cry for help has been unheard and unmet.

In Montague's case the main controlling influence in his life was slowly dying. In *The Mind of the Murderer* the psychiatrist M. Guttmacher says:

The schizophrenic murderer kills his victims in accordance with his paranoid delusions and hallucinations. The sadistic murderer kills to achieve sexual pleasure and chooses his victims with specific occupations or qualities (prostitutes, teachers, elderly women, children, or those who are chronically ill). He sees his victims as being objects for his pleasure – not as fellow human beings. His pleasure may come from abusing, mutilating, or killing his victims. He has been a loner and unable to break strong emotional ties with his mother.

The sight of Mary Ann Nichols staggering down the Whitechapel Road proudly wearing her new bonnet, vainly hanging on to the trappings of frail womanhood until the very last, was the final link in a chain of disasters which had almost certainly stretched back to his childhood. Her situation was a parody of his mother's. Can it be mere coincidence that four of Druitt's five victims were women in their mid-forties – woman who were reaping the harvest of their poverty and vice and in whose decrepit eyes he may well have imagined his own mother's fate? The act of wrenching out the womb from his victim and taking it away with him is also deeply symbolic.

Most – if not all – adult human beings who find satisfaction in the destruction of others have almost certainly experienced considerable trauma at some point in their formative years. Without knowing considerably more about Montague's childhood than we are ever likely to do it would be impossible completely to fathom the depths of his particular psyche. In Dennis Nilsen's case, the image of his dead grandfather lying in his coffin – the only person he ever really loved – impressed on his personality at the age of six a perverted appreciation of love and death that would eventually lead to a sinsiter identification with his own sexuality – a relationship between his physical and spiritual needs which would end in chaos. This is not intended to suggest that every child who sees a dead relative is in danger of becoming a psychopathic killer, but that the particular seeds of Nilsen's destruction were sown at this early age, and that, like Druitt, the key to his psychosis lay in some deprivation which was only alleviated within a relationship with one specific individual. Take that individual away and the only real link with reality is severed, with disastrous consequences.

Montague's duties at the school would probably have made it difficult for him to visit his mother during the week, but we know from his cricketing activities that he must have had more time available to him at the weekends. The significance of this is that all five of the Ripper's murders occurred at the weekend – Friday, 31 August; Saturday, 8 September; Saturday, 29 September; and Friday, 9 November. But note also the break in the pattern: the

Ripper would have been expected to attack again at least once in October, at a time when we knew that Montague had stayed with his brother in Dorset. Away from his mother the urge to kill was probably much reduced, but inevitably he would be drawn back to her and to further destruction.

Tom Cullen quite rightly says that the barrister still had his chambers in the Temple within walking distance of the East End, and he goes on to suggest that he might have done some social work in his student days at Toynbee Hall, which would have given him a familiarity with the area. Unfortunately, no records exist to support this particular point of view, as Donald McCormick is quick to point out; but, interestingly enough, he also says, 'It is true that the Temple was within walking distance of the scenes of the crimes. But if Druitt had been the killer, one would expect him to make his way back there speedily after the second murder in one night – the one in Mitre Square. Instead the killer went in the opposite direction – to the North East.'

Montague Druitt left the scene of his carnage in Mitre Square and instinctively turned the way he had come – he fled northward toward his ailing mother. In Goulston Street he stopped to wipe his hands, and reaching into his pocket he took a piece of chalk from his pocket. In a well-practised manner he left a strange cipher, which no one has satisfactorily managed to explain, before finally disappearing into the night with Catherine Eddowes's kidney and uterus.

For the past month he had been playing a grotesque game of life and death on the streets of Whitechapel, leaving a trail of broken bodies behind him for others to find. His instinct to survive was being slowly eroded by his desperate need to plunder his victims in ever more conspicuous fashion. A part of Montague John Druitt was screaming to be caught, and one day he knew he would. But the other part of his brain, which thrilled at the feel and smell of warm blood and tissue, was going to play the game for all it was worth. In the letter that accompanied Catherine Eddowes's kidney, Montague summed up his feelings in one line: 'Catch me when you can, Mr Lusk.' This was both a cry for help and an acceptance of his situation. In a month's time he would literally tear Mary Jane Kelly apart in a frantic tantrum of horror and despair. By now he must have realized that his time on this earth was running out. He could no longer keep himself secret, and sooner or later someone was bound to find out the truth.

XVI

In November 1888, Assistant Commissioner Robert Anderson wrote to Henry Matthews about the actual numbers of men who were being employed on the streets of Whitechapel. The letter was then forwarded to a concerned Queen Victoria.

In reply to the S of S's inquiry I have the honour to report that since the 8th Sept., the date of the Hanbury St murder, extra Police precautions have been taken in the district of the murders.

From that date the special 'detection' force employed; i.e. officers not in uniform, consisted of 3 inspectors, 9 sergeants, and 6 constables.

On 1st Oct. this force was augmented by 2 sergeants and 39 constables, and on 6th Oct. 10 more officers were added.

The force at present thus employed consists of 2 inspectors and 56 constables.

In addition to these, 2 inspectors and 26 constables were for some time employed in making a house to house visitation in the district of the murders.

And in connection with that visitation, strict inquiry was made respecting single men occupying separate rooms.

The Division has been augmented by 1 sergeant and 42 constables, in addition to which 7 sergeants and 70 constables have been supplied nightly from other Divisions to fill the vacancies caused by men being supplied in plain clothes as above, and to patrol the division; giving a total of 8 sergeants and 112 constables for night duty.

Special measures are in force to watch cattle boats and other ships arriving in the Thames, and also to deal with suspicious characters of every description.

Clearly the streets of Whitechapel and Spitalfields at this time were saturated with the dedicated men of the Metropolitan Police, who were constantly sending in their reports to be sifted through by their superiors. Home Office file 144/220 A4930A shows that police were still being drafted into the area in July 1889.

When retired Inspector Frederick George Abberline spoke to the *Pall Mall Gazette* in March 1903 he said, 'You must understand that we have never believed all those stories about Jack the Ripper being dead, or that he was a lunatic or anything of that kind.'

This was an understandable statement from a man who, with the help of his fellow officers, had made out over sixteen hundred separate sets of papers during the course of their investigations, with very little to show for it. But Fred Abberline was wrong. He and his men would continue their futile investigations for the next two years, with any murder of a prostitute encouraging the belief that they might yet collar Jack the Ripper, when all the time others knew only too well that the episode was over.

The Home Office above mentioned file was prepared so that Home Secretary Matthews would be able to assure the House of Commons that the police were still doing everything in their power to apprehend the man responsible for the outrages in Whitechapel; however some private papers in the same file tell a different story. On 7 December 1888 James Monro writes to an Under Secretary at the Home Office recommending that the officers employed on plain clothes duty in the neighbourhood of the Whitechapel murders should be granted an extra one shilling per day. He explains that, as many of the men came from other divisions and had to patrol at a distance from their homes, the continuous night duty would be very trying once the winter had set in. Obviously this typical concern for his men was the result of the fact that Monro had resigned himself to the possibility of the present state of affairs continuing in Whitechapel for some time – at least through the winter months, and presumably as long as Jack the Ripper was at liberty. But on 26 January 1889 he wrote again to the Home Office, saying:

> I am gradually reducing the number of men employed on special duty as quickly as it is safe to do so, but such reduction cannot be affected all at once.

This was a remarkable communication, not least because it defies misinterpretation. James Monro had to have known that the special patrols were no longer necessary, and he must have been aware that they had to be reduced without drawing attention to the fact. On 15 March 1889 – about the same time that Albert Bachert had been told to disband the Vigilance Committee – James Monro finally confirmed that special duty in Whitechapel had ceased. Just how much he knew at this time it is impossible to say, but it is clear that Henry Matthews and James Monro could justify only in private what they could never admit in public. There was no longer any need for special plain clothes detectives to continue their arduous duty, for the simple reason that Jack the Ripper was dead.

In January 1889 Montague's inquest was held with the minimum of fuss, and in February the covert activities of the Home Office were curtailed. Journalist George Robert Sims, better known to his readers as Dagonet, was the man who had precipitated Abberline's response to the drowned doctor theory in the first place. As early as 1898 Sims had consistently told the same story. In 1903 he wrote in *The Referee*:

> Jack The Ripper committed suicide after his last murder – a murder so maniacal that it was accepted at once as the deed of a furious madman. It is perfectly well known at Scotland Yard who Jack was, and the reasons for the police conclusions were given in the report to the Home Office, which was considered by the authories to be final and conclusive. . . . How the ex-inspector can say 'We never believed "Jack" was dead or a lunatic' in the face of the report made by the Commissioner of Police is a mystery to me.

Obviously Sims knew the content of the police file sent to the Home Office pretty well, which is explained in a later article on the same theme:

> No one who saw the victim of Miller's Court as she was found ever doubted that the deed was that of a man in the last stage of a terrible form of insanity. . . . A little more than a month later the body of the man suspected by the *chiefs* [our italics] of Scotland Yard, *and by his own friends* [our italics], who were in communication with the Yard, was found in the Thames. The body had been in the water about a month.
>
> I am betraying no confidence in making this statement, because it has been published by an official who had an opportunity of seeing the Home Office report. Major Arthur Griffiths, one of her Majesty's inspectors of prisons.

We looked at Major Griffiths's contribution earlier, and could see how it was virtually word for word what Sir Melville Macnaghten had included in his official Scotland Yard notes. What we now discover from George Sims is that all of this information had been available to the police at the time they made their report to the Home Office, and we have little reason to doubt Sims's word for the simple fact that Macnaghten and Sims were close acquaintances, referring to each other in their respective autobiographies as 'old friends'.

The insight we therefore glean through Sims's column in *The Referee* is due to the different perspective he is able to bring to genuine information received from his close link with Sir Melville. In 1902 he was able to tell his readers that, in the course of their inquiries, the police had reduced the number of possible Jack the Rippers to seven,

> then by a further exhaustive inquiry to three, and were about to fit these three people's movements in with the dates of the various murders when the only genuine Jack saved further trouble by being found drowned in the Thames, into which he had flung himself, a raving lunatic, after the last and most appalling mutilation of the whole series. But prior to this discovery the name of the man found drowned was bracketed with two others as a possible Jack, and the police were in search of him alive when they found him dead.

This again is entirely compatible with what Macnaghten is able to tell us in his notes, and there is no reason to suspect that George Sims's information is anything but accurate. In 1899 he had said that the name of the murderer was perfectly well known to the police, and that if he hadn't committed suicide he would have been arrested. More importantly, Sims had written as early as 2 December 1888:

> It would be strange if the accession of Mr Monro to power were to be signalised by such a universally popular achievement as the arrest of Jack The Ripper. From information which has reached me, I venture to prophesy that such will be the case.

In other words, four weeks before Druitt's body would be discovered, Sims knew that Monro was on to something. And, like Monro, he expected a speedy conclusion to the mystery that had engulfed London for the past four months.

It was not to be. But in 1914 Sir Melville Macnaghten, believing that a man called Montague John Druitt was Jack the Ripper, would state: '. . . certain facts, pointing to this conclusion, were not in possession of the police till some years after I became a detective officer'. This was Macnaghten's 'private' information which had come, not from Druitt's family, or from lower down the ranks of the police force, but from his friend James Monro. Somewhere along the line Monro had begun to realize what was going on, and not for the first time in his career he would have understood that silent and unseen wheels had once more begun to turn. But he also knew his duty, and he was prepared to bring the perpetrator of the Whitechapel murders to justice, whoever he might be. Unfortunately, at about the time that Monro finally manages to identify his quarry the suspect disappears. In a few weeks Monro would learn that the suspect had supposedly committed suicide by throwing himself into the Thames, and only much later did this upright Scot begin to suspect what had actually happened. James Monro's grandson was right. His grandfather's suspicions would have turned out to be a very hot potato indeed.

When Montague John Druitt took his last fateful train journey to Hammersmith, he expected to meet someone and he expected to return. But it was not to be. Whom had he met? The one question that should have been answered at his inquest was never asked, which is not surprising when we consider the likely answer.

Chapter 14 quoted a letter written by Prince Albert Edward Victor to his close friend Henry Wilson, in which he expressed the hope that he would be able to join his old Cambridge friends at Wilson's place in order to see the boat race. Later, he wrote again:

> My Dear Harry,
> I put off writing to you before in the hope of still being able to give a favourable answer. But I now find, very much to my regret, that I shall not be able to get away for next Saturday, which is very tiresome, for I should have much enjoyed paying you a visit at Chiswick and seeing some of my old friends again. . . .

Wilson's house in Chiswick was called The Osiers, and in an obituary on his old friend H. L. Stephen explains:

> He joined the mysterious company of the Apostles of whom nothing can be said because their very existence is a secret, and he also made a host of friends who were not leading men, and who had no particular intellectual gifts, but did possess certain common but very definite qualities which were necessary to gain his friendship . . . a Trinity fellowship in 1885 enabled him to be called to the Bar in 1888. . . . During this period he was able to carry out an idea that he had long had in his mind by establishing a 'chummery' in a picturesque little house called 'The Osiers,' in Chiswick Mall, where a succession of young men, chiefly from Cambridge, found an ideal substitute for the lonely and uncomfortable lodgings which would otherwise have been their lot, and where other friends could always find youthful and cheerful company.

Wilson's 'chummery' stood on the river at Chiswick Mall, adjacent to Thorneycroft Wharf, at the very spot where Montague John Druitt's body would be dragged ashore on the last day of December 1888.

The man whom so many had thought was Jack the Ripper was to be fished from his watery grave within a stone's throw of the house of one of Prince Albert Victor's closest friends. Barrister Henry Wilson, together with his fellow Apostles and other Oxbridge friends, surrounded Druitt's chambers at the Temple. Druitt was the man who had recently bought a return train ticket for his one-way journey to Chiswick, and he was the same man who, even as his weighted body sank into the Thames mud, had been invited to attend a royal ball in honour of the young Prince who, had he lived, would have been King of England.

When Montague John Druitt arrived at Chiswick, whom did he meet? Henry Wilson himself, perhaps? Other Apostles? What about Evelyn Ruggles-Brise, a fellow Oxford man and a cricket-playing chum who was Private Secretary to Henry Matthews and the man who had been told to give 'a hint' about the Whitechapel murders to Monro 'if necessary'. Was he the Permanent Under Secretary who had interviewed the white-eyed doctor in Woodhall's fanciful account? Did any one of these, or all, or any other faithful servants of the Crown and State take it upon themselves to rid the future Establishment of England of its current embarrassment?

For Jack the Ripper the game was up. And if we wish to be charitable we may believe that the intention was to remove him quickly and quietly to a lunatic asylum. But, whatever the plan, the events that had overtaken London in that autumn finally came to an end. Indeed, they came to an end in the only way possible for the clandestine fellowship responsible for the legacy we have all inherited.

Whether Druitt was overpowered, or whether he lived long enough to face the reality of his miserable existence, we shall probably never know. The important fact was that the danger was over for these Cambridge men; their secret was safe for a hundred years, and the Establishment which they all served was once again firmly in place on its solid foundation of wealth and privilege – at least until the next crisis. In April 1903 George Sims wrote: 'Jack The Ripper was known, was identified, and is dead. Let him rest.' Perhaps now we will.

BIBLIOGRAPHY

ADAM, HARGRAVE and LEE, *Police Encyclopedia*, Waverley Book Co., 1920.

ANDERSON, Sir Robert, *The Lighter Side of My Official Life*, Hodder & Stoughton, 1910.

ANDREW, Christopher, *The Making of the British Intelligence Community*, William Heinemann, 1985.

BARON, Wendy, *Sickert*, Phaidon, 1973.

BRIGGS, David R., *The Millstone Race*, Short Run Press Ltd, 1983.

BOYLE, Andrew, *The Climate of Treason*, Hutchinson, 1979.

BUCKLE, George Earle (ed), *The Letters of Queen Victoria: 3rd series, vol. 1*, John Murray, 1930.

CHESTER, LEITCH and SIMPSON, *The Cleveland Street Affair*, Weidenfeld and Nicolson, 1976.

CLEUGH, James, *Secret Enemy, The Story of a Disease*, Thames and Hudson, 1954.

CULLEN, Tom, *Autumn of Terror*, Bodley Head, 1965.

DANTO, Bruce L., John BRUHNS and Austin H. KUTSCHER, *The Human Side of Homicide*, Columbia University Press, 1982.

DEACON, Richard, *The Cambridge Apostles*, Robert Royce Ltd, 1985.

DEW, Walter, *I Caught Crippen*, Blackie & Son Ltd, 1938.

DILNOT, George, *The Story of Scotland Yard*, Geoffrey Bles, 1930.

DOUGLAS, Arthur, *Will the Real Jack the Ripper?*, Countryside Publications, 1979.

FARSON, Daniel, *Jack the Ripper*, Michael Joseph, 1972.

GRIFFITHS, Arthur, *Mysteries of Police and Crime*, Cassell, 1898.

HARRISON, Michael, *Clarence*, W. H. Allen, 1972.

HIRSCHFIELD, Magnus, *Sexual Anomalies and Perversions*, Encyclopaedic Press, 1946.

HYDE, H. Montgomery, *The Cleveland Street Scandal*, W. H. Allen, 1976.

JONES, Elwyn, and John LLOYD, *The Ripper File*, Weidenfeld and Nicolson, 1975.

KELLY, Alexander, *Jack the Ripper: A Bibliography and Review of the Literature*, Association of Assistant Librarians, SED, revised edition, 1984.

KNIGHT, Stephen, *Jack the Ripper, The Final Solution*, Harrap, 1976.

LESLIE, Shane, *Sir Evelyn Ruggles-Brise (A Memoir)*, John Murray, 1938.

LOWNDES, Marie Belloc, *The Lodger*, Methuen, 1913.

McCormick, Donald, *The Identity of Jack the Ripper*, Jarrold, 1959.

Macnaghten, Sir Melville, *Days of My Years*, Edward Arnold, 1915.

Masters, Brian, *Killing For Company*, Jonathan Cape, 1985.

Matters, Leonard, *The Mystery of Jack the Ripper*, Hutchinson, 1929.

Mayhew, Henry, *London Labour and the London Poor*, Penguin (this selection, 1985).

Moylan, Sir John Fitzgerald, *Scotland Yard and the Metropolitan Police*, Putnam, 2nd edition, 1934

Odell, Robin, *Jack the Ripper in Fact and Fiction*, Harrap, 1965.

Pope-Hennessy, James, *Queen Mary 1867–1953*, Allen & Unwin, 1959.

Pope-Hennessy, James, *Monckton Milnes – The Years of Promise 1809–1851*, Constable, 1949.

Rhind, Neil, *Blackheath Village and Environs, 1790–1970*, vol. 2, Bookshop Blackheath Ltd, 1983.

Rumbelow, Donald, *The Complete Jack the Ripper*, W. H. Allen, 1975 and Star Books, 1979.

Short, K. R. M., *The Dynamite War – Irish American bombers in Victorian Britain*, Gill and Macmillan, 1979.

Sims, George Robert, *My Life*, Eveleigh Nash, 1916.

Sitwell, Sir Osbert, *A Free House! or The Artist as Craftsman, being the Writings of Walter Richard Sickert*, Macmillan, 1947.

Smith, Lieut.-Col. Sir Henry, *From Constable to Commissioner*, Chatto & Windus, 1910.

Stephen, Sir Leslie, *The Life of Sir James Fitzjames Stephen*, Smith, Elder & Co., 1895.

Stewart, William, *Jack the Ripper*, Quality Press, 1939.

Thomson, Sir Basil Home, *The Story of Scotland Yard*, Grayson & Grayson, 1935.

Vincent, James E., *His Royal Highness the Duke of Clarence and Avondale: A Memoir (Written by Authority)*, John Murray, 1893.

Whittington-Egan, Richard, *A Casebook on Jack the Ripper*, Wildy, 1976.

Wilson, Colin, and Patricia Pitman, *Encyclopedia of Murder*, Arthur Barker, 1961.

Woodhall, Edwin Thomas, *Jack the Ripper, or When London Walked in Terror*, Mellifont Press, 1937.

Woodhall, Edwin Thomas, *Detective and Secret Service Days*, Jarrold, 1929.

Wynn Williams, Watkin, *The Life of General Sir Charles Warren*, Basil Blackwell, 1941.

NEWSPAPERS AND PERIODICALS CONSULTED

Acton, Chiswick and Turnham Green Gazette, *The Blackheathen*, *Cambridge Review*, *The Cricketer*, *County of Middlesex Independent*, *The Criminologist*, *Daily News*, *The Daily Telegraph*, *Echo*, *Evening News*, *Evening Standard*,

The Globe, Granta, Illustrated Police News, The Lancet, The Listener, Meteor, The Morning Post, News of the World, Pall Mall Gazette, Penny Illustrated Paper, The People's Journal, Police Chronicle and Guardian, Police Gazette, Radio Times, The Referee, St Arnaud Mercury, St James Gazette, Sala's Journal, Southern Guardian, Star, Sun, Sunday Times, The Times, Truth, Wagga Wagga Express, Weekly Dispatch.

INDEX

Aarons, Joseph, 9

Abberline, Inspector Frederick George, 17, 27, 54, 61, 71, 73, 107, 143, 150, 151, 163–4, 179–180, 181, 182, 194

Aberconway, Christabel, Lady, 62, 63, 64, 123, 124–5, 126

Abiff, Hiram, 79

Acland, Lady Caroline, 114

Acland, Reginald Brodie Dyke, 158, 159

Acton, Chiswick and Turnham Green Gazette, 176

AIDS, 35

Albert Victor, Prince *see* Clarence, Duke of

Alexander of Hesse, Prince, 174

Alexandra, Princess, 38, 49, 160

Anderson, Sir Robert, 13, 48, 54, 55, 59–62, 66, 75, 88, 89, 104, 106, 158, 193–4

Annan, Lord, 165

'Apostles' *see* Cambridge Conversazione Society ('Apostles')

Arnold, Superintendent Thomas, 27, 57, 82

Australian connection, 122, 128–9, 130–4, 135–8

Bachert, Albert, 9, 18, 143–5, 151, 167, 184, 194–5

Baring, John, 171

Barlow, Detective, 37, 49, 73

Barnett, Henrietta, 24, 28–9

Barnett, Samuel Augustus, 24

Baron, Dr Wendy, 49

Barrett, PC, 1

Bateman, Lord, 108

Baxter, Wynne Edwin, 6–8, 22, 144–5

BBC, 37, 51, 63, 79, 91, 113, 118, 129, 184

Beck, Inspector Walter, 26, 27, 54

Bedford, Edward Henslowe, 107, 158

Bell, Quentin, 116

Bell, Vanessa, 115

Birmingham Daily Post, 97

Blackheath Cricket, Football and Lawn Tennis Club, 155

bloodhounds, 85–7

Blunt, Sir Anthony, 166, 184–5

Bond, Dr Thomas, 29–30

Bowes Lyon, Hon. Patrick, 160

Bowyer, Thomas ('Indian Harry'), 26, 27

Bradford, Edward, 67

Brooke Asylum, 175, 187

Brough, Edwin, 85

Brown, Dr Frederick Gordon, 20

Browning, Oscar, 161

Burgess, Guy, 166

Burton, Jeffrey, 137

Butler, Arthur, 22

Cadosch, Albert, 69

Cambridge Conversazione Society ('Apostles'), 160–1, 162–3, 165–7, 169, 171, 173, 197, 198

Cambridge Review, The, 161–2

Cansby, Inspector, 60

Central News Agency, 13, 23, 56, 94

Chapman, Annie, 4–5, 6–8, 10–11, 21, 22, 55, 61, 68, 70–1, 74

Chapman, George (Severin Klosowski), 32

Childers, Hugh, 54

CID, 31, 55, 87, 88, 94, 99, 104, 105, 106, 107, 109, 127, 142, 149, 151, 153

Clarence, Duke of, Prince Albert Victor ('Eddy'), 28, 35, 36, 38–39, 43–4, 45, 48, 49, 51–2, 80, 107, 110–15, 119, 153, 157, 158, 159–60, 162–3, 164, 165, 168–172, 173–4, 184, 185, 197, 198

Clark, James William, 160

Clerk, Colonel, 112

Cleveland Street affair, 52, 107, 111, 158, 162–4, 185

Clough, Arthur Hugh, 160

Coldstream Guards, 2

Coles, Frances, 135, 143, 144–5, 151

Connolly, 96

Cook, Elizabeth, 42–3, 44

Cotman, Dr John, 122

County of Middlesex Independent, 154

Crawford, Henry Homewood, 20, 22, 82

Cream, Dr Thomas Neill, 32

Cricketer, The, 119

Criminologist, The, 111, 113, 118

Crippen, Dr Hawley Harvey, 27

Crook, Alice Margaret, 39, 45–6, 47

Crook, Annie Elizabeth, 36, 39, 42–7, 52, 111

Cullen, Tom, 62, 64, 119, 122, 124, 125, 184, 192

Cunningham, 95

Cust, Henry John, 160, 171

Cutbush, Thomas, 63

Daily Express, 114

Daily News, 2, 147–8, 149

Daily Telegraph, The, 11, 24, 27, 97

Dalton, Canon John Neale, 157, 160

Danto, Bruce L., 190

Davis, John, 69

Davis, R. Harding, 75

de Groot, Karen, 42

Deacon, Richard, 166–7

Deeming, Frederick Bailey, 135–6, 138

Dew, PC Walter, 27–8

Diemschutz, Louis, 15

Diplock, Dr Thomas, 154, 175–8

Donner, Gerald Melville, 124–5, 126

Donner, Julia, 125

Douglas, Arthur, 42

Dower, Alan, 131, 138

Druitt, Ann, 121, 156, 174–5, 177, 181, 187, 188, 190

Druitt, Dorothy Edith, 134

Druitt, Edward, 157

Druitt, Isabella, 133

Druitt, Dr Lionel, 122, 128–9, 131, 132–4, 137, 138

Druitt, Montague John
  and Prince Albert Victor's circle, 157–60, 162, 164–5, 171–3, 174, 184, 185, 198
  and Dr Lionel Druitt, 128–9
  and 'Juwes' message, 84
  background of, 119–21, 157, 189
  cover-up for, 153–4, 164–5
  death of, 154–5, 176–80, 182–3, 197–8
  description of, 101
  feelings for mother, 174, 187, 188–9, 190–2
  homosexuality theory, 156–7
  inquest on, 175–9
  presumed motives of, 180, 187–92
  suspicions of family, 177–8, 180–1, 183
  suspicions of friends, 99, 103–4

suspicions of Sir Melville Macnaghten, 62, 63, 64–5, 106, 110, 119, 121, 126–7, 140, 141–142, 145, 186–7
suspicions of James Monro, 196–197
Druitt, Susan Katherine, 133
Druitt, Archdeacon Thomas, 133
Druitt, William, 119
Druitt, William Harvey, 121, 141, 174, 176, 177–9, 181, 182–3, 190
Dudley, Lord and Lady, 108
Duff, James, 160
Dutton, Dr Thomas, 142

Echo, 179
Eddowes, Catherine, 16, 19, 20, 21, 24, 33, 56, 67, 69, 71, 77, 85, 87, 102–3, 192
Edhouse, Mr, 130
Edward, Prince of Wales, 92, 160, 175
Euston, Henry Fitzroy, Earl of, 107
Evening News, 6, 9, 10

'Fairy Fay', 3–4, 12
Farson, Daniel, 62–3, 64, 84, 119, 122–3, 124, 125, 126, 128, 129–132, 133, 136, 137, 138, 177, 184
Fell, Cecilia, 134
Fell, W. G., 122, 130, 133, 134, 135, 137–8
Fenian Brotherhood, 94, 95–6
Field Club, 108
Fielder, Mr, 144
Forster, E. M., 166
Frazer, Colonel Sir James, 11
freemasons, 36, 40, 79–81, 82, 83
Fry, Roger, 165

gambling clubs, 108
Garrick Club, 141, 142
Gilbank, Jane, 1–2
Gladstone, William Ewart, 94
Goldstein, Leon, 18

Goodhart, Harry Chester, 160, 169, 171, 172
Goodman, Edward John, 74
Gorman, William, 47
Gould, Maurice, 130, 131, 132, 133, 134, 135, 136, 138
Gower, Lord Ronald Sutherland, 169
Granta, 161–2
Green, Emma, 68
Grenadier Guards, 2
Griffiths, Major Arthur, 123–4, 195, 196
Guardian, 124
Gull, Lady, 114
Gull, Sir William Withey, 35, 36, 39, 48, 111, 114, 117, 158, 159, 188
Guttmacher, M., 190–1

Halse, DC Daniel, 57, 84
Hammond, Charles, 164
Hanks, PC Luke, 163
Harris, Harry, 18
Harris, W., 9
Harrison, Michael, 32, 114–18, 119, 157
Hayden, W. P., 84
Henderson, Colonel Sir Edmund, 54
Henry of Battenberg, Prince, 112
High Rips, 2–3
Hill, Rowland, 155
Hirschfield, Dr Magnus, 25
homosexuality, 107, 111, 115, 156–157, 158–9, 160–1, 162–4, 165–7
Hunter, Llewellyn (Dawson), 96
Hutchinson, George, 71–2, 73–4, 101

Ihre, Professor, 45
Illustrated Police News, 46, 74
Imperial Club, 18, 19, 102
International Working Men's Educational Club, 15

Jack the Ripper
  anatomical knowledge of, 7–8, 20–1, 30
  as doctor, 18, 34–6, 73
  as freemason, 79–81, 82, 83
  as sailor, 19–20
  as slaughterman, 20, 21–2
  as woman, 22
  cessation of activities, 30–2
  descriptions of, 17, 19–20, 70–2, 73–4, 100, 103, 146, 147
  identified as Prince Albert Victor, 35, 111–15, 159
  identified as Montague John Druitt *see* Druitt, Montague John
  identified as Sir William Gull, 36, 39, 48, 114
  identified as Kosminski, 63–4, 127, 142
  identified as John Netley, 39, 48
  identified as Alexander Pedachenko, 142, 184
  identified as John Pizer, 10–11, 60–1
  identified as Michael Ostrog, 64, 127, 142
  identified as Walter Sickert, 48–51
  identified as J. K. Stephen, 114–18, 161–2
  letters by, 13, 77–9
  organ theft theory, 6–7, 21
Jenkinson, Sir Edward, 56, 93, 94, 95, 96–7, 164
Jewish community, 9, 10–11, 16–17, 21–2, 56, 57, 59, 61–2
Jones, Elwyn, 37
'Juwes' message, 16–17, 56–8, 79–84

Kelly, Alexander, 33–4, 145, 181
Kelly, Mary Jane, 26–8, 29–30, 32, 34, 36, 39–40, 43, 48, 67, 70, 71–2, 73, 84, 87, 89, 101, 104, 110, 150, 180, 185, 192

Keyler, Mrs, 70, 73
Keynes, John Maynard, 165
Knight, Stephen, 28, 36, 37, 40, 42–51, 53, 54, 79, 80, 110, 111, 114, 115, 119, 140, 157, 158, 159, 174, 184
Knowles, A., 35, 122, 123, 128, 130, 131, 133, 136
Kosminski, 63–4, 127, 142, 159

Lacey, Frederick Henry, 156
Lancet, 5
Lawende, Joseph, 18–20, 71
'Leather-Apron', 9–11, 60
Lees, Robert James, 114
Levy, Joseph, 18
Lewis, Sara, 70, 73
Lilly, Marjorie, 40, 41, 42, 48
Lindley, Percy, 85
Listener, The, 118
Llewellyn, Dr Rees Ralph, 20, 68
Lloyd, John, 37
Loftus, Philip, 124–5
Long, PC Alfred, 56, 81–2
Long, Elizabeth, 70–1
Lonsdale, John Henry, 172–3
Lowndes, Marie Belloc, 42
Lusk, George, 9, 15, 77

McCarthy, John, 26
McCormick, Donald, 140–5, 166, 184, 192
Mackenzie, Alice, 31, 32, 79, 101, 136, 143, 185
Mackenzie, Mr, 112
Maclean, Donald, 166
Macnaghten, Sir Melville, 30, 62–5, 66, 67, 75, 89, 105, 106, 110, 119, 121, 123, 124–6, 140, 141–2, 145–6, 154, 156, 158, 165, 171, 174, 177–8, 179, 180, 181–2, 184, 186–7, 189, 195–6
MacNamara, Edward, 130, 135, 136
Manor House Asylum, 175
Marshall, William, 71

Mary, Princess (Princess May of Teck), 48, 113
Matters, Leonard, 34–5, 36, 188
Matthews, Henry, 11, 23, 24, 29, 55, 56, 84, 92, 97, 99, 104, 146, 181, 193, 194, 195, 198
Melbourne Truth, 138
MI5, 95
Mickle, David, 137
Miles, Frank, 157
Miller, Dr Jonathan, 165
Milnes, Richard Monckton, 161
misogyny, 116–17, 161–2
Monro, Charles (Charlie), 92, 109
Monro, Christopher, 91, 108–9, 110, 127, 128
Monro, Chief Commissioner James, 31, 55–6, 59, 61, 67, 84, 85, 87–9, 90–104, 105–6, 107–110, 127, 163–4, 165, 185–6, 194–5, 196–7, 198
Monro, James (Grandson), 93, 185
Montagu, Samuel, 11, 26
Moore, Detective Inspector Henry, 54, 75
Mordaunt, Lady, 175
Morden Cricket Club, 155
Mortimer, Fanny, 17–18
Moulson, PC George, 176
Moylan, Sir John FitzGerald, 127, 186
Murray's Magazine, 84

Neil, PC John, 3, 68
Netley, John, 39, 45–6, 48, 51–2
Newlove, Henry, 163–4
News of the World, 47
Newton, Arthur, 164
Nichols, Mary Ann, 3, 4, 7, 9, 20, 28, 66–7, 68, 69, 187, 191
Nilsen, Dennis, 191
North London Press, The, 107

Odell, Robin, 22–3
Openshaw, Dr Thomas, 6, 77
'Osiers, The', 197–8

Ostrog, Michael, 64, 127, 142, 159

Pall Mall Gazette, 25, 144, 179, 194
Parke, Ernest, 107, 163, 164
'Pearly Poll', 1
Pedachenko, Dr Alexander, 142, 159, 166, 184
People's Journal, The, 98, 102, 103
Perkins, Walter, 68
Philby, Kim, 166
Phillips, Dr George Bagster, 7–8, 10, 27, 33
Pickersgill, Edward, 56
Pizer, John, 10–11, 60–1
Poland, R. H., 155
police, 3–4, 54–65, 66, 67–8, 75–6, 84–9, 90–104, 127, 143, 146, 147–8, 149–50, 185–7, 194
Police Chronicle and Guardian, 4, 97
Police Gazette, 19
Prater, Elizabeth, 70
Probyn, Sir Dighton, 110

Radio Times, 91, 108
Referee, The, 195, 196
revolutionary groups, 94–8
Richardson, Amelia, 11, 69
Richmond and Twickenham Times, The, 179
Robinson, PC Lewis, 16
Rosenwater, Irving, 119, 121
Ruffels, John, 137–8
Ruggles-Brise, Evelyn, 84, 99, 172, 198
Rumbelow, Donald, 60, 61, 101, 111, 117, 120, 122, 124, 150, 189
Russell, Bertrand, 165
Russell, Mary, 1

St Arnaud Mercury, 133–4, 137, 138
St Bartholomew's Hospital, 46–7
Sala's Journal, 74
Salisbury, Lord, 28, 107
Sanders, John, 150–2, 179

Saul, John, 109
scapegoats *see* Jewish community; freemasons; homosexuality
Schwartz, Israel, 17, 18, 19, 71
Sequira, Dr George William, 20
Shaw, George Bernard, 12, 24, 97
shochet (Jewish ritual slaughterman), 21–2
Shore, Peter, 165
Sickert, Joseph, 37–52, 79, 80, 110, 114, 115, 157, 158
Sickert, Walter, 37, 38–9, 40–2, 43–4, 45, 47, 48–51, 111, 140, 141, 142, 156, 157, 174
Sims, George Robert ('Dagonet'), 195–6, 198
Sitwell, Osbert, 40, 141
Smith, Arthur Hamilton, 160
Smith, Emma Elizabeth, 1, 2–3, 4, 12, 28
Smith, Henry Babington, 160
Smith, Major Henry, 19–20, 56–7, 61–2, 83, 87, 88
Smith, PC William, 17, 18, 19, 71, 73–4
Solomon, King, 79
Somerset, Lord Arthur ('Podge'), 107, 110, 111, 163, 164
Southern Guardian, 154, 173
Special Branch, 95, 98, 102, 103, 149
Spencer, Lord John, 55, 94
Spurling, Aubrey, 155
'Stanley, Dr', 34–5, 188
Star, 3, 8–9, 12, 53, 65, 97, 147–8, 149
Stephen, Harry Lushington, 158, 160, 169, 171, 172, 197
Stephen, Herbert, 158
Stephen, James Kenneth, 114–18, 153, 158, 159–60, 161–2, 165, 170, 171
Stephen, Sir James (present), 115
Stephen, Sir James Fitzjames, 115
Stephen, Leslie, 116
Stewart, William, 22

Stoker, Bram, 72–3
Stokes, Dr Leonard, 155
Stowell, Dr Thomas, 35, 110–12, 114, 117, 118, 119, 159, 184, 188
Strachey, Lytton, 165
Stride, Elizabeth ('Long Liz'/ 'Epileptic Annie'/née Gustisson), 15–16, 24, 33, 67, 69–70, 71, 85, 98, 103
Stride, John Thomas, 16
Stride, PC Walter Frederick, 15–16
Studd, Sir John Edward Kynaston, 169, 172
Sun, 22, 63
Sunday Times, The, 48, 50
Sutcliffe, Peter ('Yorkshire Ripper'), 47
Sutherland, Dr Henry, 5–6
Sutton, Henry, 77
Swanson, Inspector Donald Sutherland, 54
Swinscow, Charles, 163
syphilis, 35, 188

Tabram, Martha, 1–2, 4, 12, 32
Tait, Lawson, 22
Tanner, Joseph Robson, 160
Taylor, Dr Joseph, 122
Tennyson, Alfred, Lord, 165
Thicke, Sergeant William ('Johnny Upright'), 10, 60
Thompson, Mr, 69
Thomson, Sir Basil, 127, 186
Thyne, Dr Thomas, 122
Tichborne Claimant case, 42
Times, The, 2, 3, 4, 5, 60, 85, 90, 91, 92, 93, 95, 103, 111–13, 147, 148, 149, 151
Toughill, Thomas, 157
Trafalgar Square riots, 54–5
Trinity College, 159, 160–1, 171
Tuke, Dr Thomas Seymour, 175

Valentine, George, 120, 154, 155–6, 177, 178, 179, 189

Veck, George, 163–4
Victoria, Queen, 15, 19, 24, 28–9,
    35, 48, 113, 117, 193
Vigilance Committee, 9, 11–12,
    15, 18, 54, 77, 143–4, 194–
    195
Vincent, James Edmund, 168–9,
    170, 172
Violenia, Emanuel Delbast, 60–1

Warren, General Sir Charles, 54–5,
    57–8, 61, 79, 81, 82–3, 84–7,
    93–4, 95, 96, 97, 102, 104,
    105–6, 107, 127, 146, 150–1,
    181
Warren, Dr, 109
Watkins, PC Edward, 69, 102,
    103
Watt, Detective, 37, 73

White, Detective Stephen, 98,
    99–101, 102–3
'White-eyes', 146–9, 151–2
Williams, Watkin Wynn, 84, 85,
    127
Williamson, Superintendent
    'Dolly', 55
Wilson, Colin, 111, 113, 129, 156,
    189
Wilson, Henry Francis (Harry),
    160, 161, 165, 168, 169–73,
    197–8
Wimborne, Lady, 174
Wimborne, Lord, 173–4
Winslade, Henry, 176
Woodhall, Edwin Thomas,
    145–52, 154, 181–2
Woolf, Virginia, 115, 116
Working Lads' Institute, 113